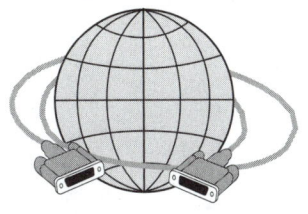

CONGRESS AND THE INTERNET

REAL POLITICS IN AMERICA

Series Editor: Paul S. Herrnson, *University of Maryland*

The books in this series bridge the gap between academic scholarship and the popular demand for knowledge about politics. They illustrate empirically supported generalizations from original research and the academic literature using examples taken from the legislative process, executive branch decision making, court rulings, lobbying efforts, election campaigns, political movements, and other areas of American politics. The goal of the series is to convey the best contemporary political science research has to offer in ways that will engage individuals who want to know about real politics in America.

Series Editorial Board

Christine L. Day, University of New Orleans
Darrell M. West, Brown University
Kelly D. Patterson, Brigham Young University
James P. Pfiffner, George Mason University
Ken M. Goldstein, Arizona State University
Rex Peebles, Austin Community College
Karen O'Connor, American University
Clyde Wilcox, Georgetown University
Rodney Hero, University of Colorado–Boulder
John J. Pitney, Jr., Claremont McKenna College
Ronald Walters, University of Maryland

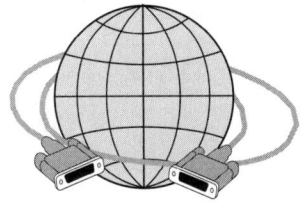

CONGRESS AND THE INTERNET

EDITED BY

James A. Thurber
American University

Colton C. Campbell
Florida International University

UPPER SADDLE RIVER, NEW JERSEY 07458

Library of Congress Cataloging-in-Publication Data
Congress and the Internet/edited by James A. Thurber, Colton C. Campbell.
  p. cm.—(Real politics in America)
Includes bibliographical references and index.
ISBN 0-13-099617-3
  1. United States. Congress—Information resources management.   2. Internet—Political aspects—United States.
  I. Thurber, James A.   II. Campbell, Colton C.   III. Real politics in America series.

JK1021 .C553 2003
328.73'00285'4678—dc21   2002011372

Senior acquisitions editor: Heather Shelstad
Associate editor: Brian Prybella
Editorial assistant: Jessica Drew
Marketing manager: Claire Bitting
Marketing assistant: Jennifer Bryant
Editorial/production supervision: Kari Callaghan Mazzola
Prepress and manufacturing buyer: Ben Smith
Electronic page makeup: Kari Callaghan Mazzola and John P. Mazzola
Interior design: John P. Mazzola
Cover director: Jayne Conte
Cover design: Kiwi Design
Cover photo: Burstein Goldman/The Stock Rep, Inc.

This book was set in 10/12 Palatino by Big Sky Composition
and was printed and bound by Courier Companies, Inc.
The cover was printed by Phoenix Color Corp.

Real Politics in America
Series Editor: Paul S. Herrnson

 © 2003 by Pearson Education, Inc.
Upper Saddle River, New Jersey 07458

All rights reserved. No part of this book may be
reproduced, in any form or by any means,
without permission in writing from the publisher.

Printed in the United States of America
10 9 8 7 6 5 4 3 2 1

ISBN 0-13-099617-3

Pearson Education LTD., London
Pearson Education Australia PTY, Limited, Sydney
Pearson Education Singapore, Pte. Ltd
Pearson Education North Asia Ltd, Hong Kong
Pearson Education Canada, Ltd., Toronto
Pearson Educación de Mexico, S.A. de C.V.
Pearson Education—Japan, Tokyo
Pearson Education Malaysia, Pte. Ltd
Pearson Education, Upper Saddle River, New Jersey

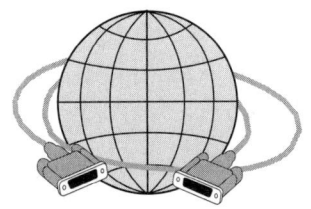

CONTENTS

ACKNOWLEDGMENTS   vii

ABOUT THE CONTRIBUTORS   ix

INTRODUCTION : CONGRESS GOES ON-LINE   1
James A. Thurber and Colton C. Campbell

CHAPTER 1
CAMPAIGNING ALONG THE INFORMATION HIGHWAY   11
Colton C. Campbell and David A. Dulio

CHAPTER 2
REPRESNETATION: CONGRESS AND THE INTERNET   31
Stephen E. Frantzich

CHAPTER 3
WE'VE COME A LONG WAY . . . MAYBE   52
U.S. Representative David Dreier

CHAPTER 4
CAN CONGRESS COPE WITH IT? DELIBERATION AND THE INTERNET   78
Donald R. Wolfensberger

CHAPTER 5
THE "WIRED CONGRESS": THE INTERNET, INSTITUTIONAL CHANGE, AND LEGISLATIVE WORK   99
C. Lawrence Evans and Walter J. Oleszek

CHAPTER 6
COMMUNICATION WITH CONGRESS: CITIZENS, E-MAIL, AND WEB SITES   123
Dennis W. Johnson

CHAPTER 7
CONGRESS, THE PRESIDENCY, INFORMATION TECHNOLOGY, AND THE INTERNET: POLICY ENTREPRENEURSHIP AT BOTH ENDS OF PENNSYLVANIA AVENUE   135
Richard S. Conley

CHAPTER 8
THE E-RATE PROGRAM: PAVING THE DIRT ROAD TO THE INFORMATION SUPERHIGHWAY   161
Jeff Gill and David Conklin

CHAPTER 9
THE INTERNET, CONGRESS, AND EDUCATIONAL OUTREACH   177
Graeme Browning

AFTERWORD: CONGRESS AND THE INTERNET: LOOKING BACK AND LOOKING FORWARD   186
Chris Casey

INDEX   193

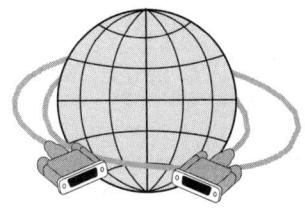

ACKNOWLEDGMENTS

As with any collaborative enterprise, this volume could not have been completed without the assistance of many individuals and organizations. First and foremost, we must thank our authors. They tolerated our exhortations to make their chapters interesting and accessible beyond the confines of academia to a broad audience. Next, we wish to thank the Pew Charitable Trusts for its grant to the Center for Congressional and Presidential Studies, the "Improving Campaign Conduct" project. This grant helped with our work on congressional campaigns and the Internet. In particular, we wish to thank all our wonderful colleagues in the Center for Congressional and Presidential Studies—Leslie McNaugher, Sam Garrett, Jennifer Arnold, and Candy Nelson—for providing invaluable support, assistance and, above all, unwavering patience in the production of this volume.

With great appreciation, we owe an intellectual debt to Vince Randazzo, former Staff Director of the House Rules Committee, for helping us during this project and for expanding our knowledge of the legislative process. His commitment to improving Congress through the expansion of the Internet and information technology in the institution is unequivocal and admirable. Special thanks go to Douglas E. Van Houweling and Robert P. Van Houweling for their advice and knowledge about the future of the Internet, Internet 2, and Congress.

We are also indebted to many people at Prentice Hall for their assistance in the development of this book, but two deserve special acknowledgment: Heather Shelstadt and Jessica Drew took exceptional care to shepherd this volume to completion. Kari Callaghan Mazzola provided editorial/production supervision, and Dana Chicchelly provided careful copyediting; both Kari and Dana contributed significantly to the volume's clarity.

Paul Herrnson, series editor of *Real Politics in America*, is owed a special debt of gratitude. His goal for the series—to convey the best contemporary political science research has to offer in ways that will engage individuals who want to know about real politics in America—is to be commended, because all too often theory and practice do not mesh on Capitol Hill. For good reason, Paul is one of the most respected congressional scholars, not only because of his careful scholarship but also for his knowledge of applied politics.

Finally, we wish to dedicate this volume to our wives, Claudia and Marilyn, who have been constant sources of encouragement, tolerance, motivation, and humor, and whose love is not contingent upon the success of our scholarship.

To the reader, we hope our efforts and those of the contributing authors will advance your understanding, appreciation, and respect for what a uniquely American institution, the U.S. Congress, can accomplish. Although this has been a collective effort, we assume responsibility, of course, for any errors of fact or interpretation.

James A. Thurber
Colton C. Campbell

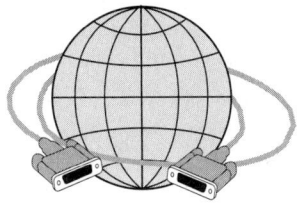

ABOUT THE CONTRIBUTORS

GRAEME BROWNING is the former Editorial Director of the Internet Policy Institute. She has covered technology policy for the *National Journal*, and has been a business reporter for the *Washington Post, Chicago Sun-Times*, and *United Press International*. Her books include *If Everyone Bought One Shoe: American Capitalism in Communist China* and *Electronic Democracy: Using the Internet to Transform American Politics*.

COLTON C. CAMPBELL is Assistant Professor of political science at Florida International University. He is the author of *Discharging Congress: Government by Commission*, and coeditor of several books, including: *New Majority or Old Minority? The Impact of Republicans on Congress; The Contentious Senate: Partisanship, Ideology, and the Myth of Cool Judgment; Congress Confronts the Court: The Struggle for Legitimacy and Authority in Lawmaking; Congress and the Politics of Emerging Rights*; and *Congress and the Politics of Foreign Policy*.

CHRIS CASEY is cofounder of CaseyDorin, a complete Web-based multimedia production company that works with congressional candidates, officeholders, party committees, businesses, and other organizations to help them better communicate with voters, constituents, contributors, and members of Congress. He is the author of *The Hill on the Net: Congress Enters the Information Age* and developed *CapWeb*, an Internet Guide to Congress.

DAVID CONKLIN is a graduate student in political science at the University of Florida.

RICHARD S. CONLEY is Assistant Professor of political science at the University of Florida. He is the author of *The Presidency, Congress, and Divided Government: A Postwar Assessment*. His articles appear in *Presidential Studies Quarterly, Political Research Quarterly*, and *Polity*.

DAVID A. DULIO is Assistant Professor of political science at Oakland University. He is coeditor of *Crowded Airwaves: Campaign Advertising in Elections*. His articles appear in *Political Science & Politics* and *Administrative Law Review*. He served as an American

Political Science Association congressional fellow for U.S. Representative J. C. Watts, Jr. (R-Oka.), Chairman of the House Republicans Conference.

DAVID DREIER is Chair of the House of Representative's Committee on Rules. He has served as co–vice-chairman of the Joint Committee on the Organization of Congress to study the operations of Congress and to provide recommendations for reform. *Business Week* has named him one of its "Digital Dozen" tech-savvy legislators in Congress, and the AEA (formerly the American Electronics Association, America's largest high-tech trade association) inducted him into its "High-Tech Legislator Hall of Fame." In 1999, he was awarded the "Cyber-Champion" title by the Business Software Alliance, and in 2000 he was named "High-Tech Legislator of the Year" by the Information Technology Industry Council (ITIC). He also won the "Founder's Award" from TechNet.

C. LAWRENCE EVANS is Professor of political science at the College of William and Mary. His books include *Leadership in Committee: A Comparative Analysis of Leadership Behavior in the U.S Senate* and *Congress Under Fire: Reform Politics and the Republican Majority*.

STEPHEN E. FRANTZICH is Professor and departmental chair of political science at the U.S. Naval Academy. He has written widely both on the impact of new technology on Congress and the political process. His books include *Computers in Congress: The Politics of Information; Political Parties in the Technological Age; American Government: The Political Game; Congress: Games and Strategies;* and *The C-SPAN Revolution*. He has served as a consultant to Congress, C-SPAN, the German Bundestag, the Carnegie Foundation, Legi-Slate, and the Dirksen Center.

JEFF GILL is Assistant Professor of political science at the University of Florida. His books include *Generalized Linear Models: A Unified Approach* and *What Works: A New Approach to Program and Policy Analysis*. He has published numerous articles in *Public Administration Review, Political Research Quarterly,* and *Journal of Public Administration Research and Theory*.

WALTER J. OLESZEK is Senior Specialist in American national government at the Congressional Research Service, and Adjunct Professor of political science at American University. His books include *Congressional Procedures and the Policy Process, Fifth Edition,* and *Congress and Its Members, Eighth Edition,* with Roger H. Davidson. He has served as policy director of the Joint Committee on the Organization of Congress.

JAMES A. THURBER is Professor of government at American University and Director of the Center for Congressional and Presidential Studies. He is currently directing "Improving Campaign Conduct," a research project sponsored by the Pew Charitable Trusts. He is editor and coeditor of *Rivals for Power: Presidential–Congressional Relations, Second Edition; Remaking Congress: The Politics of Congressional Stability and Change; Campaign Warriors: Political Consultants in Elections; Crowded Airwaves: Campaign Advertising in Elections; Battle for Congress: Candidates, Consultants, and Voters;* and *Campaigns and Elections: American Style*.

DONALD R. WOLFENSBERGER is Director of the Congress Project at the Woodrow Wilson International Center for Scholars. He is the author of *Congress and the People: Deliberative Democracy on Trial*. He served as a staff member in Congress from 1969 to 1997, working for such House members as John B. Anderson, Trent Lott, and Lynn Martin.

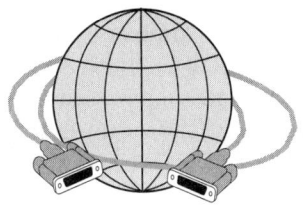

INTRODUCTION

CONGRESS GOES ON-LINE

JAMES A. THURBER AND COLTON C. CAMPBELL

In the past decade, the Internet has become an integral part of Congress, starting slowly, but becoming pervasive and necessary by the beginning of the twenty-first century. Few, however, have evaluated the impact of the Internet on the primary functions of Congress (lawmaking, representations, deliberation, education, and oversight) since Congress has entered into electronic government (e-government) along with many local, state, federal, and international levels of government. The legislative branch now relies heavily on the Internet and other information technologies to improve the efficiency of its internal operations, to link itself with constituents and interest groups, to enhance member and staff access to information useful in the legislative process, and to facilitate the publication and distribution of legislative documents.[1] But with the growth of the Internet on Capitol Hill comes a variety of opportunities, challenges, and concerns to nearly every aspect of congressional life. In short, this powerful new medium is creating revolutionary challenges and opportunities, drawing strong comparisons to the impact of television on the congressional process and the legislative way of life.[2]

Expanded congressional use of the Internet has generally coincided with the Web's growth in the private sector. Through the Web, for example, on-line users can now delve into a sea of legislative information, including the floor activities of the House and Senate, major congressional legislation, summaries and full texts of bills, all the laws Congress passed in the current session, the texts of the *Congressional Record*, committee reports, members' home pages, and historical documents such as the Declaration of Independence, the *Federalist Papers*, and the Constitution. Public demand for access to information about congressional activity and the growing volume of e-mail to Congress has brought major reforms in information technology and the use

1

of the Internet on the Hill. The volume of e-mail messages sent to Congress, for example, more than doubled from 1998 to 2000.[3] Congress was overwhelmed by "hot button" issues such as the impeachment proceedings against President Clinton and the nomination of former Senator John Ashcroft (R-Mo.) to be United States Attorney General. According to one recent analysis, the number of e-mail messages received by the House of Representatives has increased from 20 million in 1998 to 48 million in 2000.[4] This rapid increase in electronic messages to Congress reveals the demand by citizens and private-sector groups for access through the Internet to members of Congress.

Congress has also expanded its use of the Internet and electronic devices for information (e.g., <intranet.house.gov>) and document management, thereby enhancing its legislative and deliberative tasks. For example, in-house networks in the House and Senate, like corporate intranets, disseminate schedules and other information. The Senate's network is nicknamed Webster, for the Senate's nineteenth-century orator Daniel Webster. In conjunction with the Library of Congress (LOC) and the Congressional Research Service (CRS), Congress has developed a single, integrated system to organize information for all the legislative branch agencies, including the General Accounting Office (GAO) and the Government Printing Office (GPO), known as the Legislative Information System (LIS). An internal Web site for both chambers, LIS provides members, committees, leadership offices, and legislative branch agencies with a wide variety of information through the Internet that once was available only on paper. The public has access to some of this information through THOMAS (<http://thomas.loc.gov>), an Internet information system documenting congressional activity, thus making the legislative process more accessible to interested citizens and active interest groups. This Internet-based information system provides the full text of House and Senate bills as well as links to voting files, committee reports, selected hearing transcripts, and many reports from the legislative support agencies. By the end of the 104th Congress (1995–1997), 222 members of Congress, 27 committees, and 11 other congressional offices had launched Web sites on the House Web server. At the end of the 107th Congress's (2001–2003) first session, all members and committees maintained a Web presence.[5] The use of the Internet and information technology in the preparation of legislative documents, combined with increasing use of networks for exchanging text and distributing documents, has increased the speed and process of preparing bills, committee reports, and other legislative documents.

But aside from helpful on-line information, can Congress keep pace with the near instantaneous speed of the Internet and still perform its fundamental tasks, especially given the challenges and problems posed by this burgeoning technology? Will the Internet usher in a new age of representation, deliberation, lawmaking, oversight, and education on Capitol Hill? Is the Internet being forced onto Congress? Or will Congress, once notoriously Internet-phobic, make more strides toward coexistence with the new medium, streamlining its own operations and making more government information available to the public? The public has arrived via the Internet. Is Congress, the branch closest to the people, ready?

AUTOMATION VERSUS DELIBERATION

The more than seventy newly elected House members of the 105th Congress (1997–1999) were initiated into the wired legislative process when they arrived on Capitol Hill to find a cyber Welcome Wagon waiting to familiarize them with their new jobs. Each freshman representative received a laptop computer and an on-line primer on how to cope with the initial days of a new Congress, along with instructions for setting up a congressional office, ordering furniture and stationery, and boning up on parliamentary procedures. House techno-wizards even photographed the labyrinthine corridors beneath the Capitol and House office buildings and put the pictures on computer home pages, giving the lawmakers a virtual reality subterranean tour to help them navigate their way to their first committee meeting.[6]

Rather than embracing new solutions and unfamiliar procedures, Congress, institutionally, approaches uncertainty in small discrete steps, and is often sequential in action, reflecting the institution's deliberative nature. Members of Congress attribute the lack of progress in cyber areas to concerns about computer security, obsolete or incompatible equipment, and cultural opposition from an institution so steeped in tradition that Senate desks still have inkwells and goose-quill pens along with crystal sand shakers for blotting ink. "Let's face it, most of us are Industrial Age men and women trying to convert to the Information Age, and that's painful," said Senator Larry Pressler, (R-S.Dak.), a founder of the Internet Caucus, a group of House and Senate members promoting Congress's use of computers.[7] Three years after former Representative Charlie Rose (D-N.C.), then chairman of the Committee on House Administration, decided it was time for Congress to venture onto what was then being called the "Information Superhighway," both houses continued to show reluctance to move forward on making the inner workings of Congress more accessible to citizens—"netizens"—on-line. Committee chairs balked at a proposed rule change to release a range of materials in cyberspace on the same day that it unfolded on the Hill itself.[8] Specifically, these included members' voting records, Federal Election Campaign (FEC) reports on campaign contributions, financial disclosure and lobbyist disclosure reports, and others.

However, as a communication medium, the Internet, which mirrors the actual pace of legislating and lobbying, is ideal for the kind of engaged citizenship that all lawmakers supposedly want. Individual members, committees, leadership, caucuses, and legislative support groups have Web sites which usually describe key legislative activity and programs and help citizens get answers to commonly asked questions, such as how to apply to the service academies, or e-mail addresses to supplement normal surface mail. For Senator Wayne Allard (R-Colo.) electronic communication is an integral part of staying in touch with constituents; his office receives nearly 100,000 "snail mail" letters a year, and substantially more e-mails, perhaps 150,000.[9] And with an anthrax scare halting mail service at the Capitol following the terrorist hijackings and assault on the World Trade Center and the Pentagon on September 11, 2001, many legislators are urging their constituents to stay in touch using e-mail.

WIRING CAPITOL HILL

Wiring Congress to surf the Net has posed enormous logistical challenges. Technicians have laid hundreds of miles of fiber-optic wire in congressional offices, snaking the lifeline to the Internet through air ducts, steam tunnels and early-nineteenth-century chimneys. But this is just a small part of the total technological investment required to bring Congress into the modern computing age. Congress's Internet communication network itself is problematic. For several years, each lawmaker decided which computer system, if any, to buy and install in the office. This led to a congressional Tower of Babel, with some electronic messages often arriving days after being sent on one of several overlapping systems. Replacing outdated computers and software as well as hiring savvy technicians can be a luxury on Capitol Hill, given the limited annual budgets to run Washington and district offices. Senator Ben Nighthorse Campbell (R-Colo.) and Representative Joel Hefley (R-Colo.), for example, do not have e-mail addresses for their offices, placing them among a select group of lawmakers whose offices' mail operations have not joined the age of e-politics. "For our office, it's not something we're capable of doing without hiring additional staff members," said a Hefley spokeswoman.[10]

But while technology is one problem facing Internet evangelists in Congress, computer phobia is another. To some members, all of this rapid change is a bit frightening. Representative Hefley worries about getting inundated with special-interest messages, since his staff is smaller than the staffs of most members and he would have to hire another staff member to weed through junk e-mail. For Senator Campbell security concerns have prevented him from setting up an e-mail address for constituents. Representative Scott McInnis (R-Colo.) has an e-mail address, but unlike most members, it is not linked to his Web site. Rather, e-mailers from his West Slope district must visit <www.house.gov>, and click on a "write your representative" link. If they enter a zip code in his district, the letter will be directed to McInnis.

There are other prices for being so wired. A glut of easily accessible information may subtly undermine the committee system. If committees are no longer seen as the heart of the lawmaking process on specific legislative subjects, members who do not serve on those panels may feel emboldened to offer amendments or change bills in other ways. Fear is also building in some quarters that too much information, too many e-mail messages, and too much constituent contact could degrade the deliberative process, scripting actions and forcing members to react more quickly to public opinion and take fewer risks with their speeches and votes. With information moving in real time, lobbyists could potentially dial in demands straight to the House and Senate cloakrooms or, perhaps in the near future, e-mail legislative amendments straight to the floor. Congress has already witnessed the power of the Internet, along with the potential pitfalls, when in 1998, as Federal Reserve Chairman Alan Greenspan testified before Congress on the economy, an aide with a laptop computer was slipping him notes on how his comments were moving the stock market. He could tailor his words and tone accordingly.

CONGRESS ENTERS ITS THIRD CENTURY

Congress has arrived on the Internet but, like the legislative process itself, the results are somewhat haphazard, occasionally impractical, and highly political. The direction of computer links, for example, is predominantly unilateral, flowing from leadership or committee chairs to rank-and-file members.[11] Members representing higher proportions of minorities and rural residents tend to have lower-quality Web sites in terms of overall features, constituent services, and technical sophistication than do members representing higher proportions of whites and urban constituents.[12] This raises new questions regarding representation. In the past, for example, debates revolved around whether lawmakers should be delegates or trustees, with the focus on public policy. There were also questions of symbolic representation. Could whites, for example, represent blacks? Could men represent women? These questions were mostly subsidiary to the delegate-trustee issue. Although legislators' interpretations of representation vary widely, they all agree that it rests on the principle of geography and population, a sensible idea when land was the basic productive resource. The Internet, however, is a realm without geography. Today, virtually everything a lawmaker does falls under the rubric of representation.[13] Therefore, are members of Congress with technically sophisticated Web sites somehow better representing their constituencies or vice versa? If so, then the Internet is expanding the concept of representation, providing yet another way for constituents to better know their representative or senator.

Like most things on Capitol Hill, the Internet is subject to partisan politics. At the start of the 104th Congress, during the legislative infancy of the

Internet, lawmakers squabbled over who controlled the information within various Internet destinations across Capitol Hill. Controversy erupted when the House Oversight Committee adopted new "netiquette" rules listing just the Web pages of the majority on congressional committees from a central menu.[14] Republican lawmakers said they could exercise this kind of control because they viewed a Web page like a committee report that accompanies legislation, and because the majority has to pay for resources such as the stationery that committee reports are printed on and, now, for the technical expertise necessary to provide information on the Web. Democrats argued that the regulation was a maneuver by the Republicans to manage, limit, and decide what the public received from the Web.

Irrespective of partisanship, on both sides of the aisle, as computer technology invades House and Senate offices, some members have taken to it like digit heads, organizing videoconferences with their constituents and designing interactive Web pages—graphic links to the worldwide computer network—that function the way members' newsletters used to, allowing lawmakers to adopt a folksy tone with sound, video clips, messages, even their favorite cookie recipes. Others have not yet thrown away their typewriters. Most are struggling somewhere in between. In a slight twist of irony, Senator Strom Thurmond (R-S.C.), born a year after Guglielmo Marconi first transmitted Morse code over the Atlantic, was plugged in with his own home page well before former House Speaker Newt Gingrich (R-Ga.), the self-proclaimed "cyber speaker," was with his.[15]

Midway through October of 2001, members of Congress and their staff moved out of their offices in the Capitol complex for the first time since 1814. Banned from their offices while biohazard experts cleaned up the anthrax contamination, lawmakers were forced to use makeshift arrangements in order to conduct normal legislative business. Some members hung around their homes, making fundraising calls and doing what congressional-related work they could. "I have a computer here and Internet hookup, so I'm sending e-mails off," said Representative Dave Weldon (R-Fla.).[16] In most cases, folding tables and computers accommodated displaced Hill people in temporary offices at the Government Accounting Office (GAO), three-quarters of a mile away from the Capitol, where each House member was allotted two 10-by-15-foot offices.[17] This prompted House Majority Whip Tom DeLay (R-Tex.) to offer a broad interpretation of what defines Congress. "The Congress is not a building," he said. "Congress is wherever the elected representatives gather to make decisions for the American people."[18] After the tragedy of September 11 and the anthrax attacks, Congress became keenly aware of the dangers of terrorism and the use of an E-Congress. Several hearings were held in the House in 2002 on the use of an E-Congress in emergency situations. The newly created Subcommittee on Technology and the House of the U.S. House of Representatives Committee on Rules is a vocal point for the study of E-Congress. It has general responsibility for measures related to the impact of technology on the process and procedures of the House and has held hearings on E-Congress and using advanced technology to conduct congressional operations in times of emergencies. The Committee on House Administration also held a special hearing on May 1, 2002, called "E-Congress? Hearing for Conducting Congressional Operations in Emergency Situations." The Internet can work to realize such a vision: Committees broadcast their proceedings in live audio format over the Internet; interactive video, teleconferencing, and other technology collect testimony from witnesses who may be located in other parts of the nation; witness testimony is transmitted over the Internet, and cable television viewers may e-mail questions to witnesses; chat rooms are virtual Town Hall meetings; Dear Colleague Letters are sent electronically; and because of the anthrax attack on Congress, constituent mail is being scanned and sent electronically to House offices on an experimental basis as of June 2002.[19]

ORGANIZATION OF THE BOOK

The next ten chapters analyze the emergence and impact of the Internet on Congress, both positive and negative. The contributors address the procedural and cultural impact of the Internet on the legislative process; how the use of the Internet affects the conduct of communication and business on the floor, in committees and offices, and among members; the advantages and disadvantages of computer-based communication and interaction between lawmakers and their constituents; how the Internet is used to shape Congress's policy agenda; the impact of Internet lobbying on Congress; how the Internet is used as a campaign tool; and how the Internet influences civic engagement with Congress. Although still relatively new to Capitol Hill, the Internet is fast becoming a normalized aspect of the legislative way of life. Where members of Congress once used their Web sites mainly for advertising their legislative accomplishments,[20] or communicating to their constituents,[21] today these electronic portals are more intricately connected with lawmaking.

In the opening chapter, Colton Campbell and David Dulio analyze the political uses of the Internet (both internal and external, positive and negative) in congressional elections. These uses include Internet campaigning, public attitudes toward and beliefs about the Internet as an electioneering tool, legislative restrictions on the use of the Internet by incumbent members of Congress running for reelection, and the regulation of Web-based activity by the Federal Election Commission.

Stephen Frantzich organizes the second chapter around a series of inherent differences between the congressional and the Internet perspectives on the world, with each set of assertions followed by detailed examples and empirical data from the congressional realm to support the assertions. For example, Congress and its members are, by design and practice, geographically based, sensitive to political passions measured by effort, desirous of controlling information retrieval and format, and tasked with mediating values. The Internet and its most common users are potentially disrespectful of geography, accustomed to low-effort communications, routinely used to free-form information-gathering techniques, and are more comfortable with facts than battles over values.

U.S. Representative David Dreier (R-Calif.), chair of the House Rules Committee, shows us in Chapter 3 how the Internet increasingly occupies one of the largest slots in a cluttered legislative calendar. He outlines some of the policy problems the Internet presents to lawmakers, such as privacy, e-government, and taxation.

In Chapter 4, Donald Wolfensberger explores the vast, unknown stretch of territory lying between representation and deliberation, with particular emphasis on how the Internet affects the deliberative nature of Congress. Possible trends are already appearing on Capitol Hill along with hints from various sources about the emerging shape of this latest phase in the mass communications revolution. The historical perspective of how other communications innovations were initially greeted on the Hill, compared to their actual impact, helps us ponder the future impact of the Internet on congressional deliberation.

C. Lawrence Evans and Walter Oleszek, in Chapter 5, look at the multifaceted impact of the Internet on the way decisions are made in Congress. They consider the influence of communications technology within and between offices, committees, and party leaders, including the "message agenda" of each party. Additionally, they review how new technologies are allowed in or introduced to Congress. They conclude with an assessment of how the Internet has reshaped congressional governance.

In Chapter 6, Dennis Johnson analyzes two key challenges facing Congress: the overload of e-mail from constituents and congressional Web sites as communication tools. Much of the research in this chapter is derived from the "Congress Online Project," a two-year study that looks at ways in which Congress has improved communication with constituents and the general public. While e-mail messages to Capitol Hill are now up to a million messages a day, this is not so much a technological challenge, Johnson suggests, as it is a management challenge. Many congressional Web sites, for example, leave much to be desired when actually analyzed by citizens.

Richard Conley's Chapter 7 explores the respective roles of the White House and Capitol Hill in the development and regulation of the Internet from 1993–2000. No single paradigm adequately explicates executive and legislative actions on Internet policy. The concept of "policy entrepreneurship" does, however, cast light on the distinguishable roles played at the opposite ends of Pennsylvania Avenue. This analytical perspective aides in reconciling charges of "policy chaos" with the reality that the 1990s witnessed significant progress toward the delicate balance between governmental promotion of information technology development and regulation of the Internet.

INTRODUCTION   9

In Chapter 8, Jeff Gill and David Conklin look at the details of the E-rate program, an important piece of legislation Congress has passed with regard to the Internet, and examine why it endures in a seemingly hostile political environment. A component of the 1996 Telecommunications Act, E-rate works as a grant mechanism in which organizations, mostly public schools, apply based on local economic conditions and specific educational needs. The E-rate program is a classic and emblematic example of constituency politics in Congress, with the structure of political support among members displaying both traditional and familiar patterns.

Graeme Browning, in Chapter 9, examines how Congress and its members use the Internet for educational outreach. Electronic mail to constituents, the use of palm pilots and laptop computers, and Web casting committee hearings are just a few of the many devices now available to lawmakers for educating and responding to constituents, interest groups, and other political actors in the lawmaking process. Concurrently, these devices present new challenges to an institution that heeds tradition, particularly the Senate, where laptops continue to be banned from use on the chamber floor.

Finally, the afterward by Chris Casey assesses where Congress is at regarding the Internet and looks ahead to where it is going by examining where it has already been. Although it has often moved slowly, almost ten years have passed since Congress first began using the Internet. Milestones that Congress has passed on the Information Superhighway are reviewed, and reflections on the lessons learned and their implications for the future use of the Internet by Congress are discussed.

NOTES

1. See Jeffrey W. Seifert and R. Eric Peterson, *House of Representatives Information Technology Management Issues: An Overview of the Effects on Institutional Operations, the Legislative Process, and Future Planning*, Congressional Research Service Report No. RL31101, August 28, 2001, Washington, D.C.
2. See Chris Casey, *The Hill on the Net: Congress Enters the Information Age* (Boston: AP Professional, 1996); and Anthony G. Wilhelm, *Democracy in the Digital Age: Challenges to Political Life in Cyberspace* (New York: Routledge, 2000).
3. Katy Saldarini, "E-mail Is Overwhelming Congressional Offices," *Government Executive Magazine*, 20 March 2001, <http://www.govexec.com>.
4. George Washington University and the Congressional Management Foundation, *E-Mail Overload in Congress: Managing a Communication Crisis*, Congress Online Project (March 2001), <www.congressonlineproject/email.html>. See also <www.american.edu/ccps>.
5. Seifert and Peterson, *House of Representatives Information Technology Management Issues*, p. 11.
6. Eric Schmitt, "After the Election: For Bewildered House Newcomers, Help Is Just a Mouse-Click Away," *New York Times*, 10 November 1996, p. 30.
7. Quoted in Eric Schmitt, "Capitol Hill Takes to Cyberspace, Though in Fits, Starts, and Stumbles," *New York Times*, 10 July 1996, p. A-12.
8. *Washington Post*, "Congress on the Net," 30 September 1996, p. A-22.
9. Quoted in Mike Soraghan, "Delegates Have Yet to Join E-Mail Age: Campbell, Hefley Worry about Spam," *Denver Post*, 17 October 2001, p. A-15.

10. Ibid.
11. Dongwook Cha, "Internet Communication Structure in U.S. Congress: A Network Analysis" (presented at the Annual Meeting of the American Political Science Association, San Francisco, Calif., August 30–September 2, 2001).
12. R. Sam Garrett, "Congress and the Digital Divide: Are Minorities and Rural Americans Underserved by Congressional Web Sites?" (presented at the Annual Meeting of the Southern Political Science Association, Atlanta, Ga., November 7–10, 2001).
13. Eric M. Uslaner, "Representation," in *The Encyclopedia of the United States Congress*, vol. 3, eds., Donald C. Bacon, Roger H. Davidson, and Morton Keller (New York: Simon & Schuster, 1995).
14. Linton Weeks, "House Web Server Leaving Minority off the Menu; Oversight Panel Defines Majority's Internet Rights," *Washington Post*, 1 July 1996, p. A-15.
15. Gebe Martinez, "Congress Now Posts Its Politicking on Internet," *Los Angeles Times*, 4 September 1996, p. A-1.
16. Quoted in Amy Keller and Paul Kane, "Hill Works through Closures," *Roll Call*, 22 October 2001, <www.rollcall.com>.
17. Adam Clymer, "Cramped and Scattered, Congress Resumes Work," *New York Times*, 24 October 2001, p. B-9.
18. Quoted in Juliet Eilperin, "Away from the Hill, but on the Job," *Washington Post*, 22 October 2001, p. A-17.
19. Sean Piccoli, "Hill Samples 'Third Wave,'" *Washington Times*, 13 June 1995, p. A-8.
20. Diana Owen, Richard Davis, and Vincent James Strickler, "Congress and the Internet," *Press/Politics* 4 (1999), pp. 10–29.
21. Scott E. Adler, Chariti E. Gent, and Cary B. Overmeyer, "The Home Style Homepage: Legislator Use of the World Wide Web for Constituency Contact," *Legislative Studies Quarterly* 23 (1998), pp. 585–595.

CAMPAIGNING ALONG THE INFORMATION HIGHWAY

COLTON C. CAMPBELL[1] AND DAVID A. DULIO

Elections provide defining experiences for newly elected members of Congress—lessons for both winners and losers—and models for those contemplating future races.[2] In the past, campaigns were party-driven contests in which much of the campaign was conducted face-to-face, with volunteers and local parties supporting candidate activity.[3] But with the advent of television, and the growth in the number of eligible voters in elections, the mass media age of televised campaigning was born,[4] changing the way candidates are elected. Are political campaigns undergoing another sea change in the wake of the Internet?

In growing numbers U.S. House and Senate candidates are campaigning along the Information Superhighway. Where campaign Web sites once were little more than digital yard signs,[5] today they are employed to solicit contributions, send targeted messages that can include harsh attacks on opponents, and reach specific types of voters to engineer the most efficient victory with the least public involvement.[6] The most familiar example of a successful use of the Web for electioneering purposes may be Senator John McCain's (R-Ariz.) 2000 presidential campaign, which raised more than $2 million for his primary bid and recruited 26,000 volunteers.[7]

In this chapter we explore the political uses of the Internet in congressional elections—both positive and negative—that are internal and external to the institution. We begin by discussing Internet campaigning. Internet users are disproportionately white and well-educated, with high incomes; they also tend to be registered voters.[8] The Internet is particularly good at tailoring information to the needs of these kinds of individuals, allowing candidates access to an elite audience with high voting norms.[9] This, in turn, has the potential for enabling candidates to promote more efficient targeting of voters that may yield the most support per dollar spent,[10] provided voters use the Internet for election purposes.

We then discuss public attitudes toward and beliefs about the Internet as an electioneering tool. When it comes to voting for congressional candidates, how important is the Internet as a source of information about the election? What are the implications of digital voting? Does it increase participation in congressional elections? Arizona and California, for example, pioneered computerized voting in 2000 when they allowed various voters to cast their votes electronically in their primary and general elections. While Arizona's test led voters to cast nearly 40,000 votes—more than 46 percent of the total—through cyberspace,[11] it was quickly challenged in the judicial arena because it increased the electoral access of affluent persons who owned computers over poorer voters.[12] Are such experiments the future?

We conclude by discussing legislative restrictions on the use of the Internet by incumbent members of Congress running for reelection and the regulation of Web-based campaign activity by the Federal Election Commission. Congressional offices may use their computer systems to generate outreach mail on selected topics to selected audiences, similar to the congressional frank. These electronic mailings are targeted to constituents who have written and expressed an interest in a topic, or to names from lists "harvested" from other sources, such as voter registration and association memberships. Lawmakers are also increasingly sending downloadable video e-mail messages to constituents. In 2002, for example, Senate Democratic hopeful Susan Parker e-mailed a controversial video clip to 130 Alabama union members, a move that successfully targeted specific voters at a fraction of the cost of television ads. The e-video, which showed a union president tearing up Honduran-made t-shirts emblazoned with her opponent's campaign slogan, generated publicity for minimal cost, and proved popular with the union members.[13]

CONGRESSIONAL CAMPAIGNS AND THE WILD, WILD WEB

Computer usage has clearly spread to campaigns. The modern congressional campaign headquarters is no longer a rented storefront decorated with bumper stickers, posters, and bunting. Increasingly it has an annex open any hour of the day or night, at an address starting with www.[14] However, the use of the Web is not yet universal. More Senate candidates than House candidates, more nonincumbents than incumbents, and more candidates in competitive races than those in one-sided contests use the Internet to communicate with voters.[15] But are candidates' Web ventures netting more consumers than traditional campaigning? Do they affect electoral outcomes? The use of the Internet in campaigns is still in an early stage of development, with the most significant use being the traditional realm of campaign fund-raising.

CANDIDATE-CENTERED WEB SITES

Web sites require marginal start-up costs for a candidate, are subsequently easy to maintain, are able to convey a great deal of information quickly with little effort, and are used to mobilize voters with their interactive nature. Generally, congressional campaign Web sites are repositories of information, including the candidate's biography and issue positions, favorable media coverage, a schedule of events, a directory that provides headquarters and staffing information, an area to facilitate voter involvement in the campaign, and negative information on the opposition.[16] Good campaign Web sites are updated regularly throughout the campaign cycle with clearly displayed icons that direct viewers to other areas of the site. They provide on-line arenas that enable individuals to volunteer for campaign activities, and to make on-line contributions, which can be integrated into the campaign's computerized volunteer and finance databases.[17] Some Web sites encourage activists to write op-ed articles, send letters to the editor, or call radio talk shows by providing the names, addresses, and telephone numbers of local media outlets. Some also provide voters with directions to their polling place. Still others develop "electronic precincts," the political version of multilevel marketing in which a campaign volunteer brings in a handful of other volunteers, who in turn bring in more. Hypothetically, the first volunteer, the e-precinct captain, may be rewarded with special briefings, on-line video presentations, an opportunity to meet the candidate, and real-world recognition.[18]

The Internet is particularly good at tailoring information to the needs of the person requesting it, allowing candidates access to an elite audience with high voting norms.[19] E-mail addresses, for example, are efficient and inexpensive ways for candidates to reach voters and prod them to get to the polls. Sending (and forwarding) a message electronically costs a fraction, compared with a letter or telephone call. A growing number of congressional campaign Web sites permit the user to sign up on the campaign's e-mail list. The most commonly used method asks donors and constituents to mail a check directly to the candidate by way of "snail" or surface mail. Others allow donors to download and print a form to be filled out in longhand and then returned to the candidate's headquarters. Still others request pledges, asking the donor to fill out an on-line screen and pledge to mail in the check or a credit card number with a signature.[20] Particularly elaborate Web pages take advantage of secure transaction technology known as a secure socket layer (SSL) that permits on-line contributions using a credit card.[21]

PARTIES ON THE NET

State and local party committees use the Web to compliment traditional party activities, such as attracting volunteers, raising money, mobilizing activists, and registering voters (see, for example, Table 1.1, on page 14, for

Internet activities). State party Web sites often promote particular candidates, with most providing direct links to their home pages. Most state and local parties tailor their Web sites to attract Internet surfers by highlighting a national issue and coaxing the user to support their candidates,[22] or by taking out banner ads on other strategically important Web pages. Due to the relative newness of the Internet, however, many party Web sites are generic. According to one estimate, by 1998, a majority of state and local parties spent less than $1,000 on Web site development.[23]

TABLE 1.1   STATE PARTIES AND THE INTERNET*

INTERNET TECHNOLOGY IN STATE PARTIES	DEMOCRATS	REPUBLICANS
Have a party e-mail address	100%	79%
Utilize an electronic mailing list	67	39
Have a party Web site	67	68
Have integrated voter e-mail addresses into their databases	32	18

STATE PARTIES AND INTERNET ACTIVITY	DEMOCRATS	REPUBLICANS
Volunteering/Member solicitation	57%	57%
Voter registration	25	26
Election Day reminders	50	32
Persuasion mailings	45	32
Fund-raising	20	47
Mobilization for rallies	55	26

INTERNET VOLUNTEERS AND DONATIONS	DEMOCRATS	REPUBLICANS
Have attracted volunteers with their Web site	85%	74%
Have received donations	35	37

STATE PARTY SPENDING ON WEB SITE DEVELOPMENT	DEMOCRATS	REPUBLICANS
Less than $1,000	55%	68%
$1,001–$5,000	25	11
$5,001–$10,000	0	5
$10,001–$25,000	5	5
More than $25,000	5	0

*Information based on survey of fifty-nine state party organizations conducted in February of 1997.
Source: Noah J. Goodhart, "The New Party Machine: Information Technology in State Political Parties," in *The State of the Parties*, ed. John C. Green and Daniel M. Shea (Lanham, MD: Rowman and Littlefield, 1999).

Political Web sites once deemed experimental are coming under increasing scrutiny from both political parties, with both sides looking at the medium with equal intensity. In 2000 the Democratic National Committee spent $1 million to upgrade the software and operation in state parties to allow them to build their professional resources, to invest in a high-tech infrastructure, and to implement new practices.[24] "Whichever party can figure out how to most effectively and efficiently communicate through the Internet," claimed then Democratic National Committee Chair Joe Andrew, "will be the party that will dominate the future."[25] One area in which the Republican National Committee has embraced the Internet is in recruitment of and checking on potential candidates. According to the committee's political director, "the Internet has been a huge and tremendous help. When we recruit a candidate, one of the things we always do is an Internet search and a LEXIS-NEXIS search just to find out as much about them as we can. And that always has either confirmed what we've heard or sometimes thrown up some red flags."[26]

USING THE INTERNET AS A SOURCE OF CAMPAIGN INFORMATION

The elections of 2000 firmly established the Internet as a source of election news and information, but survey results paint a less-than-optimistic picture for this medium as a major campaign tool in future election cycles. Based on data derived from a national survey of 1,005 Americans, eighteen years of age or older,[27] roughly half (48 percent) of those surveyed reported being on-line and using the Internet. Of these, only 28.5 percent indicate using the Web to access information about politics, candidates, or political campaigns. When these individuals are evaluated as part of the entire sample, the number of individuals using the Internet for political purposes among the entire population decreases. All totaled, only 13.8 percent of respondents report actively using the Internet as a medium for acquiring political information.

Little evidence suggests that the general electorate currently take the Internet seriously as an electioneering medium. When compared to more traditional campaign sources—such as television, radio, newspapers and magazines, and candidates' campaigns, political parties, and their network of friends, family, and coworkers—survey results indicate that the Internet ranks last as a valuable information source (see Table 1.2 on page 16). For example, when asked how important different sources of information are for obtaining political information, over 80 percent of all respondents reported that newspapers, magazines, and television are important sources of information, with slightly more than 50 percent saying the same about the Internet. Even less prominent sources like community organizations (i.e., churches, parent-teacher organizations, or the League of Women Voters), labor unions, and business groups fared better than the Internet. This pattern also holds among Internet users as a group; more individuals who actively go on-line report that mass media–based sources are more important than the Internet as conduits of political information. As indicated in Table 1.2, among this group, newspapers and magazines, television, radio, parties' and candidates' campaigns, and community organizations are mentioned with greater frequency; fewer than 66 percent of those surveyed and who are on-line believe the Internet to be an important source of election information.

Those most likely to take advantage of Web-based information over the course of an electoral cycle, and who cast a vote on Election Day (i.e., likely voters and individuals who are well-informed about politics), report with the same frequency as the full sample who see the Internet as an important information source.[28] Only slightly more than half of all likely voters surveyed (57.6 percent)—as well as self-described well-informed individuals (56.8 percent)—view the Internet as an important tool for accessing information about elections (see Table 1.2). Moreover, likely voters are no more inclined than

TABLE 1.2 IMPORTANT SOURCES OF INFORMATION AS DEFINED BY THE GENERAL PUBLIC, MARCH 2000*

INFORMATION SOURCE	ALL RESPONDENTS[a]	INTERNET USERS[b]	LIKELY VOTERS[c]	WELL-INFORMED VOTERS[d]
Newspapers and magazines	86.2%	88.5%	87.6%	86.4%
Television	84.0	81.2	83.6	84.1
Political parties' and candidates' campaigns	79.4	79.5	87.1	81.4
Community organizations	76.0	73.9	78.1	76.4
Radio	75.2	73.9	76.0	75.3
Friends, family, and coworkers	75.2	70.5	73.2	73.6
Labor unions and business groups	62.0	56.5	58.7	61.6
Internet	56.5	65.6	57.6	56.8
Percentages based on sample size	N = 1,005	N = 488	N = 277	N = 794

*Percentages reflect the respondents who reported that the information source was either "very important" or "somewhat important" for collecting information about the election.
[a]These figures are based on the total sample of respondents.
[b]These figures are based on those in the sample who said that they were Internet users.
[c]Likely voters were determined by respondents' answers to a series of questions.
[d]Well-informed voters are self-identified.
Note: Percentages do not include those respondents who answered "Don't know," or refused to give a response.

nonlikely voters to see the Internet as an important source of information (57.6 percent of likely voters classified the Internet as important compared to 56 percent of nonlikely voters). Comparatively, however, they are much more likely than their nonlikely voter counterparts to see parties' and candidates' campaigns as important sources of information (87.1 percent compared to 76.5 percent).[29]

The only substantial and meaningful differences in the evaluation of the Internet as an information tool lie between age cohorts. Two-thirds of individuals between the ages of eighteen and thirty-four report using the Internet to learn about elections, compared to 56 percent of those between ages of thirty-five to forty-nine, and 47 percent of those fifty years and older. Nearly one-third of the latter group indicates that the Internet is not important at all, compared to just 14 percent of the youngest age cohort. Interestingly, those members of the electorate between the ages of eighteen and thirty-five determined to be likely voters in this survey are no more likely than those unlikely to vote to say that the Internet is an important source for election information. So as young individuals in the electorate become older and more likely to participate in politics, the Internet may assume a larger, more important role as a source to educate voters. Similarly, this young cohort may lead even younger cohorts that are *more* dependent on the Internet onto the electoral scene.

Political discourse over the role of the Internet in politics centers on it being a new source of information void of the "spin" that regularly accompanies candidate- or group-sponsored television commercials and direct mail. But such an assumption that political information contained on the Internet is purely informational, consumed by a hungry public, is flawed. Internet material is just as prone to spin as television advertisements or direct-mail literature. Moreover, the survey data suggest that the Internet is not an information source that many turn to for information concerning their voting decisions. A general evaluation and rating of the Internet is not the same as a personal inventory of what activities respondents see themselves undertaking on-line.

WEB-BASED ELECTIONEERING ACTIVITIES

A fairly lucent representation of the Internet as an electioneering tool is seen when examining the types of political activities individuals perform on the Net and, more importantly, the frequency with which they perform them during an electoral cycle. Few take advantage of the Internet in this regard, as just 30 percent of those surveyed report they would actively use the Internet to get information about a candidate or acquire information about campaign issues. Less than 10 percent of respondents using the Internet reportedly will use the Web to communicate with a candidate (8.4 percent), volunteer for a campaign (4.5 percent), or donate money to a campaign (3.3 percent).[30]

TABLE 1.3   POTENTIAL POLITICAL ACTIVITY ON THE INTERNET, MARCH 2000

ACTIVITY	INTERNET USERS[a]	LIKELY VOTERS[b]
Get information about candidates	35.3%	41.0%
Get information about various issues	31.1	32.4
Forward a voting-related e-mail to a friend	18.0	25.7
Communicate or "chat" with others about issues	14.7	14.3
Communicate or "chat" with a candidate	8.4	8.6
Volunteer for a campaign	4.5	6.7
Donate money to a campaign	3.3	5.7
Percentages based on sample size	N = 448	N = 277

[a]These figures are based on those in the sample who said that they were Internet users.
[b]Likely voters were determined by respondents' answers to a series of questions.

A similar pattern is found among likely voters, although greater percentages of these individuals say they would use the Internet to be active in each of the different activities (see Table 1.3). For example, 41 percent of likely voters said that they used the Internet to gather information about candidates during the election of 2000, compared to only 35.3 percent of all Internet users. However, when likely voters' responses as to whether they planned to take advantage of the Internet are compared to nonlikely voters, differences surface. Likely voters are more likely to report their intent to use the Internet to gather information about candidates.[31] Likely voters also are more inclined to forward a voting-related e-mail to a friend or colleague.[32]

ACTIVATING VOTERS OVER THE INTERNET

Despite the use of the Internet as an information source and a tool for electioneering, the general public is both resistant to and skeptical of using the Internet to register and to vote. Roughly 40 percent of the entire sample surveyed say that using the Internet to register individuals is a "good idea," with less than a third saying the same about allowing people to vote on-line. Nearly 85 percent express concerns about fraudulent behavior taking place on the Web if it is employed as a voting tool. This kind of skepticism and doubt is not unwarranted considering the opportunity for "hackers" to contaminate lists of registered voters or Election Day vote totals. Even though current technology allows for "secure servers" and encryption devices to transmit credit card numbers and personal information through telephone and fiber optic lines, many Americans seem unready to entrust their vote to Web-based technology, especially in the aftermath of questionable conduct on Election Day 2000 in places from Palm Beach County, Florida, to St. Louis, Missouri.[33] Indeed, less than a third of all individuals in the survey say they would use the Internet, if available, to either register to vote or cast a ballot (28.2 percent and 25.3 percent respectively).

A silver lining in these data is that while the Internet's impact on individuals' access to political information is marginal, with many shying away from expanding the Net to permit election registration and voting, this new medium may be a way to expand political participation for those who otherwise are left behind on Election Day, namely those unregistered to vote who are automatically disqualified and nonlikely voters. Obviously, those who are not registered cannot vote on Election Day. For individuals who avoid registering because of various administrative burdens,[34] the Internet may alleviate some of these problems. This is particularly the case with first-time registrants, those who move frequently (e.g., college students), or those who must re-register because they have been purged from the rolls.[35] Individuals in the sample who were *not* currently registered to vote, for example, were much more likely than currently registered voters (64.6 percent to 46.6 percent respectively) to say that voter registration via the Internet was a good idea (see Table 1.4).[36] Those individuals not currently registered were also more likely to favor using the Internet to vote than were those who were already registered to vote (50 percent compared to 34 percent).[37] While nonregistered individuals are just as concerned about the possibility of fraud in this process (85.9 percent said they were at least somewhat concerned), they also are more willing to employ the Web as a campaign tool and become active. For example, 34 percent of all nonregistered individuals in the sample say they would use the Internet to register if it were available, compared to just 27 percent who were already registered,[38] and over a third of all nonregistered respondents say they would actually use the Web to cast a ballot on Election Day, compared to only 23 percent of those currently registered.[39]

TABLE 1.4 USING THE INTERNET TO REGISTER VOTERS (BY REGISTRATION STATUS)

	ARE YOU CURRENTLY REGISTERED TO VOTE?	
USING THE INTERNET TO REGISTER TO VOTE IS A . . .	NO	YES
Good idea	64.6% (84)	46.6% (341)
Bad idea	35.4 (46)	53.4 (391)
Total	100.0% (130)	100.0% (732)

Note: Fisher's Exact test – p = 0.000.
Note: Numbers in parentheses are cell Ns.

Additionally, those individuals who do not meet the criteria used to classify respondents as likely voters are more inclined than those who are classified as likely voters to report using the Internet as a good idea, both to register (54.3 percent compared to 36.7 percent) and to vote (50.4 percent compared to 25.4 percent).[40] Nonlikely voters report that they are not as concerned about fraud as are likely voters (84.1 percent and 90.7 percent, respectively, say they are at least somewhat concerned). Conceivably, this explains nonlikely voters' greater propensity to say that they will use the Internet to register to vote and to cast a ballot electronically. Close to 30 percent of all those identified as nonlikely voters say they are inclined to use the Internet to register and to vote, compared to only 21 percent and 16 percent (respectively) of likely voters.[41] In sum, the potential benefit of the Internet as an electioneering tool is that it can help to encourage the participation of those who are both locked out of and turned off to the process.

CONGRESS AND THE INTERNET

The Internet has certainly impacted how the average citizen can interact with Congress. People now have greater access to lawmakers[42] and to information about the legislative process. Individual members, committees, leadership, caucuses, and legislative support groups have Web sites that describe key legislative activity and programs and help citizens get answers to commonly asked questions, such as how to apply to the service academies, how to arrange a visit to Capitol Hill, how to contact the office, or how to research legislation. At the beginning of the 104th Congress (1995–1997) there were very few e-mail addresses for House members and no House committee Web sites. The House processed virtually all legislative information through paper-based systems. Use of paper and ink as a method of communication was so entrenched that the electronic files were actually discarded once the paper documents were created. Internet-savvy lawmakers, spearheaded by former House Speaker Newt Gingrich's (R-Ga.) futuristic proclivities, helped to move Congress on-line in the 1990s. "As more people use the Internet as a way to communicate, do business, and educate our children," declared Representative Richard A. White (R-Wash.), "we in Congress need to make sure that we are using this new medium as a way to communicate with our constituents. By posting committee reports, voting records, and other documents on the Internet we will give the public access to the same information we in Congress have."[43]

Today, all members have gone on-line and each standing committee has allocated disk space on the Web server for the purpose of providing access to congressional information.[44] Table 1.5 and Figure 1.1 illustrate the growth in overall House Web sites and the proliferation of reported Web site hits between 1995 and 2000. Where only 91 House members and 5 committees built

TABLE 1.5 CHRONOLOGY OF HOUSE WEB SITES

	MEMBER	COMMITTEE
104th Congress		
1995	91	5
1996	222	8
105th Congress		
1997	338	19
1998	409	19
106th Congress		
1999	431	21
2000	438	22

Source: Prepared by House Information Resources, U.S. House of Representatives, October 13, 2000.

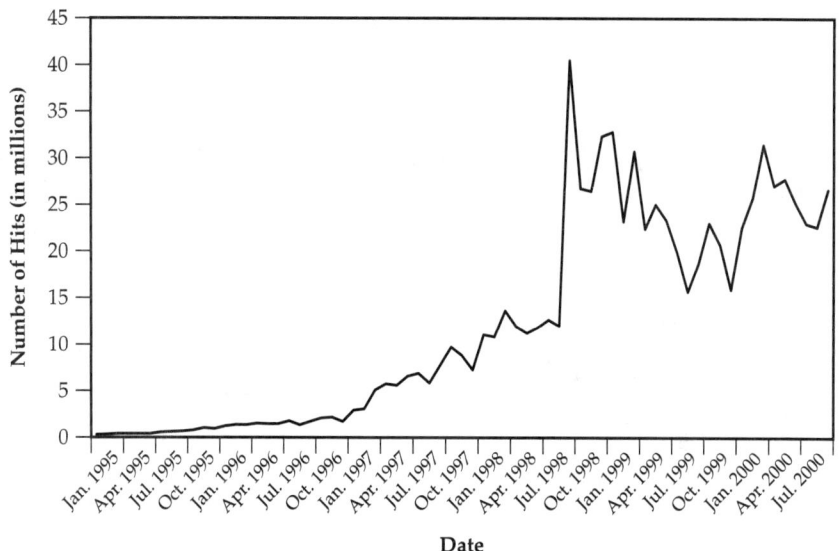

FIGURE 1.1 WEB HITS ON <WWW.HOUSE.GOV> HOSTED SITES

Source: Authors' tabulation from data provided by House Information Resources, U.S. House of Representatives, October 13, 2000.

Web sites in 1995, all 438 members and 22 standing committees reported having Web pages in 2000.[45] At the start of the 104th Congress, when Congress first went on-line, 168,175 Web hits were reported on House-hosted sites. Near the end of the 106th Congress (1999–2001), 26,567,014 hits were reported, following a high of over 40 million hits during the start of the Clinton impeachment and delivery of the Starr Report to Capitol Hill in 1998.[46]

The uniqueness and speed with which e-mail enables communications has changed the dynamics of how news is disseminated from lawmakers. The traditional cornerstone of congressional publicity is the franking privilege, which is the right of members to send out mail at no cost to them with their signature—or frank—instead of a stamp.[47] The majority of these mass mailings are general-purpose newsletters blanketing home states or districts, often upbeat accounts of the legislator's activities. While intended to facilitate official communication between elected officials and their constituents—current franking laws confer wide mailing privileges but prohibit use of the frank for mail unrelated to official congressional business, activities, or duties—in recent times members have found that the aggressive use of the frank can aid in their quest for reelection.[48] In the Senate, existing rules regarding electronic communications parallel franking regulations, and the assumption is that this new format of direct mass mailings violates political challengers' right to compete for office free of government-imposed handicaps. In the House, however, proponents counter that the Internet is a distinctly separate medium from surface or "snail" mail, advocating loosened regulations in terms of mass e-mails.[49]

SENATE

In the Senate, during the sixty-day period immediately preceding the date of any primary or general election (whether regular, special, or runoff) for any national, state, or local office in which a senator is a candidate, no member may place, update, or transmit information using his or her Web site, unless the candidacy in the election is uncontested. Similar to franked mail, senators are prohibited from transmitting electronic mail through the Senate Internet Server, which consists of the FTP Server, Gopher, and World Wide Web, sixty days before the date of the member's primary or general election unless it is in response to a direct inquiry. The use of the Web for personal, promotional, commercial, or partisan political/campaign purposes is prohibited, nor may senators, or committee chairs and officers of the Senate, post to the Web information files, which contain matter relating to their official business, activities, and duties. And official records, such as bills, public laws, committee reports, and other legislative materials, may not be posted unless otherwise approved by the Secretary of the Senate.[50]

Additionally, e-mail may not be transmitted by a member during the sixty-day period unless it is in response to a direct inquiry. No senator may place or update on the Internet server any matter on behalf of a senator who is a candidate for election sixty days preceding the election, unless the candidacy of the senator in such election is uncontested. Senators under such restrictions must indicate on their home page that pursuant to Senate policy their home page may not be updated for the sixty-day period immediately before the date of a primary or general election (the words "Senate Policy" must be hypertext linked to the Internet services policy on the U.S. Senate Home Page).

A senator's home page may not refer or be hypertext linked to another member's site or electronic mail address without authorization from that member, and any links to information not located on a Senate Internet server must be identified as a link to a non-Senate entity.[51]

Senators are prohibited from posting on or linking to their Web sites political matter, which "specifically solicits political support for the sender or any other person or political party, or a vote or financial assistance for any candidate for any political office."[52] Nor may individual Web pages post matter that mentions a senator or an employee of a senator as a candidate for political office, constitutes electioneering, or advocates the election or defeat of any individuals. Senators are prohibited from linking their home page to a political party page that is used for posting matter that is purely personal and unrelated to the official business activities and duties of the sender. This includes any article, account, sketch, narration, or other text laudatory and complimentary of a senator on a personal or political basis rather than on the basis of performance or official duties; reports of how or when a senator or family member spends time other than in the performance of, or in connection with, the legislative, representative, and other official functions; and any transmission expressing holiday greetings.[53] Promotional matter, such as the solicitation of funds for any purpose is also prohibited, as well as the placement of logos or links used for personal, promotional, commercial, or partisan political/campaign purposes.

House

The House has been less receptive to such preelection blackouts on the Internet. In June of 2000, the House Committee on Administration considered a resolution and tasked the committee's staff to revise unsolicited mass communication restrictions to include electronically transmitted messages. Currently, members must obtain an advisory opinion from the House Franking Commission[54] prior to sending out five hundred or more unsolicited communications regardless of format. The resolution under consideration would have amended franking regulations, relieving House offices from getting franking advice from the Franking Commission prior to sending out *five* or more unsolicited e-mails to constituents who have individually subscribed to receive periodic e-mail updates. Accordingly, the e-mail would still adhere to all of the franking regulations, and members would submit copies of the subscribed e-mail update to the commission at the time of transmission.

At the heart of discussion in the Committee on Administration was a proposal that all mass e-mail communications contain three disclaimers. The first would acknowledge the congressional office from which the communication is sent. The second would affirm that the recipient resides in the congressional district and that the e-mail is sent under the member's name, not forwarded by someone else; if not, the recipient would be instructed to remove his or her name from the mailing list. And the third would confirm that if the recipient were a media entity that it served the congressional district. Of particular concern were the format and content of these disclaimers. "We don't have to put that on the newsletters we send out," charged Representative Vernon J. Ehlers (R-Mich.). "Why in the world do we want to require a very officious statement of that nature on the e-mails we send out?"[55] Ehlers went on to say the following:

> I don't know about others, but in Michigan, where I live in Grand Rapids, I send my communications out to many other areas of the State because much of what I do affects the State of Michigan. It is not just my district. I don't work just for my district; I work for my State. In fact, I work for my country. And I don't see why I am not allowed to send mass e-mail communications outside of my district to the media.[56]

Representative Steny H. Hoyer (D-Md.), supported this viewpoint, suggesting that such reporting requirements went beyond "that which is necessary or appropriate in terms of dissemination of the information" (*House Committee on Administration* 2000, 20). "I am on the Appropriations Committee, and I consider myself responsible for more than just the 5th Congressional District." Committee Vice Chairman John A. Boehner (R-Ohio) expressed concern that the resolution would prompt members to ignore the rules, or to force them to send e-mail to their campaign to distribute. "We have taken all of the franking rules and just applied them carte blanche to e-mail," he said.[57]

Another snare during debate involved the proposed restriction of mass e-mail communications ninety days before an election, in sync with House franking rules. Representative Ehlers was first on the committee to express reservation:

> My office and I know many offices are now doing this, with the e-mail they send out, an e-mail newsletter every Friday, which just summarizes what happened that week.
> It is not partisan; it is just simply an informational summary of these bills that were taken up; this is the result of the bills. And my constituents are finding that useful; the e-mail list is growing. I think my constituents and your constituents, if you do the same thing, will find it a bit strange that, suddenly, three months before the election, they are not allowed to hear from me about what the Congress has done in a non-partisan way.[58]

When solicited to respond, a committee staff member indicated that he and other staffers held numerous discussions internally and within the House about potential abuses of e-mail. "I think that, clearly, e-mail is a different medium and the per unit cost drives perhaps some different behavior, and we want to try to open up that process to do that," the staff member said.[59] "We had discussions with members to say that in the case of, for example, Mr. Ehlers in Science wanting to communicate with a broad science constituency across the country, not limited by a ninety-day blackout period, for example, that that communication consent came, in effect, from a Science Committee as opposed to in his individual office."

After a few more questions, the committee unanimously moved to send the proposal back to staff, and the motion to reconsider was laid upon the table, effectively killing any chance that the regulation would be amended.

REGULATING WEB CAMPAIGN ACTIVITY

Campaign regulations written before the Internet came of age threaten to stifle Web politicking in modern elections.[60] In a series of opinions handed down since 1996, the Federal Election Commission (FEC) has found numerous problems with Web-based electioneering, and has enacted several rules to address these problems. Election Web-site operators, according to the FEC, even if they are just individual voters, must now identify themselves on-line. Web sites operating independently of official campaigns must register with the FEC if they spend $250 or more, including costs of a PC used to build and maintain a site, software, and the Internet connection used to keep the site live. And corporations, already banned from contributing directly to campaigns, are prohibited from providing forums in which candidates can express their views.

The early part of the 2000 New York senatorial race between then–First Lady Hillary Clinton and then–New York mayor Rudy Guiliani illustrates some of these issues. While traditional candidate Web sites were created and maintained by the two candidates, a number of creatively named ones, such as HillaryNo.com (sponsored by the "Friends of Guiliani") popped up to take aim at the candidates. An anti-Guiliani Web site deviously dubbed YesRudy.com offered mouse-clickers a decidedly different take on the mayor's all-but-certain Senate bid than his official site, RudyYes.com. Unlike HillaryNo.com, however, which wasted little time in getting to its negative message, the new anti-Guiliani page was a subtler, almost sneaky affair. Developed by a California-based group, RT Mark, the spoof site virtually mirrored the mayor's official site, with its photos, icons, and layout. Even Guiliani's signature was identical. Only in the text did the sites veer from one another, such as when the mayor seemingly boasts of having made New York "a vital hub . . . that increasingly focuses the world's wealth in a few million white hands."[61]

Other groups came in with other sites devoted to forwarding their favored candidate. Among the issues intertwined here is one that has been termed "cybersquatting," which simply refers to an individual or group that purchases an Internet domain name that is similar to or exactly like another individual's name. In this case a group purchased a domain name similar to Guiliani's official site. There is nothing illegal about this, of course, as they filed in accordance with the FEC guidelines. As the director of Guiliani's political committee, Bruce Teitelbaum, said, "We spoke to lawyers who specialize in this kind of work. They said there is absolutely no recourse we have."[62] Although it is not any different from an outside group getting into a race and running a deceptive television commercial, whether it is ethical is another story—as Teitelbaum remarked: "It snookers people in."[63]

Conclusion

The Internet is many things simultaneously—a broadcast medium; a gigantic bulletin board; a collaboration tool for businesses, government, nonprofit groups, and political organizations; and a huge post office for electronic mail[64]—and has impacted nearly every aspect of congressional life. This powerful new medium is creating revolutionary challenges and opportunities, drawing strong comparisons to the Guttenberg Press as a prodigious tool for political change.[65] It is fast becoming an instrument for citizens seeking to organize with like-minded people, to petition government, and to speak out on elections.[66] Similarly, candidates can interact with voters through Internet chatrooms.

The Internet is lowering the cost of entry into campaigns by allowing candidates to create "virtual" headquarters in cyberspace, reducing the need for the expensive hardware of a traditional organization: offices, furniture, fax and copy machines, stationary, and postage. But in many ways, the Web is a difficult fit for congressional campaigns and candidates who are slow to adapt. Politics remains a geographically based domain, in which members of Congress are selected for states or districts, and voters still expect them to ask for voter support. "All politics are local," former House Speaker Thomas P. (Tip) O'Neill (D-Mass.) was fond of saying. Candidates must use styles and address issues in ways that have long appealed to voters of their districts and states. But the informal World Wide Web is a realm without geography.[67] Unlike television or radio, it is hard to use the Internet to proactively seek out and activate a passive audience. On the Internet, the audience must already be motivated and searching for information.

While an increasing number of campaigns have experimented with on-line contributions, the results are scant at best. Few have experience with the Web. Instead, they must experiment and learn, then, in the next iteration, use the medium more fully.[68] Those campaigns that effectively adopt existing technologies and applications do so with little or no adaptation to the political environment. In many instances, campaigns are using the Internet to fight the same ground war they have always fought, and if the results are not fruitful, they simply discard the Internet as somehow ineffectual.

While not entirely conclusive, the survey data suggest some preliminary findings. First, those in the electorate who are politically active, and who are on-line, are likely to take advantage of the Internet as a campaign tool. However, these individuals are predisposed to favor a particular candidate or an established position, and thus use the Internet to seek information about their candidates. Second, young individuals are more likely to utilize the Web as an electioneering tool than their older cohorts. But until those who place a heavy reliance on the Internet in their daily lives become a larger part of the electorate who participates in large numbers, the Internet will conceivably have a small, if not negligible, effect on elections. An indication of this trend is that likely voters (as well as those who self-identify themselves as being well-informed) also report that they will utilize the Internet to volunteer or to make a campaign donation in greater numbers than all Internet users. Overall, however, those who use the Internet view it as an additional resource to campaign activity, rather than an unearthing medium.

The benefit of the Internet as an electioneering tool may be that it can help encourage the participation of those who are locked out of and turned off by the process.[69] Only if Internet-savvy individuals become the norm among the voting public will the Internet then become a key component of congressional elections. The resistance to using it by both likely and registered voters is probably attributed to the fact that this demographic already actively participates in elections. But this is not surprising, considering that individuals who register to vote have already taken sufficient steps—even if it means simply filling out a form while waiting in line for a driver's license—to become eligible to vote. They will, therefore, need less assistance to use the Internet in future congressional elections than those who are guaranteed to be shut out of the process.

Ironically, a strange juxtaposition exists regarding the Internet and congressional elections. Great care and attention is devoted to regulating what members of Congress may do with their home pages and electronic communication. However, empirical data suggest that these regulations may be premature. Future congressional elections may benefit from recent congressional action to outline Web-based activity.

Notes

1. The authors express their appreciation to the Pew Charitable Trusts and the Center for Congressional and Presidential Studies at American University for use of the survey data (see <www.american.edu/ccps> for further analysis of the survey), as well as Jay Eagen, Chief Administrative Officer of the U.S. House of Representatives, and Dr. John Pontius of the Congressional Research Service for their valuable assistance and support.
2. Roger H. Davidson and Colton C. Campbell, "The Irony of the 105th Congress and Its Legacy," in *Politics in an Era of Divided Government: Elections and Governance in the Second Clinton Administration*, ed. Harvey L. Schantz (New York: Garland Publishing, Inc, 2000).
3. Paul S. Herrnson, *Party Campaigning in the 1980s* (Cambridge: Harvard University Press, 1988); and Paul S. Herrnson, *Congressional Elections: Campaigning at Home and in Washington*, 3rd ed. (Washington, D.C.: CQ Press, 2000).

4. Robert J. Dinkin, *Campaigning in America: A History of Election Practices* (Westport, CT: Praeger, 1989); and Stephen K. Medvic, *Political Consultants in U.S. Congressional Elections* (Columbus, OH: Ohio State University Press, 2001).
5. Chris Casey, *The Hill on the Net: Congress Enters the Information Age* (Boston: AP Professional, 1996).
6. Steven E. Schier, *By Invitation Only: The Rise of Exclusive Politics in the United States* (Pittsburgh, PA: University of Pittsburgh Press, 2000).
7. John Mintz, "Political Groups Scramble to Find E-Mail Addresses of Likely Backers," *Washington Post*, 22 October 2000, p. A-21.
8. Michael J. Martinez, "Who Are Internet Users?" *abcnews.com*, 1998, <abcnews.go.com/sections/tech/DailyNews/www.survey980714.html>.
9. Jim Drinkard, "E-Politics: How the Net Is Transforming Grass-Roots Campaigns," *USA Today*, 31 August 1999 (accessed on LEXIS-NEXIS, October 27, 2000); and Schier, *By Invitation Only*.
10. Schier, *By Invitation Only*, p. 102.
11. Paul S. Herrnson, "Elections Are More Than Just a Game," in *Playing Hardball: Campaigning for the U.S. Congress*, ed. Paul S. Herrnson (Upper Saddle River, NJ: Prentice Hall, 2000); and Richard Wolf, "Arizona Voters Click into History," *USA Today*, 10 March 2000, p. A-3.
12. Ben White, "Candidates' Web Ventures Are Netting Fewer Consumers, Pew Survey Shows," *Washington Post*, 3 December 2000, p. A-28.
13. Sarita Chourey, "Incumbents Still Shunning Online Campaigns," *The Hill*, 3 April 2002, p. 13.
14. Tina Kelly, "Candidate on the Stump Is Surely on the Web," *New York Times*, October 19, 1999 (accessed on LEXIS-NEXIS, October 27, 2000).
15. Herrnson, *Congressional Elections*, p. 214.
16. Ibid.
17. Ibid.
18. Kelly, "Candidate on the Stump Is Surely on the Web."
19. Drinkard, "E-Politics"; and Schier, *By Invitation Only*.
20. Mary Clare Jalonick, "Bringing in the Bucks on the Web," *Campaigns & Elections* (April 2000), pp. 48–49.
21. David A. Dulio, Donald L. Goff, and James A. Thurber, "Untangled Web: Internet Use during the 1998 Election," *Political Science and Politics* 32 (1999), pp. 53–59. For other studies and links related to this topic, see <www.american.edu/ccps>.
22. John Kenneth White and Daniel M. Shea, *New Party Politics* (New York: Bedford-St.Martin's, 2000), p. 203.
23. Ibid.
24. Emiliene Ireland and Phil Tajitsu Nash, "Campaign 2000: Parties Vie for Internet Dominance," *Campaigns & Elections* (October 1999), pp. 1–7.
25. Quoted in ibid.
26. Ibid.
27. This survey was developed by the Center for Congressional and Presidential Studies at American University and administered by Yankelovich Partners, Inc. The research is part of the "Improving Campaign Conduct" project at CCPS, which is funded by a grant from the Pew Charitable Trusts. More information about the survey may be found at <www.campaignconduct.com>.
28. This is a special group of individuals given that they were determined to be likely to vote in the election that was more than eight months away. Likely voters were modeled with the help of Yankelovich Partners, who administered the survey, in order to be careful only to include those who were the most likely to be active members of the electorate in November.
29. Fisher's Exact test – p = 0.000; table not reported.
30. These figures are only for those individuals who said that they currently used the Internet.
31. 41 percent to 33 percent respectively, Fisher's Exact test – p = 0.09; table not reported.
32. 25.7 percent compared to 14.4 percent of nonlikely voters, Fisher's Exact test – p = 0.01; table not reported.
33. Questionable activity in Florida refers to accusations by many African Americans that election officials prevented them from casting a ballot through intimidation and notices that they were not legally registered, and that their ballots were not counted fairly. On November 7, 2000 in St. Louis, Missouri, a court decision to keep polling places open later than usual was struck down by a higher court at the request of state officials.

34. Raymond E. Wolfinger and Steven J. Rosenstone, *Who Votes?* (New Haven, CT: Yale University Press, 1980).
35. The United States, unlike many European nations, places the burden of registration on the individual. In other nations where registration is handled by the state, similar problems do not exist. See, for example, Douglas J. Amy, *Real Choices/New Voices*, 2nd ed. (New York: Columbia University Press, 2002).
36. Fisher's Exact test – p = 0.000.
37. Fisher's Exact test – p = 0.000; table not reported.
38. Fisher's Exact test – p = 0.09; table not reported.
39. Fisher's Exact test – p = 0.000.
40. p = 0.000 in both Fisher's Exact tests; table not reported.
41. p = 0.000 for both Fisher's Exact tests; table not reported.
42. Thomas Edsall, "In Congress, They've Got Mail—Far Too Much of It," *Washington Post*, 19 March 2001, p. A-5.
43. *Congressional Record*, 104th Cong., 2nd sess., June 13, 1996, E1087.
44. Representatives initially stored their Web sites on servers maintained by the House Information Resources, which did not allow the use of complicated computer coding because of security and stability concerns. The House Administration Committee has written new rules allowing members from both parties to use servers maintained by private companies, which have the ability to host the latest technology safely.
45. The Senate first offered on-line services to members and committee offices in the 103rd Congress (1993–1995). In June of 1993 the first of these services was brought on-line, providing senators with the ability to send and receive e-mail over the Internet. By November of the same year, the Rules Committee approved the establishment of a Senate FTP/Gopher site for members' and committees' use. These capabilities provided Senate offices the ability to post information such as press releases as well as to communicate with constituents over the Internet.
46. U.S. Congress, House of Representatives, Information Resources 2000. These figures are total "hits" to House Web sites, which can be misleading, since they count each time someone accesses or returns to a page, not how often they visit an entire site.
47. Roger H. Davidson and Walter J. Oleszek, *Congress and Its Members*, 7th ed. (Washington, D.C.: CQ Press, 2001).
48. Ibid.
49. U.S. Congress, House Committee on Administration, *Campaign Reform and Election Integrity Act of 1999*, 106th Cong., 1st sess., H. Rept. 106-295, 1999.
50. U.S. Congress, Senate Committee on Rules and Administration, *Internet Services Usages Rules and Policies*, 104th Cong., 2nd sess., July 22, 1996.
51. Ibid.
52. Ibid.
53. This promotion does not preclude an expression of holiday greetings at the commencement or conclusion of an otherwise proper transmission.
54. The House Commission on Congressional Mailing Standards was established in 1973 for the principle of congressional self-regulation. The Franking Commission was created and authorized to hear and decide cases concerning abuse of franking privilege as well as to issue regulations and to provide counsel and instruction to members and their staff.
55. House Committee on Administration, *Campaign Reform and Election Integrity Act of 1999*, p. 18.
56. Ibid., p. 19.
57. Ibid., p. 21.
58. Ibid., p. 22.
59. Ibid., p. 23.
60. Will Rodger, "Net Parody Exposes Holes in Election Laws," *USA Today Tech Report*, <www.usatoday.com>, July 28, 1999; Will Rodger, "Regs Hinder Online Campaign Support," *USA Today Tech Report*, <www.usatoday.com>, July 28, 1999; and Will Rodger, "Net Election Stumping Runs Afoul of Laws," *USA Today Tech Report*, <www.usatoday.com>, October 27, 2000.
61. Quoted in Dave Saltonstall and Michael O. Allen, "Web Payback for Hizzoner," *New York Daily News*, 15 August 1999, p. 29
62. Quoted in Adam Nagourney, "Parody on the Web Mocks Guiliani's Senate Hopes," *New York Times*, 14 August 1999, p. B-3.

63. Ibid.
64. Kevin A. Hill and John E. Hughes, *Cyberpolitics: Citizen Activism in the Age of the Internet* (Lanham, MD: Rowman & Littlefield Publishers, 1998).
65. U.S. Congress, Senate Committee on Rules and Administration, *Political Speech on the Internet*, 106th Cong., 2nd sess., S. Rept. 105-226, 2000, p. 1.
66. Bruce Bimber, "The Internet and Political Mobilization: Research Note on the 1996 Election Season," *Social Science Computer Review* 16 (1998), pp. 391–401; and Bruce Bimber, "The Internet and Citizen Communication with Government: Does the Medium Matter?" *Political Communication* 16 (1999), pp. 409–428
67. Drinkard, "E-Politics."
68. Dulio, Goff, and Thurber, "Untangled Web."
69. Marc Strassman, "An Internet E-Ballot for Democracy: Feasible and Cost-Effective, Electronic Voting Could Empower Citizens," *Los Angeles Times*, 31 January 1999, p. B-17.

REPRESNETATION

CONGRESS AND THE INTERNET

STEPHEN E. FRANTZICH

One can almost hear the crunch of metal as one ancient institution (at least in the political realm) and new technology collide. For all the promises of cyberdemocracy-enhanced political linkages, in some ways, the interface of Congress and the Internet is a match made in hell. Divorce is not possible, but tensions are inevitable. The basic premises and operating procedures of Congress and the Internet diverge widely. Congress and its members are by design and practice geographically based, sensitive to political passion as measured by effort, desirous of controlling information retrieval and format, and tasked with mediating values. The Internet and its most common users are by design and potential disrespectful of geography, accustomed to low-effort communications, habituated to free-form information gathering, and are more comfortable with facts than battles over values.

What happens when seemingly incompatible institutions attempt to co-exist? Technologies do not impact on stable institutions, like two rudderless ships colliding at night, according to inexorable laws of nature and physics. Members of institutions take evasive measures and adapt technologies for their personal and institutional benefit. Kenneth Laudon put it as follows:

> Information technology is a malleable tool whose ultimate social meaning, content and consequences are highly subject to the influence of specific political values and interests that inform its use.[1]

In the early days of computerization in Congress, grand plans to use the technology to rationalize congressional working procedures often ran headlong into political realities. After spending over $10 million on the Committee Information and Scheduling System (COMIS), which created a matrix matching every member's committee schedules to avoid conflict, it became clear that committee chairs did not necessarily want to reduce conflicts. Missing members from the opposition party may well facilitate a committee decision. Chairs refused to input their scheduling plans and the program lay unused.[2] Many of the "good ideas" for technical fixes were bypassed in favor of immediate needs with practical political payoffs. Correspondence management became the king of the hill during early computer applications because it helped solve the real need to tame the mountains of incoming mail and to provide individual members a service crucial to their political survival.[3]

The Internet is another extension of the wave of technological options to which Congress has been forced to react over its history. The major difference seems to be the acceleration of the speed at which new options appear and the limited life cycle of many applications. A decade ago gopher systems ruled the roost as the efficient way to distribute new information in textual form. The day in the sun for gophers was little more than a nanosecond in human history. Betting on the wrong technology is particularly embarrassing and politically dangerous for public institutions, which face both direct dangers to their operational capabilities and the indirect dangers of being called into account for misusing public funds. Given their average age and the focus of efforts required to get into Congress, few members have significant personal experience with the Internet. They need to be convinced that the benefits of use by the Congress are real and the risks are manageable. The emphasis of this paper will be on the potential impact of the Internet on representation: the process by which members "re-present" (present a second time) the interests of the citizenry. It specifically excludes a discussion of numerous other methods of using the Internet, such as policy research, internal communication, and specific political campaign applications. Although on the functional level most of the technology use (including the Internet) in Congress is a staff function, the term "members" will be used in an expansive sense to include individual members and their staffs as they work together as a team. The paper is organized around a series of inherent differences between the congressional and the Internet[4] perspectives on the world, with each set of assertions followed by detailed examples and empirical data from the congressional realm to support the assertions.

THE INTERNET DISCONNECTS: CONGRESS, THE INTERNET, AND "ILLEGAL FUNCTION CALLS" OVER THE BACK FENCE VERSUS THE NETWORK NEIGHBORHOOD

CONGRESSIONAL PERSPECTIVE: GEOGRAPHICAL REPRESENTATION

For both practical and philosophical reasons, Congress was designed to represent the interests of individuals and groups in geographic constituencies. Members were expected to re-present (present a second time) the wishes of their legally (and geographically) defined constituents who held sway over potentially errant members with their votes. On the practical side, it was assumed the individuals living in a particular geographic area would share many of the same political interests making these interests easier to represent. The limits of communication and travel also argued for geographic representation. Members were expected back in their districts regularly to "soak and poke,"[5] absorbing constituent interests as directly as possible. Until very recently, with the advent of e-mail and cell phones without roaming charges, the cost of communications technologies were related to distance. The model was to have the representative go to the people more than vice versa.

Recognizing human nature and the infinite variety of political interests and desires, Madison and others intentionally made the task of representation more difficult by successfully arguing for relatively large geographic constituencies for the House of Representatives. In *Federalist No. 55*, Madison argued that House constituencies should be large enough to insure "free consultation and discussion," but not so large as to produce the "confusion and intemperance of a multitude." In *Federalist No. 10*, he argued that since factions were inevitable, government must be structured to garner the benefit of competing factions and that individual representatives would be forced to "refine and enlarge the public views."[6]

The Senate was designed to temper the passion of House constituencies and to represent the interests of the states as geographic and political entities. With the shift from state legislative to direct election of senators in 1913, it could be argued that senators simply became "big representatives" responsible to a larger constituency. In the contemporary Congress, the pattern is well established that on the most basic level, members of Congress are elected *from* geographic constituencies to *re-present* (present a second time) interests of those living in those constituencies.

It is true that some members of Congress favored with secure electoral fortunes have the freedom to go beyond the interests of their geographically defined constituency on selective issues; however, the beck and call of communications from those constituents remains a practical necessity and a sense of duty. In Richard Fenno's words, "the electoral goal is achieved—first and last—not in Washington but at home."[7] As the old colloquialism goes, most members of Congress soon realize they must "dance with them that brung you."[8] Members who lose touch with their geographic constituencies do so at their own political peril.

Internet Perspective: The Triumph Over Geography

The Internet supercedes the relevancy of geography as cost and time of increased distance is irrelevant to the user. E-mailing a colleague down the hall, while perhaps seemingly strange to some, feels and looks the same as e-mailing someone thousands of miles away. The protocols for e-mail addresses make it impossible to effectively screen such messages to capture only those from a particular constituency. Unlike a zip code or postmark, there is no way to assure certain identification of the constituency from which an e-mail actually originated.

The most outspoken proponents of congressional offices taking e-mail seriously argue that "congressional offices have exacerbated the problems they face [with e-mail] by failing . . . to take advantage of available technologies and strategies that could significantly ease the burdens."[9] Existing sorting and data-entry software could be used to prioritize e-mail and automate data entry from those communications. Essentially the technology could be used to undo what other technology spawned.

While using technology to counter technology seems like a form of justice, it begs the larger question of how political activism arises from the Net. In the past, geographic communities often spawned political activity based on personal experience and face-to-face communication. Individuals with complaints about government shared them with friends and neighbors. In some cases, aggregation of interests developed geographically. If a critical mass of concern developed, a viable interest group might be formed. Interest group entrepreneurs took on the task of combining local units into national organizations. Alternatively, disparate individual demands reached congressional offices. If similar concerns emerged, the member of Congress aggregated those from the geographic constituency into his or her version of "what the people want."

The Internet, on the other hand, is the world of politically active virtual communities rather than geographic communities. It is an extension of the kind of checkbook aggregation of political interests facilitated by computer-based, direct-mail techniques. Vitiating the need for face-to-face mobilization, interests can gain support and resources directly from individuals no matter where they geographically reside and press their case for political change with little regard to geography.

For some, the projected promise is tantalizing:

> . . . [N]ew media technology hails a rebirth of democratic life. It is envisaged that new public spheres will open up and that technologies will permit social actors to find or forge common interests. People will actively access information from an infinite, free, virtual library rather than receiving half-digested "programming," and interactive media will institutionalize a right of reply.[10]

Interests and political preferences are aggregated around desires. Internet factions tend to become both more numerous and more intemperate as like-minded souls can exchange their views without the niceties of having to temper them for face-to-face interaction with their geographic (and potentially more diverse) neighbors. There seems to be no technological vehicle for tempering the more strident and extreme positions facilitated by the Internet.

The geographic problem goes well beyond the "simple" issue of inadvertently representing another member's U.S. constituents. E-mail disregards national boundaries with the same abandon it skips over domestic constituency boundaries. It is forbidden by U.S. law and tradition for foreign nationals to lobby Congress. Many of the lobbying organizations which have most effectively used the Internet are international, such as Amnesty International, Friends of the Earth, and the International Coalition to Ban Land Mines.[11] While the interorganizational sharing of information and strategy is legitimate, these groups must be careful when they begin involving themselves in domestic fund-raising for candidates or communication campaigns directed at elected officials.[12] The elected officials must protect themselves from charges they are illegally or illegitimately catering to foreign interests.

Traditionally, members of Congress do respond to some interests not totally associated with their geographic constituencies by using surrogate measures of an interest's importance and relevancy. The act of organizing is a clear sign that an issue is of importance to someone. The ability of a traditional interest group to extract resources (time, money, and effort) from affected individuals often becomes their "ticket" to congressional consciousness. Members at least implicitly assume that "any group taking the effort to organize and communicate must have something today." Interest groups help push the door open with financial support. Whenever possible, local constituents are used as "door openers" to make appointments with key legislators. A geographic constituent asking to accompany the lobbyist from an interest group of which he or she is a member indicates the local implications of broader policy alternatives. Grassroots communication campaigns using calls, visits, and letters are joined by "astroturf" (fake grassroots) barrages stimulated and coordinated by organized interests. More formally, informed lobbyists often provide high-quality information and are explicitly invited to testify on policy, especially when they represent a large and active interest group. The Internet is clearly another tool organized interests can capitalize on.

The relative low cost of creating and activating virtual communities on the Internet, which supercede geographical or political boundaries, denies members of Congress the shortcut, clue-measuring effort by which they have long helped define importance. The information presented by a virtual community interest may well be as important or relevant as that from a traditional interest group, but there are no accepted yard sticks to evaluate its quality or legitimacy. Most members have met with union, civil rights, business and/or professional groups within their districts, making it easier to give a human face (preferably of a geographic constituent) to abstract policy demands. Virtual communities, not organized geographically, have a more difficult time seeming relevant in the geographic mind set of contemporary members of Congress who by necessity and proclivity think in geographic terms about "my constituents" in "my district."

The member of Congress who opens himself or herself to the unmediated messages from the Internet has little idea as to what constituency they are attempting to represent. As members of Congress begin to realize that relatively small groups bound together by e-mail can make a lot of political noise, they may well "begin to believe that the nets are populated by fringe groups"[13] alone. This could further dampen their interest in catering to the wishes of these groups.

THE CONGRESSIONAL GEOGRAPHIC MANAGEMENT OF THE E-MAIL DRAGON

Members of Congress encourage and react favorably to communications from geographic constituents and often establish sophisticated procedures for screening out communications from outside the geographic district. For traditional mail, zip codes and addresses serve as signals for appropriate and inappropriate incoming mail. "Misdirected" mail is often sent to the appropriate geographic member with a "buck slip," getting it off the staff member's desk and out of the member's potential consciousness.[14]

Some members either ask for a zip code or require potential communicators to register their bonafide status as a constituent before sending an e-mail. The registering process has the added advantage of helping the member create an information-rich database of interested citizens with whom they might want to communicate further on the issues in which they have shown concern.[15] Recognizing the importance of a legitimate local connection, a number of the special-purpose sites linking to congressional e-mail such as <www.congress.org> (maintained by Capital Advantage) require that e-mail correspondents fill out a block of identification questions which include address and zip code before their message is forwarded.

To help individuals find their Representative and to identify a sender's location, the House created a "Write Your Representative" Web page, which also serves as a geographic screen. Constituents use their zip code to identify their representative. This would transfer them to a Web form and the message is sent directly to the Representative from that zip code. The downside is that this system accepts externally generated e-mail. Some offices have adopted a system called CitizenDirect, which allows the congressional office to post responses to incoming e-mail on a Web site. Like "Write your Representative," CitizenDirect cannot accept normal e-mail.[16] So far, the price of efficiency and geographic targeting serves to reduce the incoming flow of e-mail, which may in fact be intentional.

At least in the short run, congressional offices are likely to either pay little attention to e-mail in general due to its lack of fit with their geographic outlook, or use whatever means available (labor intensive or technologically supported) to separate e-mail into the geographically "relevant" and "irrelevant."

Cold Sweat versus Key Punching: Evaluating the Input Connection

Congressional Perspective: Passion and Individual Representation

A key aspect of representation lies in responsiveness to incoming messages generated by constituents suggesting desired courses of action. The willingness to take up a constituent's call to arms is a combination of an informal measure of preference and passion. Members look at constituent communications as a surrogate measure of voting intention more than a source of neutral information or expert testimony. They assume that the more effort put into communicating an idea or position, the more likely that the member's utilization of that idea or supporting that position will serve as a key factor in the constituent's next electoral decision.

On the political battlefield, constituent messages are like incoming missiles. E-mail messages in this battle are small caliber projectiles lacking appropriate targeting and the firepower of most other techniques of communication. With limited resources, congressional offices use shortcut techniques to evaluate those messages requiring attention and response. Few members feel beholden to respond for the sake of responding. The subtext of an effective message to Congress lies in imparting the impression that the constituent not only is interested in the issue, but also that its disposition will impact on future political activity. An individual taking the time and effort to write a detailed "cold sweat" letter outlining the implications of a policy choice on their life does not have to explicitly say "and, I will take your official response into account at the next election." Members of Congress "are inclined to associate the costliness of the means of communication with the likelihood of voting."[17] As two observers put it, the passion behind e-mail is hard to measure:

> Internet messages come quickly and silently. . . . Congressional offices have a more difficult time telling individually written e-mail messages from cookie cutter e-mail campaigns, because there are fewer clues as compared with paper-based communications, where handwriting looks different from printing, hand-addressed envelopes look different than mass-addressed envelopes, and signatures look different from typed names.[18]

Congressional offices have an informal hierarchy of effort required to communicate. A personal visit from a distant constituency trumps a personal letter; expensive overnight mail trumps regular "snail mail"; a letter trumps a postcard; a personal postcard trumps a preprinted postcard provided by an interest group.

While the vast majority of members now have Web sites, relatively few advertise their e-mail address and many are hesitant about encouraging direct e-mail communication through their site.

INTERNET PERSPECTIVE: PASSIONLESS NET

While the Net may facilitate activation of individuals deeply interested in narrowly defined causes, there is limited ability to measure the passion of the sender. The low cost of e-mail communication cheapens its perceived importance, and the ease of forwarding encourages mass mailings. Even if a member of Congress is not familiar with the methods of spamming, he or she and his or her staff recognizes the equivalent of political junk mail. Thousands of identical e-mails scream "interest group–stimulated campaign; watch out," and have no more impact than thousands of low-effort tear-off postcards from an organization's newsletter. To paraphrase Marshall McLuhan's "the medium is the message," in politics, "the apparent effort is the message."

AN EMPIRICAL NOTE

In-depth measurement of the impact of various means of communicating with members of Congress is well beyond the purpose of this paper, but an initial foray into gathering empirical evidence is insightful. Members of Congress often justify their arguments and highlight their representative function by referring to their constituents. A quick search of the *Congressional Record* from 1992–2000 indicated forty-six references to "my mail," with thirty of the references reporting specific constituent desires on legislation. During the same time period, only four members referred to "my phone calls," and only one to "my e-mail," when reporting substantive preferences of corresponding constituents. Perhaps reflecting staff skill and priorities for e-mails, one member reported, "I had hoped to be able to share with you some of my e-mails, but apparently my computer is not working and we cannot get them printed out."[19]

AN ATTEMPT AT INFLUENCE

During the impeachment process, "Censure and Move On" created a Web site for a "flash campaign" designed to inundate Congress with a petition message encouraging action less than impeachment. Recognizing the geographic bias, messages were automatically routed to member offices on the basis of zip codes. Censure and Move On garnered over one-half million petition responses and significant media attention. Measuring actual effect is impossible, but one set of analysts argued that, "the petitions helped create a backdrop of support for congressional Democrats who might have appeared as being purely partisan supporters of the President."[20]

"CHECK YOUR CABLE SIGNAL" ERROR: THE OUTPUT CONNECTION

CONGRESSIONAL PERSPECTIVE: CONTROLLED DISSEMINATION OF MEASURED INFORMATION

Congress is a receiver and disseminator of information on both the individual member and aggregate level. As a disseminator, Congress has traditionally relied on the commercial media to present their individual and collective stories. Congress and its members have long had a love–hate relationship with the traditional media. As Congress increasingly viewed media coverage as inappropriate, they began to take an "if you can't fight them, join them approach," and adopted a broadcast mode of thinking about information dissemination. Broadcasting (whether in print or electronic mode) is built on a one-to-many model of imposing its message and attempting to capture a largely *inadvertent audience*. The audience has chosen to attune to something, but stands ready to be enticed by clever presentation or grabber headlines. As Congress recognized their lack of control over content and a commercial media that would not tell their story the way they wanted, members became their own publishers, producing newsletters they hoped would stand out from the piles of junk mail arriving every day in the average home. This was a first step in their goal of countering some of the damage done by the media. As television became the public's medium of choice, Congress agonized over how to capitalize on a medium which many felt was being used to their disadvantage.[21] They eventually became their own broadcasters by providing a tightly controlled television signal, which privately-financed C-SPAN then broadcast more widely. While many older members brought up in the days of station and program loyalty could not understand the spasmodic pattern of younger viewers who watch television with the remote ready to click from one program to another, their hope was that at least as people flipped through the channels, they would get drawn in by the content of congressional debates.

In many ways, the Internet audience, as compared with the television audience, is more *intentional*. One can still broadcast, but the Internet places the initiative more on the shoulders of the potential recipient of the message. The audience Congress is attempting to reach is searching for something specific, although they may not know where to find it. The analogy of "surfing" the Net implies a choice of "waves" to ride, giving potential users control over when one gets off and on. The use of search engines and the click of the mouse moves users from one site to the next. There is less inadvertent receptivity to a broadcast message and little loyalty to a particular site. On the surface, clicking the mouse and clicking the remote may seem like identical peripatetic behavior, but the purpose defines the unique character of each. Individuals use the Internet to seek information, while what appeals to the television viewer is much more variable. The trick for Congress and its members in utilizing the Internet to get their information out is to lure interested Web surfers to their sites and keep them there long enough to transfer the desired information.

After conducting a poll and content analysis of congressional Web sites, one set of media scholars concluded that the congressional response to the opportunities of the Internet has

> lagged behind that of other social institutions. Congress has not made full use of the possibilities offered by new computer-assisted communication technologies. Members of Congress seem more troubled than excited about using e-mail, and as a result have treated it as merely an extension of regular mail, rather than taking advantage of its potential for quick and efficient communication.

They go on to point out that despite the fact that by 1996 over two-thirds of House and over 90 percent of Senate members have home pages, they "do little more than safely advertise the members that maintain them."[22] Congressional Web sites offer an opportunity for members to get around the traditional media which at best ignores Congress (especially individuals members) and which at worse presents Congress and its members in a negative light. Web sites are under the control of the member and serve as positive bulletin boards advertising that member's virtues. The 1996 survey of member Web sites indicated that the most popular components of both House and Senate members sites were biographies (over 90 percent), press releases (over 60 percent) and descriptions of sponsored legislation (over 40 percent).[23] They found relatively little discussion of the substance of legislation or alerts about upcoming decisions. In general, members used their Web sites "to present themselves as attractive, approachable and helpful public servants."[24]

The one area in which Congress made more practical use of technology is for the internal distribution of information about schedules and legislation. The congressional *Intra*net, linking members and their staffs, may well be the most immediate cause for change in congressional communications patterns. There are fewer surprises for lawmakers and their staffs concerning impending legislation and its scheduling. Users of the congressionally designed and operated THOMAS system can search all proposed legislation's full text to monitor possible activity in areas of concern. Knowing about scheduled hearings and other legislative action provides members and their staff with the "heads-up" information they need to insert themselves into the decision-making process. Much of this information is also available to individuals and interest groups outside of Congress, facilitating their potential participation.[25]

On the aggregate (committee and chamber) level, Congress thinks in terms of official documents and controlled distribution. Members of Congress and their staffs recognize that information is a power resource which, if shared, declines in value. Procedures establish mechanisms for assuring proper content and timing of distribution. Members of Congress implement their right to "revise and extend their remarks" in the *Congressional Record*, so it more faithfully records what they *wanted* to say as opposed to what they did say. Tradition and legal rulings have maintained that this "corrected" version of history is the basis for legislative intent. Real-time distribution of information and/or the ability to easily edit content runs counter to concern over control. In the traditional print era, the cost and effort of producing documents facilitated tighter control. The problem of institution-wide change is exacerbated by the fact that information in Congress is "owned" by a number of entities. The House and the Senate are separate bodies with different traditions and rules. Committees control their own reports, often not distributing committee testimony until after a policy decision is made. Institutional standards on what information to distribute, in what form, and under what time schedule is more of a political question than one of technology.

Ideally, members of Congress would like individuals to enter the congressional information realm through one official portal and have access to official documents in a predetermined format. They continue to see themselves as a traditional one-to-many publisher, holding the official "copyright."

THE INTERNET PERSPECTIVE: NOMADIC INFORMATION GATHERERS, INSTANT INFORMATION, AND OPEN ARCHITECTURE

Searching the Web on the Internet is a largely idiosyncratic, nonhierarchical process with the expectation of finding a combination of almost real-time information and historical background. As is often the case, the terminology reflects reality. Traditional "re-search" implies "searching again" following time-tested patterns of bibliographies, tables of content, and indexes. On the Web, "re-searching" becomes "searching." This is a much less directive verb. The "Web" nomenclature is particularly revealing since it exemplifies a many-to-many communication pattern with multiple crisscrossing paths. Untangling a spider web is often only child's play relative to untangling the paths an individual traversed through Internet Web links. Unlike rigid seekers of *the* truth following well-defined data collection techniques with a known ultimate outcome, Web information seekers exemplify Marshall McLuhan's "nomadic gatherers of knowledge."[26] Rather than following a hierarchical searching pattern, the nomads come upon information more idiosyncratically and then follow multiple links to specific topics or issues. In the process, they are often diverted into information realms they had not previously considered and become sources themselves as they forward material to others or capture it to their own Web site. The "open architecture" philosophy of many Internet activists asserts the right to use, transform, and distribute whatever they find on the Web. The fact that congressional information "has already been paid for by the public" and is not copyrighted gives further impetus to this presumed right. This "snatch and grab" or "right-click acquisition" approach scares those wishing to control information. Web information seekers not only don't enter the information realms in clearly predictable ways, but once there they often have the power to download what they find, edit it, and send it on its way without the cost of traditional publication technologies. The newly transformed information may well look official, but is out of the control of the originator and may convey an entirely erroneous intent. All of this scares those in Congress who desire control over "their" information. The development of low-cost "spoof sites" with the official look will only exacerbate congressional fears.

Evidence from the Field

Members have only partially accepted the potential for e-mail communication. While most members allow incoming e-mail through their Web sites and from a variety of noncongressional sites which offer "write your representative" utilities, staff members point out that "I don't know any office that responds to e-mail by e-mail."[27] The general pattern is to send an auto response via e-mail indicating the message was received, and then send the response via a regular hard-copy letter. This allows outgoing mail to go through the normal screening process to assure that what goes out over the member's name faithfully represents the message the member wants to communicate.

An Empirical Test: Finding Congressional Information

Search engines provide a key tool for accessing Web-based information. Unless one consults a Web directory or makes a good guess as to a likely address, finding a particular Web site can be a hit or miss proposition. Is it "House.org," "Houseofrepresentatives.gov," or some other formulation? Attempts to use the Internet to find information about Congress will depend on the visibility of congressional sites on search engines and links from other popular sites. Although attempts are being made to create universal portals for government information, there is no widely accepted beginning point to find congressional sites. Unless one makes a lucky guess on a URL, search engines vary in how easy it is to get into the official congressional sites. As Table 2.1 shows, a quick test of various search engines indicated wide variations in access, but a relatively high success rate in finding official sites.

An Example of Access: A Starr Illuminating the Future or a One-Shot Shooting Starr?

"The release of the Starr Report [September 1998] signaled the coming of age of a new technology that is going to play a commanding role in politics. Communication is the vehicle of politics and the Internet is the most powerful political vehicle yet built."[28] Release of the report on the Internet with its anticipated titillating accounts of the president's sexual misadventures bypassed the traditional filters and generated Web site–clogging traffic. America Online reported 800,000 downloads in the first twenty-four hours. The

TABLE 2.1 SEARCHING FOR OFFICIAL WEB SITES

SEARCH TERMS	OFFICIAL SITE	SEARCH ENGINES RESULTS*		
		MSN	GOTO	ALTA VISTA
"+house+representatives"	www.house.gov	#1	#2	#2
"+u+s+senate"	www.senate.gov	#1	#2	#1
"+u+s+congress"	www.house.gov or	#3	#4	> #10
	www.senate.gov	#4	> #10	> #10
	www.congress.org**	> #10	#1	> #10
	Library of Congress with links	#1	> #10	> #10
"THOMAS"	thomas.loc.gov	#1 and #2	> #10	#9, indirect link

*location in search results
**private site with access to congressional sites

House Web servers jumped from an average of 66,000 hits per hour to three million.[29] Using the Internet, numerous commercial and noncommercial sites picked up the report and made it available on their sites almost instantaneously. Traditional media used the electronic version in the Web to print all or part of the report in newspapers and magazines. More people downloaded the Web version than bought the almost instantly published book form.[30] The decision to distribute on the Web shattered traditional divisions. Many Republicans who traditionally support limiting pornography saw release of the report with its explicit sexual content to their political advantage in the impeachment battle. Many Democrats, on the other hand, took on the equally nontraditional wariness of free speech arguing that its release showed "no sensitivity, no interest in the impact of . . . its pornographic disclosures on the minds and attitudes and mental well-being of children," according to Representative Bobby L. Rush (D-Ill.).[31] The irony of Congress having passed legislation (The Communications Decency Act) which would have disallowed using the Internet to distribute such information was not lost on many observers. While it cannot be shown that publishing the report on the Internet necessarily moved the impeachment process forward, it certainly showed how the Internet could speed up the distribution of information and almost erase the traditional filtering of information.

ACCESS TO OFFICIAL RECORDS: PRINCIPLES IN PRACTICE

Congress has long been careful about sharing information. It took the initiative of private vendors such as LEGI-SLATE, LEXIS-NEXIS and *Congressional Quarterly* to provide public access to the *Congressional Record* and to bill status information. For a number of years the battle revolved around the definition of the word "document," with those opposing access arguing the laws requiring public access of documents did not apply to records in electronic form. While the official THOMAS system launched in 1995 was a giant leap forward in using the Net to provide information, it intentionally lacks public access to valuable information to which the public has a right. For example, to find individual voting records of members, you need know the roll call numbers of the relevant bills. There is no capability to analyze voting patterns such as party loyalty or voting by gender or race. Committee and subcommittee votes are completely inaccessible as are the annual financial disclosure statements of members.

At each stage of expanding public access, the congressional predisposition has required the advocates of openness to shoulder the burden of proof. The continuing battle over Web access to policy research from the Congressional Research Service (CRS) is a prime example. The advocates argue that the public has the right to the research they have already paid for through taxes. In Senator John McCain's (R-Ariz.) words, "For FY1999, the American taxpayers will pay $67.9 million to fund CRS' operations. . . . The CRS products can play an important role in educating the American public. Public access to these documents will mark an important milestone in opening up the federal government."[32] Opponents in Congress raise a number of objections. They are concerned about copyright infringement, disruption of CRS efficiency with new public demands being made on individual CRS analysts, funding constraints, fear of disseminating internal documents which have not gone through peer reviews, and constitutional limitations on distributing information under the "Speech and Debate" clause.[33] Proponents argue that each of the concerns can be ameliorated, or that they pose no greater threat than the current extensive distribution of CRS products to the public in hard-copy form. To cut through the marshaled arguments of the opponents, Senator McCain was asked, "Could it be that members of Congress want to control information about themselves and don't want to be scrutinized?" He responded directly, "Exactly."[34] So far the opposition has stalled action at the committee level. As the public waits for CRS access, they are limited to selective Web access on a few "rogue" congressional sites[35] and access through commercial vendors who often sell outdated versions of reports. Many CRS insiders expect "we will lose this battle, and virtually all reports will be on the Net by the end of this year (2001)."[36]

Members of Congress recognize that information access and framing is a powerful resource. In a highly partisan environment like Congress, it is no surprise that those in power would attempt to control access. Majority party rules require that Web sites for the minority be accessible only through the official majority party committee site. The surfing public is thus guaranteed at least initially to get the majority party perspective first, before accessing the minority party committee site which may well question the list of glowing accomplishments presented by the majority.[37]

Timed Out by the Machine

Congressional Perspective: The Cooling Saucer

Congress was not designed nor has seldom worked as a rapid response mechanism. Representative government filters passions through elected officials whose role is to weigh and evaluate ideas more dispassionately. Traditionally this has been one of the unique roles of the Senate. The longer terms of its members and its initial indirect election were designed to protect it from the pressure to act in a quick, intemperate manner. Although the conversation may well be apocryphal, tradition has it that George Washington explained his support of the Senate to Thomas Jefferson by asking, "Why did you pour your coffee into your saucer?" When Jefferson responded, "To cool it," Washington responded that, "We pour legislation into the senatorial saucer to cool it."[38] Throughout much of our history, The Senate has served as the brake on popular passions. For example, in recent years, it was the Senate that slowed down much of the Republican "Contract with America" that House members saw as their mandate after the 1994 election.

Congress was not designed to act quickly. Being somewhat removed from the desire for immediate gratification—which is likely to grasp the public—is seen as a virtue rather than a fault. Slow redundant consideration of competing views is seen as the forge for better outcomes.

The desire to avoid being rushed into judgment can easily turn into an excuse for not providing timely information to the public. Lacking timely information hampers the ability of the public to influence policy decisions before they are made. Accountability means considerably less if it is solely after the fact. As Gary Ruskin of the Congressional Accountability Project argues, the Internet should be used to "allow citizens to impact bills *while they are in the process*" (italics added).[39]

The Internet Perspective: Real Time—Real Influence

Marshall McLuhan's argument that "instant information creates involvement" was intended to apply to television, but applies even more to the Internet. E-mail utilities allowing one to determine whether a message has been opened assures that no one can say, "I never got your message." From instant messaging, to chat rooms and on-line stock or news alerts, denizens of the Net expect immediate information and immediate response.

The Congressional Response

Many congressional procedures are an intentional attempt to counter the assertion that "faster is better." Members of Congress recognize that e-mail communications are definitely quicker to generate and likely to be more intemperate. As Charles McGrath put it, "Most of us have either sent or received an electronic jolt that would have benefited from the cooling down period afforded by the traditional drawer-yanking search for an envelope and fumble for a stamp."[40] Sharp and unguarded comments over e-mail have even spawned their own label: "flaming." On the receiving end there may well be some temptation to respond in kind. Instant messages seem to deserve instant responses. The potential for speeding up the demand/response cycle is exacerbated by companion technologies. The once remote deliberations of Congress and its committees are now broadcast in real time by C-SPAN. It is certainly feasible for an interested citizen to watch an ongoing debate and "fire off" (notice the intemperate but widely used terminology) an e-mail prior to the final vote in an attempt to influence its outcome.

Responding to e-mail with a regular letter allows for a cooling-off period for the sender and time for quality control by the congressional office. Fear over providing immediate access to documents (testimony, bill drafts, proposed amendments, etc.) reflect logistical concerns, the desire to assure quality control, and the fear of generating too much interest in potentially extraneous material. While transparency of the "people's houses" sounds desirable and inherently democratic, the encouragement of more voices could well cripple the deliberative process. Congress has attempted to provide a safety net of necessary information without opening every legislative nook and cranny to full and real-time review.

THE "FORMATTING ERROR" PROBLEM

CONGRESS'S FIXATION WITH FORMAT

Congress and its members clearly fall into the oral and textual tradition. They think in terms of complete speeches and documents structured in intentional ways to make a point. Members are accustomed to attending committee mark-up sessions where they go through the text line-by-line from beginning to end. Perhaps reflecting the dominance of legal training, formalized logical arguments predominate in floor speeches and committee reports.

THE INTERNET: TRIUMPH OF SUBSTANCE OVER FORMAT

The Internet is increasingly multimedia-oriented, revealing a conversion of formats in which the user gathers information in visual, audio, graphic, and textual formats all on the same screen. "Reading" a Web site is seldom a top to bottom exercise. Hot links encourage users to delve into the document at various levels. Seldom do two people experience a Web site in the same way. Simple page turner Web sites where the designer retains control are likely to turn off most Web surfers. Members of Congress are less experienced with the "grammar and syntax" of making visual and graphical arguments which increasingly dominate the Web. The increasing use of charts and graphs on the floor since the arrival of C-SPAN does indicate that members are willing to accommodate to technology and are educable. Making arguments on the Internet requires a way of thinking that is alien to many members of Congress and their staffs. It will be a long time before there is a critical mass of individuals in society skilled in the grammar and logic of Web presentation. Congress is unlikely to be at the forefront of organizations that can draw the most talented Web designers.

"REFINE YOUR SEARCH" LOGIC

CONGRESSIONAL DELIBERATION

Members of Congress see their task as amalgamating a wide range of inputs—including constituent communications, expert advice, and personal experience—and bringing them to bear on tough issues concerning the values government should promote. Whether we as a society should spend more on national defense as opposed to education is less a question of facts and more one of which output is more valued. Seldom is there a clearly "right" answer, since values preferences are goals over which reasonable people can rightly disagree. Facts are more ammunition on the value battlefield than ironclad reasons to choose one value over another. Congressional deliberation is an iterative process, with proposals generating reaction from those whose values were not accommodated, who then often create counterproposals in hope of creating a winning coalition behind them. The process is complex and takes time. The options between which members choose are seldom ones of "good" versus "bad," but rather between "better" versus "worse." In analyzing the problems of factions, "Madison does not argue that faction is caused by lack of information or expertise, which the vast resources of the Information Revolution could cure. Neither partisan interests or collective passions are brought on by ignorance."[41] Most members of Congress would agree that their major problem is not lack of information, but rather differing views of the world and the lack of skill and will to reach the necessary compromises. In making their decisions, members of Congress need information, but their needs are less for facts, and more for who in their constituency holds which values and how strongly they hold them. They seek solutions that are good enough to seem better than the worse alternatives rather than seeking unobtainable perfection. Success in the political realm often depends on satisfying enough of the value preferences of one's base of support to win the next election.

In the wake of the terrorist bombings and anthrax scare on Capitol Hill, the House Administration Committee held a hearing (May 1, 2002) on the feasibility of using the Internet to create a virtual Congress. While there was some support for an e-Congress as a last resort, considerable concern was expressed over diminishing the deliberative quality of Congress.

The Internet: Self-Evident Truths and Completing the Program

The vast reach and flexibility of the Internet lead to a feeling that better and more efficient decision making simply lies in wait for creative utilization by open-minded decision makers. In those realms where the driving criteria for a good decision is based on facts, the Internet promises to make it much easier to find those facts, communicate them widely, and force the "right" decision. In those realms where facts are less important than value preferences, Internet proponents see it as an instant preference tabulator, facilitating a shift from representative democracy to a purer form of plebiscitary democracy in which elected officials are either unnecessary or serve a dramatically reduced role. Instant polling over secure lines on binding referenda is portrayed by some of the futurists as the ultimate democratic triumph of the technological age.

The Reaction to Political "Instant Messaging"

Just because something can be done does not justify doing it. The concept of an Internet-facilitated, national plebiscite to achieve pure democracy brings shudders to most observers both in and outside of Congress. Members of Congress may be seen as a suspect class on this issue since their livelihood is at stake, but they and others point out a number of philosophical and practical barriers unlikely to be subject to either a sociological or technological fix.

Complexity and Agenda Setting The issues Congress faces are complex, arguably beyond the level of interest and/or capability of most voters. The process by which they reach the decision stage requires management and control. Whoever has the right to call for a plebiscite and outline the alternatives holds more power over the outcome than those who participate in the actual vote. It is possible to frame questions and alternatives in such a way as to almost predetermine voters' choices.

Digital Divide Technological and motivational barriers, as well as resource limitations, are guaranteed to facilitate the participation of some and discourage similar involvement by others. Who is involved in the plebiscite will determine the outcome. Political self-interest will unleash massive efforts by organized interests to target supporters and get them involved, expanding the fragmentation of political discourse we already experience.[42]

Deliberation versus Responsiveness Politics of necessity is a process of deliberate coordination and compromise, processes not likely to be facilitated by instant plebiscites and their promise of responsiveness. The public is both ill-equipped and lacks the ongoing interest to participate effectively in the wide range of policy choices facing government. Political systems need individuals with the knowledge, will, and political protection to make tough choices. Public guidance and periodic control at the margins through elections keep such decision makers within boundaries. A Congress filled with supercharged delegates responding to the blowing winds of instant plebiscites provides little hope to improve policymaking. We can search for ways to make the system more responsive, without making it irresponsible. In the mixed desire for deliberate decision making and responsive decision making, direct democracy sacrifices too much of the necessary deliberation.

BACK TO THE FUTURE

Throughout history the positive potentials of new technologies have been oversold and their dangers deemphasized. Each wave of new technology confronted by Congress has spawned speculations—often faulty—about their transforming power over the institution and its members.

Five basic rules seem to emerge to temper our confidence in making bold predictions. First, Congress and its members are amazingly adaptable to technological change. In most cases the denizens of Congress have found ways to tailor new technologies to their individual and collective benefit more than simply being the victims of their application. Second, new technologies tend more to strengthen current power holders than to empower others. Third, creative use of new technologies by a few risk takers will push the envelope of applications and serve as guideposts for others. Once the downside of new applications are worked out, others will copy the once-new applications, turning once-cutting-edge applications into standard operating procedures.[43] Fourth, new technologies seldom impact on institutions and processes in isolation. Multiple and often interrelated potential causes of change make sorting out the actual causes difficult. And, finally, the challenge of understanding new technologies is hampered by our short-term perspective on how the next wave of technologies will look. Just about the time we get a handle on the impact of the Web and the Internet, they will have fallen by the wayside as technological dinosaurs such as gopher systems and carbon paper.

Congress will inevitably continue lawmaking, representing, educating, and performing oversight. The Internet has considerable *potential* for facilitating these tasks by providing more information and increasing Congress's ability to communicate its efforts and decisions to broader audiences. Too heavy reliance on the Internet will affect whose problems get represented on the lawmaking agenda and, to a degree, what gets overseen. Replacing one group of information "haves" with another changes, but does not necessarily improve, representation. Perhaps the greatest immediate potential of the Internet lies in its ability to educate the congressional and wider community by providing low-cost, easy-to-access, and timely information. The potential contribution of the Internet to thoughtful deliberation is less likely, except to the degree that it improves the information base from which congressional deliberators begin their work.

The clearly identifiable disconnects between traditional congressional perspectives and the opportunities inherent in the Internet do not imply that the Internet is doomed to failure as a potential influence on Congress and its members. Congressional utilization of the Internet, at least in the foreseeable future, will be more dependent on the ability of potential users to adapt its application to the congressional perspective more than Congress adapting to the Internet perspective.

NOTES

1. Kenneth Laudon, *Computers and Bureaucratic Reform: The Political Functions of Urban Information Systems* (New York: John Wiley, 1974), p. 311.
2. Stephen E. Frantzich, *Computers in Congress: The Politics of Information* (Beverly Hills, CA: Sage Publications, 1982), pp. 129–130.
3. Ibid., p. 168.
4. In this paper, the term "Internet" is used expansively to include more specific applications such as Web pages and e-mail.
5. Although Richard F. Fenno, Jr. (*Home Style*, Boston: Little, Brown and Company, 1978, p. xiv) used this term to describe his research approach, it also is a good description of what members of Congress do as they travel around their constituencies asking open-ended questions and seeking insight as to how things are going.
6. See Michael J. Malbin, "Congress during the Convention and Ratification," in *Contemplating the People's Branch*, ed. Kelly D. Patterson and Daniel M. Shea (Upper Saddle River, NJ: Prentice Hall, 2000), pp. 21–22.
7. Fenno, *Home Style*, p. 31.
8. Supposedly, advice given to a young prom attendee that switching dates at the prom is unacceptable. One owes loyalty to the one responsible for getting you there.
9. Kathy Goldschmidt, et. al., "E-Mail Overload in Congress: Managing a Communications Crisis," Congress Online Project conducted by George Washington University and the Congressional Management Foundation, <http://www.congressonlineproject.org/email.html>.
10. Cathy Bryan, Roza Tsagarousianou, and Damian Tambini, "Electronic Democracy and the Civic Networking Movement in Context," in *Cyberdemocracy: Technology, Cities and Civic Networks*, ed. Roza Tsagarousianou, Damian Tambini, and Cathy Bryan (New York: Routledge, 1998), p. 5.
11. See Stephen Frantzich, *Citizen Democracy: Political Activists in a Cynical Age* (Lanham, MD: Rowman & Littlefield, 1999), p. 187.
12. Wayne Rash, *Politics on the Nets* (New York: W. H. Freeman, 1997), p. 105.
13. Ibid., pp. 160–161.
14. See Stephen E. Frantzich, *Write Your Congressman: Constituent Communications and Representation* (New York: Praeger, 1986), p. 32.
15. Rash, *Politics on the Nets*, p. 143.
16. Daniel Bennett and Pam Fielding, *The Net Effect: How Cyberdemocracy Is Changing the Political Landscape* (Merrifield, VA: 2-advocates Press, 1999), pp. 135–136.
17. Rash, *Politics on the Nets*, p. 8.
18. Bennett and Fielding, *The Net Effect*, p. 129.
19. *Congressional Record*, 105th Cong., 2nd sess., June 3, 1998, H3034.
20. Bennett and Fielding, *The Net Effect*, p. 37.
21. See Stephen Frantzich and John Sullivan, *The C-SPAN Revolution* (Norman, OK: The University of Oklahoma Press, 1996).
22. Diana Owen, Richard Davis, and Vincent James Strickler, "Congress and the Internet," *Press/Politics* 4, no. 2 (1999), p. 27.
23. Ibid., p. 23.
24. Ibid., p. 25.

25. Critics do point out that the public version lacks timeliness and reports more on what *has* happened than what is actually in the process and open to influence. See David Corn, "Filegate.gov: The Biggest Congressional Scandal of the Digitial Age: Politicians Aren't Putting Public Docs on the Net, and No One Seems to Care," *Wired Magazine*, November 2000, <http://www.wired.com/wired/archive/8.11.govdocs.html>.
26. Marshall McLuhan, *Understanding the Media: The Extensions of Man* (New York: McGraw-Hill, 1965), p. 358. This idea has been extended by Melvin Dubnick in "Educating Nomads: Narratives and the Future of Civic Education" (paper presented at the Annual Meeting of the American Political Science Association, Boston, MA, September 3–6, 1998), <http://www.dubnick@mediaone.net>. For a more detailed discussion, see Stephen Frantzich, *Cyberage Politics 101: Mobility, Technology, and Democracy* (New York: Peter Lang Publishers, 2002).
27. Consensus of key staff participants in the Woodrow Wilson Center/Stennis Center roundtable discussion on "The Information Age Congress and Deliberations," January 22, 2001.
28. Bennett and Fielding, *The Net Effect*, p. 16.
29. See Donald R. Wolfensberger, *Congress and the People: Deliberative Democracy on Trial* (Baltimore, MD: Johns Hopkins University Press, 2000), p. 229.
30. Bennett and Fielding, *The Net Effect*, pp. 21-22.
31. Ibid., p. 19.
32. *Congressional Record*, 105th Cong., 2nd sess., July 20, 1998, S8558.
33. Ibid., S8559.
34. Corn, "Filegate.gov: The Biggest Congressional Scandal of the Digitial Age."
35. Representatives Martin T. Meehan (R-Mass.) and Christopher Shays (R-Conn.), two of the advocates of public access, are participating in a sanctioned test of providing selective CRS issue briefs on their sites. A number of committees also have included selective briefs.
36. Author's interviews with CRS staff.
37. Owen, et al., "Congress and the Internet," p. 13.
38. See Suzy Platt, *Respectfully Quoted* (Washington, D.C.: U.S. Government Printing Office, 1984), p. 60.
39. Corn, "Filegate.gov: The Biggest Congressional Scandal of the Digitial Age."
40. Charles McGrath, "The Internet's Arrested Development," *New York Times Magazine*, 8 December 1996, p. 85.
41. Arthur Isak Applebaum, "Failure in the Cybermarketplace of Ideas," in *Democracy.com: Governance in a Networked World*, ed. Elaine Ciulla Kamarck and Joseph S. Nye (Hollis, NH: Hollis Publishing, 1999), p. 29.
42. See Steven Schier, *By Invitation Only: The Rise of Exclusive Politics in the United States* (Pittsburgh, PA: University of Pittsburgh Press, 2000).
43. See Goldschmidt, et al., "E-Mail Overload in Congress." This study identified offices using "best practices" in managing e-mail and attempts to outline the lessons for other offices and Congress as a whole.

WE'VE COME A LONG WAY ... MAYBE

U.S. REPRESENTATIVE DAVID DREIER

On the opening day of the 104th Congress (1995–1997) in January 1995, the House of Representatives enacted what many considered to be the most sweeping institutional reforms in nearly fifty years. A number of academics and political commentators wrote books and papers, and held conferences throughout the country on the significance of those reforms on deliberation and accountability in Congress. But arguably the one change that has had the most profound impact on the way Congress does business was not part of that opening day package of reforms. It was the widespread introduction of electronic mail and the Internet, and it has only been recently that observers have begun to examine the effects of these technologies on the institution. As Ken Weinstein of the Heritage Foundation noted before my subcommittee: "Congress's efforts to bring itself on line in the age of the information superhighway were an important, albeit largely unheralded, part of the reform efforts [of the 104th and 105th Congresses]."[1]

By now, we are all familiar with former House Speaker Newt Gingrich's (R-Ga.) quote about making information "available to any citizen in the country at the same moment that it is available to the highest paid lobbyist." At the time the Speaker made that statement, it is doubtful that anyone fully appreciated the technical constraints that Congress faced in turning his vision into reality. Updating the technological infrastructure of an organization as large and decentralized as the Congress was and continues to be an enormous undertaking. The resources dedicated to new technologies, and the familiarity of lawmakers and staff with their practical use, were limited.

As the Computer and Information Services Working Group of the House Oversight Committee wrote in a 1997 report:

> The U.S. House of Representatives was intrinsically a "paper-based" institution. Electronic legislative information, committee documents, and documents from the Library of Congress, Congressional Budget Office, Government Accounting Office, and other organizations all existed on separate computer systems or in hard-copy storage. Even though electronically stored, most documents were only available for mass distribution in hard-copy format, and there was no common architecture, language, or format by which documents could be easily integrated, shared, electronically distributed, or viewed among offices or organizations. Electronic mail systems (E-mail) in Member and committee offices were available, but many existed as islands of technology. Communicating electronically among offices was clumsy and difficult, even for offices that were next door in the same building. Access to most legislative information was accomplished through the use of primitive computer equipment accessing a mainframe program first written over fifteen years ago. No common computer platforms existed.[2]

When you look back to where we were just a few years ago and look at where Congress is today, it is clear that the institution has made a remarkable transformation into the Information Age. According to estimates by the Committee on House Administration and the Legislative Branch Appropriations Subcommittee, the infrastructure of the House network has been substantially upgraded, at a cost of approximately $1.5 billion over the past six years. Support and training of congressional staff has drastically improved, and the institution's presence on the Internet has been expanded to provide the public with unprecedented access to House documents, electronic communications to their representatives, and audio and video streaming of committee hearings. We can say with certainty that Congress is a very different institution because of the Internet and its related tools.

How Far We've Come: Technology Use in the House since 1995

Prior to 1995, the U.S. House of Representatives was almost exclusively a "paper-based" institution. While computers and electronic document production applications were used, they were largely limited to stand-alone computers or text-only "dummy terminals" not connected to any House-wide network and the mass distribution of documents was possible only through hard-copy means. Only fifty-six House members had Internet access and there were virtually no personal office or committee Web sites. Electronic connections between members' Capitol Hill and district offices were limited with fewer than thirty legislators using high-speed network connections. Finally, the House supported nine disparate and effectively uninteroperable e-mail systems.[3]

Things began to change quite rapidly with the opening of the 104th Congress. At the direction of former Speaker Newt Gingrich and Representative Bill Thomas (R-Calif.), the then–Chairman of the Committee on House Oversight (now the Committee on House Administration), the House began an ambitious program to upgrade all of its computer systems. In short order the House made significant headway. The House adopted a set of Internet e-mail standards ensuring full interoperability, and by the end of the 104th Congress, 655 member and supporting offices had connections to the Internet, 222 members had high-speed network connections between their Washington, D.C. and district offices, and more than 222 member offices and 27 full committees had established Web sites on the House Web server.[4] In addition, on January 5, 1995, Gingrich, Thomas, and the Librarian of Congress, Dr. James H. Billington, unveiled the THOMAS Web site, a comprehensive database allowing the public unprecedented access to members of Congress and legislative information including roll call votes, the *Congressional Record*, bill text, and more.

In addition to these upgrades in the infrastructure of the House information technology system, the House began to investigate and study early on the procedural impacts of technology on the legislative process and the House as an institution. In early 1996, I organized the *21st Century Congress Project* to assess the potential implications of future technology utilization on the legislative process and to recommend proposals for change. Its first hearing, held on May 24, 1996, aptly enough incorporated video-conferencing technology along with television, e-mail, and the Internet to create the first fully interactive congressional hearing. Subsequent hearings of the subcommittee have further investigated this topic, including examination of the experiences of a number of state legislatures and their utilization of technology.[5] As part of the project, the subcommittee also released a number of reports on technology and its real and potential impact on the U.S. House.[6] At the beginning of the 105th Congress (1997–1999) in 1997, the House Rules Committee recommended a new rule stating that "each committee shall, to the maximum extent feasible, make its publications available in electronic form." Its passage marked the first Internet-related procedural change to House activities and saw quick results as committees began to require testimony in electronic format for publication to their Web sites along with meeting and hearing schedules, hearing transcripts, and other committee information and publications.

Today, Internet use by Congress is part of the everyday working environment. Every member and standing committee has a Web page, e-mail is often the standard method used for communicating and sharing documents between offices, Capitol Hill and district offices are wired for high-speed Internet access, and the use of audio and video streaming technology, especially by committees, is becoming more and more common. The public has around-the-clock access to their representatives through e-mail and Web sites and the unprecedented availability of congressional proceedings activities and legislative publications via THOMAS and other related Web sites gives them a clearer picture than ever of the activities of Congress. Add to this the fact that lawmakers and their staffs are becoming more tech savvy and demanding, and it would be hard to name any other government entity anywhere in the world that uses technology better than the United States Congress to both improve efficiency and productivity internally and provide transparency and access externally.

How Congress Uses the Internet

With the continuing expansion of the Internet into everyday life in Congress, congressional offices have varied in their application of this technology. In general, however, over the past few years Internet use by member offices and committees has grown rapidly in two primary areas: *Internal Use*—legislative/policy research and communications; and *External Use*—constituent/press communications and services.

In addition, the growing use of technology has resulted in a real impact on the systems and staffing requirements of member and committee offices. While the House itself provides a significant level of hardware and software maintenance through its supporting offices, many offices find themselves demanding or requiring services beyond that provided by the House. In addition, as members and committees come to rely more on these technologies, they also find themselves requiring staff that is proficient in its use, including personnel specifically dedicated to maintaining and supporting their computer equipment and applications. While the position of Systems Administrator is sometimes a secondary position relegated to another staffer, many offices, in order to sufficiently support the hardware and software they use, now require a dedicated and experienced staffer whose sole responsibility is maintaining and supporting the office's computer equipment, Web site, and other IT systems. As offices continue to rely on these technologies more, this position will only become more important.

Legislative/Policy Research and Communications

As a research tool, the Internet is quickly becoming the standard on which congressional staff rely. Until just recently office personnel were forced to depend on hard-copy delivery services provided by such entities as the Congressional Research Service (CRS), Congressional Budget Office (CBO), Government Printing Office (GPO), and others. While some electronic research tools were available (e.g., LEXIS-NEXIS), their cost and/or limited content restricted their usefulness. The Internet has made such research, once a timely and labor-intensive effort, straightforward and has greatly increased productivity in this area. For example, until recently, legislative staff spent a majority of their time responding to constituent comments, questions, and requests. Today, the Internet and other tools, including massive database-driven

Constituent Management Software (CMS) packages, have greatly reduced the time required to fulfill these duties, freeing staff for more involvement in legislative and policy planning. The resources and documents of all the above-listed organizations—plus those of the entire executive branch and public policy research organizations—and more are now available literally at the click of a button. In addition, improvements in Internet search engines have made Web-wide searching vastly superior to anything heretofore available.

In addition to the Internet itself, other commonly used office applications have made it possible to enhance and supplement electronic documents with links to additional information. Word processing software, e-mail, scheduling programs, and more have all been designed so that users can append Web pages as "clickable" links. Electronic documents can now be shared within and between offices via e-mail including these links, allowing staff to include and share supporting information found on the Web. Finally, the growing usage of such software as Adobe Acrobat® is allowing staff to access, produce, edit, and share documents electronically in the same format in which they are produced. This is especially important when considering the visual representation and formatting of legislative documents.

As mentioned above, e-mail has allowed member, committee, leadership, and supporting offices to share documents and other information on a larger and more rapid scale than previously possible. E-mail, scheduling software, and other related applications are used at all levels and have had a tremendous impact on the ease and efficiency of everyday life in a member office. Rare is any activity that has not been coordinated, scheduled, discussed, or studied through the use of some electronic communications application. In March 2001 alone, nearly nine million internal e-mails passed between House staffers.[7] Increasingly, documents previously mass-produced and distributed throughout the House are now sent electronically, providing significant labor and material savings in an era of cost-cutting. This trend promises to grow as publishing and related software applications adopted by the House continue to simplify and expedite these activities.

Finally, the House continues to expand and improve on the publication and management of legislative documents. According to a recent CRS memorandum:

> [A planned new electronic document management system (DMS) in the House] is part of a Hill-wide effort to facilitate publication of legislative documents on the Internet, provide for more current retrieval of legislative information, and allow for more rapid exchange of documents without having to convert them to different formats. This will enable Congress through a single source to have immediate access to core legislative documents, receive information on actions taken in committees and on the floor, and link to a wide range of information resources that are relevant to issues on the legislative agenda. Similarly, by rapidly making much of this information available via THOMAS, there will be greater public access to ever-increasing quantities of legislative information.[8]

In a relatively short period of time, the U.S. House of Representatives has gone from a largely "paper-based" institution to one that increasingly relies on the Internet and other related electronic communications technologies. Virtually every activity in the House, from administrative and support functions through the various stages of the legislative process, has been affected in one way or another by these technologies. Overwhelmingly, these effects have been positive, with visible increases in productivity and efficiency at all levels. And while the House will never be at the "cutting edge" of technology adoption, it will continue to implement the tools necessary to improve the internal functioning of the institution to the extent that they take into account and support the vital importance of the deliberative process that gives Congress its unique nature.

CONSTITUENT/PRESS COMMUNICATIONS AND SERVICES

Member and Committee Web Sites Starting with the 104th Congress, every member and committee was provided with the opportunity to maintain an official Web site on House-maintained servers. As evident from Table 3.1, at the end of the 104th Congress, 222 members had an official Web site. Together, these sites were accessed approximately 850,000 times per month. Today, every member and standing committee has an official Web page and together they are accessed over 43 million times per month.[9] Of these, most are hosted by servers maintained by the House while a few, mostly leadership, sites are served and maintained on office-owned or privately contracted equipment.

Side-by-side with the growing use of Web sites by lawmakers and committees is the manner in which they are developed and maintained. At the start of the 104th Congress, a significant number of member sites were developed and sometimes maintained by supporting House, not member office, staff using a basic template design. Today, however, the overwhelming number of sites are developed and maintained by office staff themselves, the results being a wide variance in the design style and content of sites. Whatever the case, these Web sites have quickly grown into an important part of the member's and committee's communications and constituent service toolbox.

A critical function of any member's office is illustrating the member's work and legislative service on issues important to his or her district. Prior to the advent of the Internet, members relied almost exclusively on labor-intensive outlets such as Town Hall meetings and other public appearances to maintain

TABLE 3.1 MEMBER WEB-SITE ACCESS

CONGRESS	MEMBER WEB SITES	ACCESS PER MONTH
104th (1993–1995)	222	850,000
107th (2001–2003)	440	43,000,000

Source: House Information Resources.

visibility. Newsletters and other related mailings were often, and continue to be, used for the same reason. The local print, television, and radio media remained the other available avenue for such activities, but this method includes the obvious lack of control that is so important. The Internet has changed this. While personal, hands-on appearances and related activities will remain indispensable, the Internet has allowed legislators to speak directly to constituents, in their own words, without any filters, at any time of the day, through Web sites and related technologies that can be updated at a moment's notice without the time-related and other costs that go into traditional hard-copy mailings.

At their most basic level, member Web sites provide a source of general information on the member and his or her legislative activities including a bio, district information, floor statements, sponsored bills, and press releases. On an active, frequently updated Web page, this serves as an around-the-clock brochure *highlighting* the member and his or her service. In addition, the member Web site allows the member to directly present information in a manner free of any outside filters. While political and campaign content or links are prohibited, the member Web page plays an important part in *promoting* the member's legislative activities and policy agenda. At this level, the member Web pages serve not only as a basic informational resource, but as a tool *advocating*, in the member's own words, their work. As the Internet continues to grow in usage, this unfiltered and member-controlled source of information will continue to grow in value as constituents, the press, and other people and organizations come to rely on it, and as members continue to come to terms with and appreciate its benefits and possibilities.

Along with legislative service, the other important function of a member of Congress is in the constituent services arena. While each member has staff in Washington, D.C., to assist with their legislative and policy activities, they also have personnel—most often located in their district office(s), and who often outnumber legislative staff—whose primary role is in working directly with constituents and local government officials who have problems, concerns, or questions regarding any of the various federal agencies. At any moment, these staffers may be handling dozens of matters including Social Security and veterans benefits delays, student loan issues, immigration and naturalization assistance, passport requests, and postal delivery or Internal Revenue Service (IRS) complaints. In addition, these staffers assist constituents planning trips to Washington, individuals interested in purchasing a U.S. flag, and high school seniors interested in service academy appointments. Any member who values a strong constituent service record comes to rely greatly on these staff resources.

Prior to the advent of the Internet, members of Congress and the constituents they serve were often limited to regular, often East Coast, business hours when attempting to request or receive information from federal agencies. As a member representing the Los Angeles area, I recognized early on the frustrations this can cause. For each request made, the member office was often forced to contact multiple agencies or organizations for the information and then forward it on to the constituent, oftentimes leading to considerable delays. The amount of time spent handling "the basics" (e.g., providing constituent release forms for casework issues, answering frequently asked questions, taking constituent tour and flag requests) is often significant and can sometimes limit the time available for handling more substantive, time-critical matters.

The Internet has changed this. Now, via the member's Web page, a constituent can submit an electronic tour or flag request, apply for a service academy nomination, learn how to apply for a small business loan, become a U.S. citizen, get a passport, or obtain Social Security benefits whenever he or she wants, regardless of whether or not the member's Washington or district offices are open. This usage of the Internet as a tool saves both the constituent and the member's staff time, allowing them to fulfill basic needs on their own and providing more "quality time" for those requests that require more in-depth attention and personal contact. As more of this information is made available on-line and as various e-commerce tools of the business world are applied throughout government, the effective member Web site will continue to include these services and provide constituents with an increasingly important source of valuable information.

While member Web sites vary across the board, not only in design and focus but in content as well, they have become generally useful in providing the public with information and tools that highlight the member's service to his or her district and constituents. They have become an extremely valuable communications and public relations instrument in promoting the member's activities, and as a tool they offer time-saving, self-help information and assistance to the public on matters concerning federal agencies and other issues. This source of information will only grow in importance as Web use becomes commonplace and constituents continue to seek, and expect to find, such information on their representative's Web site.

Committee Web sites have similarly grown in use. As with member sites, the design and content of committee sites vary widely but each has attempted to provide its audience with helpful and informative material covering its activities including, in most instances, the views of the minority membership. Unlike member office sites whose primary target audience is their own direct constituency, the audience of a committee site is focused primarily on those who follow the specific issues within its legislative jurisdiction. While this audience certainly includes the general public, especially when concerning "major" issues, it is most often made up of groups and individuals, including lobbyists, government officials, interest groups and others, who follow and often seek to influence in one way or the other, specific legislation and other matters before the committee. For example, the House Committee on Agriculture's audience primarily includes those groups and individuals focused on such matters as farming, food safety, conservation, and other related issues. Other committees have a very different role and, therefore, a very different audience. The audience of the Rules Committee, for example, as the committee that sets the ground rules for legislative debate on bills coming to the House floor, is often made up of members themselves and their staff, executive branch employees, and outside groups and individuals tracking various legislation. For example, in May 2001 alone, the Rules Committee Web site received almost 200,000 requests from within the House as well as over 16,000 from the U.S. Senate, approximately 3,000 each from the Congressional Budget Office and Department of Justice, over 1,000 each from the U.S. Securities and Exchange Commission, Department of State, and Department of Education, and approximately 20,000 each from nonprofit organizations (.*org*) and educational institutions (.*edu*) (House Information Resources 2001). Internationally, the committee site received almost 2,500 requests from Germany and over 1,000 from Japan during the same month.[10] The House Rules Committee Web site also provides valuable background reports and briefs on its site about congressional rules, procedures, processes, and legislative terms in language that is easy for the average citizen or student to understand. This information is used by a number of colleges and universities around the country as an information resource for American government and political science courses.

A look at the various committee Web sites shows the extent to which the rule requiring publications to be available in electronic form has been implemented. Standard information on committee sites include hearing schedules, transcripts and written testimony, jurisdictions and procedure information (e.g., committee rules, jurisdiction, oversight plan, history, and so forth), and committee reports, prints, and other publications.

Recently, many committees have begun to offer even more information via their Web sites. A number of them regularly broadcast audio or video feeds of hearings over the Internet and some offer e-mail subscription services for committee hearing announcements and other information. Again, this information has provided the public with unprecedented access to the activities of House committees and is another example of the largely unheralded reforms taken up by Congress.

As the bodies where much of the legislative "footwork" is accomplished, committees will continue to look for tools that help them fulfill their responsibilities in an era of increased cost cutting. At the beginning of the 104th Congress, for example, the House moved to cut committee staffs by one-third and the yearly battles to increase committee funding, no matter how small, remain pitched. Today, committee Web sites play not only an important role in providing important and relevant information to their users, but have helped increase productivity in committee offices. Prior to their availability on committee Web sites, staff spent much of their time on the phone answering questions about hearing schedules, the availability of committee reports and other publications, and other related activities. Today at the House Rules Committee, the productivity increases have been quite significant, with many more hours per week now available for actual legislative work since the availability of this information on the committee Web site. For example, in April 2001, a relatively slow month for the committee with only three pieces of legislation before it, the Amendment Log-In Form on the Web page, which allows lawmakers to print out the form required for submitting their proposed amendments to the committee, was used over forty times. Previously, each such submission required the involvement of Rules Committee staff. Another example covers the issuance of special rules for each piece of legislation. Prior to the posting of this information on the Web site, which includes the amendments made in order by the committee for that specific bill, committee staff often took over one hundred phone calls from those, including legislators who submitted amendments, requesting the information. It is estimated that these calls have been reduced by over 75 percent now that the information is immediately posted to the committee Web page. These applications have proven invaluable to the limited resources of the Rules Committee. Other committees have reported similar savings.

With a relatively minor and unheralded change to House rules, two significant results came about. The first, to be expected, was that information heretofore largely inaccessible to the public was posted on committee Web sites for all the world to see. Hearing schedules and transcripts, even live coverage, were no longer only available to lobbyists and other individuals and organizations "inside the Beltway" but to interested citizens coast to coast. Along with other Web sites such as THOMAS, this has provided the public with an unprecedented view and access to the inner workings of their government and increased their ability to monitor and participate in the legislative process. Another result, perhaps less planned but significant nonetheless, has been increased committee staff productivity. The simple posting of committee schedules, hearing transcripts, and committee publications on their Web sites has resulted in substantial decreases in direct information requests that must be answered and fulfilled by committee staff. Taking into account the committee staff reductions passed at the beginning of the 104th Congress and limited increases in committee budgets, these savings have played an important role in freeing up valuable committee staff resources for important legislative and policy-planning responsibilities. As additional information is made available on committee Web sites and their use becomes more widespread, the positive effects from both of these consequences will continue to grow and illustrate the ability of technology to play a vital role in informing and educating the public on their system of government in a continued era of cost savings.

E-Mail and Related Electronic Communications Another fast growing Internet-related application used by members and committees is e-mail and related electronic communications tools. Again, its use across offices varies widely, but it has had an overall positive effect on the sharing of information within and among offices, and with their constituents.

In addition to its use as an internal communications tool, e-mail's other obvious application has been with constituent and press communications. In this respect, there is an even wider variance in its application across offices, but its impact has been significant nonetheless.

E-mail has made communicating with one's elected representatives easier and faster than ever before. Overwhelmingly, the vast majority of electronic constituent communications is incoming from constituents as opposed to outgoing from members, with 48 million e-mail messages reaching House offices in 2000.[11] According to a recent study conducted by George Washington University and the Congressional Management Foundation, this number continues to grow by an average of one million messages per month.[12] While a significant number of these communications are legitimate and thoughtful constituent-written items, a large and growing number of them are produced by individuals and organizations engaged in practices more akin to "spamming" than anything else. Like the growth in advocacy group–coordinated postcard and fax campaigns, these practices have forced offices to adopt procedures to help ensure that direct constituent communications and services are not adversely affected, while at the same time making sure that this new method of communication is treated no differently than other more traditional means.

Member offices have two general methods for accepting and managing constituent e-mail. They can choose to have either a public e-mail address or a form-based Web mail system. Each system has its own advantages and disadvantages and each has been adopted in one way or the other across most member offices.[13]

Offices providing a public e-mail address offer the easiest method for contacting a member electronically. With e-mail, individuals can contact their own or multiple lawmakers at the same time with a single message, allowing them to create personal distribution lists using their e-mail software package. Depending on the platform, this also allows people to attach documents to the e-mail being sent. Approximately 255 members have a public e-mail address allowing constituent contact.

The downside of this method is just as clear as its advantages. Short of the constituent including his or her street address within the e-mail, there is no viable way of confirming whether or not he or she is an actual constituent. In addition, the creation and use of distribution lists easily supports the practice of "spamming" and other activities that make managing these communications difficult at best. With some offices accepting public e-mail receiving as many as 8,000 messages a month,[14] it is easy to see why this has become a concern. Given that a majority of these come from nonconstituents only serves to highlight the problem even more. While some offices have successfully automated their e-mail response procedures to an extent, others have begun to reconsider this system altogether. In any instance, this situation has led many offices to install electronic mailbox management filters that, when unable to determine their origin, simply delete the e-mail unread altogether.

The system preferred by many offices is based on an on-line form where the communication is sent via a Web page to an established, usually hidden, e-mail account. Today, approximately 155 members use this system instead of having a public e-mail address. In most instances, this system requires an individual to enter in his or her name, street address, e-mail address, and other information before they can submit their message. Depending on the system and procedures in place, this method allows electronic communications to be automatically or manually sorted as coming from a constituent or nonconstituent based on the information entered. This method prevents individuals from spamming using distribution lists and, by forcing the entry of personal information with the message cuts down on the overall number of e-mail messages from nonconstituents and advocacy organizations engaged in mass e-lobbying and related activities. Offices using this method receive approximately 300 communications a month, with the overwhelming number of them from constituents.

The overall advantages to using this system are that, as indicated above, by requiring individuals to fill in a certain amount of information prior to their message or comments, the quantity of incoming messages is far more manageable than that in many offices with a public e-mail–address-only system. In addition, the quality of the items, as measured by their origination from an actual constituent of the member, far surpasses offices using a public e-mail address. While a certain level of automation and filtering is available with the public e-mail address system, the overall volume of incoming messages, including those unverified as originating from constituents, continues to present management problems with that system.[15] While I initially maintained a public e-mail address, the volume of messages from nonconstituents and the amount of spam and "junk mail" that I received made response management quite difficult and led me to switch to a Web form–based method of electronic communications. Since then, I consistently receive a steady stream of incoming messages from constituents and have yet to receive a single piece of spam-like e-mail. My constituents have been overwhelmingly positive in their view of this system and my office is now able to more efficiently manage and respond to their questions, comments, and suggestions.

The primary downside to the Web mail system is the possible "annoyance" factor that individuals attempting to regularly use the system may develop. While Web forms can be developed to remember the user's information and automatically fill in the required material, this would arguably defeat the purpose of the form and verge on permitting spam to at least the one member using the form. This procedure, however, would still prevent multiple member spamming. In general, however, most individuals come to appreciate the purpose of the Web form system when explained to them—that it is a system developed to allow the same, near-instantaneous communications as e-mail, while helping to ensure that messages from actual constituents are handled expeditiously and spam-type messages are filtered out.

One area in which an increasing number of member offices are applying electronic communications applications externally is in the use of electronic list services (listservs), e-mail newsletters, and, in a handful of instances, video newsletters. Similar to traditional member newsletters, these electronic communications services allow constituents to "subscribe" to them, usually via the member's Web page. Though the House does not provide for these services internally, lawmakers have turned to outside vendors and off-the-shelf software applications to provide a service that is becoming increasingly popular among constituents. While in many instances, these e-newsletters are simply electronic versions of the hard-copy newsletters sent out by the member, they are increasingly being used to provide exclusively electronic monthly or even weekly updates of congressional activities including bills sponsored by the member, legislative action on the House floor, and other updates on official House business. These electronic newsletters fall under the same House franking regulations as traditional mailings, including the regulation stating that mass mailings of over 500 identical pieces cannot be sent out "less than 90 days immediately before the date of any primary or general election (whether regular, special, or runoff) in which such Member is a candidate for public office."[16] Interestingly, in the Senate, a similar sixty-day rule applies to the updating of member Web sites themselves while House regulations do not apply to "Web sites and other electronic bulletin boards that post information for voluntary public access."[17] Given that these mass electronic communications services have little to no per-item cost following initial installation of the required software and hardware, it seems likely that they will continue to grow in use and may at some point become a functional answer to the increasing problem of how to most efficiently and effectively respond to constituent e-mail.

House committees are also increasingly turning to these types of electronic communications services in order to allow people to receive e-mail notices including committee hearing announcements, news releases, and other information. While these announcements are usually posted on the committee Web site, they are more effective as an active method of providing the information as opposed to their passive placement on the Web site that still requires people to look for it themselves. In the case of committee meeting announcements, this procedure has proven extremely helpful and effective.

Another fast-growing application of electronic communications is the use by House committees of streaming audio and video technologies over the Internet. Today a majority of the standing committees of the House provide audio or video streaming of their hearings. Most, due to cost limitations, are limited to audio-only Webcasts, but a few committees, most notably the committees on Science, Government Reform, and International Relations, have made significant technical infrastructure investments that allow them to Webcast in video as well. While certain hearings have always been covered by C-SPAN and other broadcasters, this new technology allows committees to air every hearing, making them available to a far wider audience on a regular basis than ever before imaginable. While issues such as bandwidth limitations and high-speed access availability have restricted the successful widespread application of this technology over the Internet in general, its use continues to grow.

Systems Management and Staffing Requirements The House of Representatives provides and supports a significant amount of the technologies on which member and committee offices rely. These include the backbone system through which members and staff send and receive e-mail, browse the Web, and other Internet-related applications. In addition, House-maintained servers house the vast majority of member and committee Web pages. Finally, the House provides supporting information, including a set of minimum standards, on computer and related equipment that offices may purchase from outside vendors. In many instances, however, member and committee offices themselves make the decisions on what computer equipment to purchase and have the added responsibility of servicing the equipment. While vendor support contracts cover a significant portion of this equipment, the final decision and responsibility for a growing number of technological tools fall on the offices themselves.

Personal computers and, increasingly, laptops have quickly become the primary tool on which member office personnel rely daily. While the House provides a list of minimum required hardware standards for such equipment, it is up to each office, often through third-party vendors, to choose, purchase, install, and maintain their own hardware and related software. As these systems become more complicated, more is required of those supporting them. Again, while vendor support contracts cover a great deal of this, a growing number of offices are finding it increasingly important to have in-office personnel who can, at a minimum, help troubleshoot problems.

In addition to the basic set of hardware and software found across all offices in general, a growing number of legislators are demanding the use of other tools (discussed earlier and widely found elsewhere), including videoconferencing, audio and video Web streaming, electronic newsletters, and more. While in some of these instances the House offers support, there are a number of others where the office is left to purchase, install, and maintain the equipment on its own or through an outside vendor. Internet streaming services offer the most vivid example of this. While this technology is not currently supported by the House, a number of member offices and, especially, committees, have begun to offer streaming audio and/or video from their sites. While this technology is expensive, offices have noted its usefulness in communicating beyond the simple written word via the Internet and have made the decision, on their own, to develop and administer streaming services. In a number of instances this has involved contracting out to third-party vendors, at least initially, but many offices manage this technology in-house. As this technology grows in popularity, the growing bandwidth requirements and other issues will at some point force the House to decide on support procedures for it or risk access and other problems that member offices, committees, and their constituents will not accept.

These and other related technology uses by member and committee offices have led to the growing need for experienced and dedicated technology staffers not only in House supporting offices, but also in member offices. As the use of these tools continues to grow, the demand for support staff will as well. Already, members of Congress have increasingly come to realize the important need for such individuals in their offices as they continue to implement and use the newest gadgets and tools. From Web site design and management through office network administration, the skill requirements for these positions will continue to grow and track that of the private sector. Already the House spends more money and resources on training staff in these technical-related areas than in legislative or procedural-related ones. The ability of member and committee offices to hire and retain these individuals will only continue to grow in importance, for while the House will continue to support a significant portion of these systems, their demand and implementation in congressional offices will vary widely and force members and committee offices to depend on in-office personnel to best apply and support them.

IMPACT AND IMPLICATIONS: THE TECHNOLOGY PARADOX

While the Internet and related technologies have had an overwhelming impact by offering the public unprecedented access to, participation in, and understanding of Congress, it has also raised some valid and serious concerns. Congress is not a one-dimensional institution. It has many functions and responsibilities—among them to deliberate, legislate, educate, and communicate. Each of these functions and responsibilities is affected differently by institutional change. Where technology may improve the efficiency of Congress's internal operations and enhance its ability to publish documents, track legislation, and communicate with constituents and with each other, it also has the potential to undermine Congress as a deliberative institution.

Electronic Democracy

E-mail, Web pages, and other tools of the Information Age have allowed information to flow faster than ever before and have increased the calls from many corners for Congress to respond to this by streamlining the legislative process in order to make it more directly and rapidly responsive—calls that run counter to the very core of our system of representative democracy. One observer notes the following:

> American democracy is about to change. . . . It will involve deeper, more structural, even seismic shifts that will move this country away from its traditional reliance on "representative democracy" towards newer, emerging forms of "direct democracy." . . . [The] rapid emergence of interactive communications technologies . . . [along with a] growing frustration with institutions of "representative democracy" . . . will increasingly converge in the immediate future, possibly in an explosive manner, to transform our American system of electoral

democracy into something very different than what we know today.... The framework of this new form of *electronic democracy* is already beginning to emerge. There seems no stopping it [emphasis in the original].[18]

If this trend continues and "electronic democracy" does indeed loom ever-larger in our system of governance, Congress may be forced to devise new procedures or mechanisms to check the popular passions of the moment and insure that reasoned debate can continue in an environment free from the undue influence of powerful but narrow interest groups armed with the latest communications technologies bent on fomenting a second, electronic Shays Rebellion.

Already we have seen one consequence of this in the fact that real decision making in Congress has increasingly moved behind closed doors. Today the rapid and widespread dissemination of information allows interest groups to more easily galvanize grassroots forces that, in turn, force lawmakers to solidify positions before consensus can be reached. To avoid this scrutiny, more and more activities are taking place outside of the formal process and procedures of the institution, including informal task forces and conference committees where Congress's open meeting rules do not apply. Ironically, the very technologies that have provided the public with unprecedented access to the official workings and functioning of the institution have at the same time forced some of those activities beyond its reach.

DOCUMENT PREPARATION AND PUBLICATION

One clearly significant impact that technology has had on the activities of Congress is in the preparation and publication of legislative documents. For example, House Legislative Counsel (Leg Counsel) uses electronic publishing applications and e-mail to draft bills and amendments and distribute them to member and committee offices. The use of the Adobe Acrobat® (.pdf) format permits the electronic drafting, editing, and proofing of legislative documents while maintaining the necessary layout and formatting of the material. This allows documents at the various stages of the drafting process to be quickly transmitted back and forth between Leg Counsel and the member or committee offices without any loss of the material's original visual representation.

While this has been significant in that it has increased the speed and efficiency of the legislative and bill drafting process, it has also raised some substantive and serious concerns as well. First, there is always concern over the security of the transmission of legislative documents in their unfinished state. While Leg Counsel maintains a separate e-mail server and all information is transmitted internally through the House, there is still concern over the accidental release to the wrong member office or even the public or press of such material in its unfinished stages. Once e-mail is sent, there is virtually no way to stop or retrieve it.

A second related concern is in the validation and authentication process as this material is transmitted back and forth electronically. Even with the coming implementation of digital signature technology, a number of questions and concerns will remain to be answered. For example, there will remain the question of authorized access to the electronic signature. How will congressional offices ensure that only authorized staffers have access to digital signature technology? Who will have the authority to digitally sign documents for a member or committee chair? Are current rules governing the requirements for member signatures adequate in an electronic environment?[19] These and other questions are becoming more critical as the House continues to develop and implement advanced document preparations systems.

The speed with which legislative material can be drafted, from start to finish, has also raised concerns as to the reduction in quality control measures and the deliberative process as a whole. In addition, the ability to quickly edit or add text to legislative documents has been related to the growing length and complexity of legislation. For example, in 1956, the legislation authorizing the national highway system was only 32 pages. The bill to improve that system in 1998 totaled 403 pages. In 1956, a 403-page bill would have taken months to put together. Just because we can prepare such a lengthy and complicated piece of legislation in such a short time does not mean we have produced a better product. Arguably, the speeding of the process can serve to mask the fact that there has been little time to analyze or validate the content. "As legislative text moves seamlessly from initial drafts through final publication," notes one CRS analyst, "one loses the time between each stage of the process that historically has been available for further consideration of the wording and for performing quality control."[20]

The electronic preparation and publication of legislative documents for matters of internal efficiency has also seen a corresponding move to make the material available to the public over the Internet as quickly as possible. Members' floor statements can be found on their Web pages almost immediately after being made. Committee Web sites often include witness testimony and hearing transcripts just as fast. In addition, all of these documents can include links to other information elsewhere on the Web and corrections or additions can be made at a moment's notice. None of these, however, are considered "official" congressional documents. The growing and widespread posting of such "unofficial" information on official congressional Web sites raises a number of important questions that are just now being considered. If these materials are to be considered "official," then who is ultimately responsible for the control of its content? Can links to material even be considered a "document"? What responsibilities are there for long-term archiving of the electronic versions of this information? What will the role of such entities as the Government Printing Office (GPO) be in the future as Congress continues to move towards the use of electronic means for preparing and publishing legislative documents? And as legislators, committees, and the House as an institution continue to provide more proceedings through audio and video coverage, what steps will need to be taken to establish standards and criteria for the relationships between the printed, on-line, and multimedia versions and their consideration as "official" records of Congress?

Finally, while Congress has implemented reforms and policies that give the public unprecedented access to the official activities and publications of the House via the Internet, we have seen increasing expectations for on-line access to additional documents as well. For example, CRS reports have long been available to the public when requested through and provided by their member of Congress. These reports are also available in electronic form via a congressional Intranet, for members and staff only. For a number of reasons, CRS and the Library of Congress have decided not to place these documents on THOMAS or some other publicly accessible Web site. Recently, however, legislation has been introduced which would require CRS to do just that.[21] Proponents of the legislation correctly point out that CRS products are produced at taxpayer expense and they provide valuable information that will help educate the public about the complicated nature of the issues facing Congress. While CRS's concerns about potential litigation, public lobbying over content, and the erosion of candid advice to lawmakers are legitimate, it is doubtful that making these reports available to the public over the Internet will undermine the deliberative nature of Congress as envisioned by the Founding Fathers. It is likely that they will be put on-line sometime in the near future. In fact, a number of members and committees, including the House Rules Committee, have begun to make them publicly available on their Web sites.

A number of people and organizations have gone a step further, however, demanding that such documents as bill drafts, chairmen's marks and draft amendments, and draft conference reports be made available on-line "as soon as they are printed or made available to lobbyists or members of a committee or subcommittee."[22] While the argument exists that making these documents publicly available would increase public trust in the system and permit enhanced citizen input into the process, it is also true that, as a CRS analyst notes, "the time gaps that have traditionally existed as drafts were revised, bills marked up, and committee and conference reports prepared—time which is often used to reach compromise, eliminate errors, and consider alternatives—may be lost if electronic versions of bills are rapidly composed and placed on Web sites."[23]

The House is in the process of developing and implementing a new document management system that will further enhance the means by which legislative documents can be prepared and published, both internally and for public consumption. While these tools will continue to perform a needed role, and the demand for continued enhancements will be strong both internally and externally, it will be just as important, if not more so, for the House to develop the necessary rules and guidelines for the technology's use as it pertains to the overall legislative process and all its components. As these technologies are developed, it will become increasingly important to the institution itself that these guidelines be developed and defined so that it is the legislative and deliberative process that drives the implementation of these tools, and not the technology that is allowed to define the process.

COMMITTEE ACTIVITIES

The premise of the committee system in Congress, that lawmakers serve on committees to gain expertise on issues important to their constituents and that members generally rely on the judgment of the committees when legislation is considered by the full House or Senate, has served well since the very first Congress. Today, however, the Internet and other related tools allow legislators, other committees, and staff to bypass these specialized bodies and gain immediate access to a wealth of documents and information heretofore unavailable with such ease, making the premise for serving on a standing committee questionably obsolete. As this trend continues, and the committee system, as the authority figure for matters within its jurisdiction, loses its primary *raison d'être*, we will likely see increasing amounts of legislation authored by members in areas where they heretofore lacked the "expertise" or experience that came from sitting on a certain committee. The rapid and widespread availability of information that the Internet and supporting technologies have provided has doubtlessly had an impact at the committee level and will most likely force a reexamination of the roles and responsibilities of the committee system in the near future. But it has certainly provided individual members the ability to more independently come to informed conclusions on matters before the House and has allowed them to participate in a far wider range of policy and legislative matters of local, national, or international concern.

Another area of concern for committees that has been raised by the increasing use of technology is in their regular proceedings. As committees have increasingly begun to broadcast the audio or video coverage of their hearings over the Internet, it is only a matter of time before lawmakers begin to question the necessity of physically attending hearings. Already committees have held hearings involving witnesses appearing via remote video conferencing. While current House rules prohibit proxy voting (House Rule XI, Clause 2[f]) and require a majority to be physically "present" before a measure or recommendation can be reported (House Rule XI, Clause 2[h][1]), the pressure will inevitably build to allow members to remotely listen in on hearings, e-mail questions to colleagues to be asked, or demand remote attendance rules for quorum requirements and even voting.[24] Already some members have proposed, unsuccessfully, remote voting allowances from their district under such circumstances as serious illness or family emergency. While these options may offer a solution to some of the difficulties facing a member and are clearly technically possible, the consequences may be even more damaging. The deliberative process in the House relies in large part on regular interaction between and among legislators. For all its possibilities, no technology exists that can reproduce the consensus building engagement that occurs during the face-to-face, physical sharing of ideas and passions that is at the core of the legislative process. This is a vital concern that the advocates of these proposals must seriously consider.

A number of other regular committee activities are being reexamined in light of the growing use of technology. The House is being forced to question the entire legislative document publication process. Committees, like Congress as a whole, have historically required written, hard-copy publication of its official documents. Among other things, House rules require committees to:

- adopt written rules governing its procedures—Rule XI, Clause 2(a)(1);
- provide witnesses with a transcript copy of his or her testimony—Rule XI, Clause 2(k)(9);
- submit a report on its activities—Rule XI, Clause 1(d)(1); and
- consider as read a proposed report if available to members for at least twenty-four hours—Rule XI, Clause 1(b)(2).

To what extent does the electronic posting or publishing of these documents suffice to fulfill the necessary requirements? How will the audio or video components of committee activities be incorporated into these rules? What standards will be necessary to provide for archiving the electronic versions of this material? These and other similar questions are at the heart of the discussion concerning the new electronic environment Congress increasingly finds itself in.

One recent item that vividly illustrates some of the questions and concerns facing House committees in an ever-increasing electronic environment is that of the audio and video broadcasting of committee hearings. As noted above, a number of committees have undertaken significant hearing room infrastructure upgrades in order to broadcast their hearings over the Internet. These upgrades have included various computer hardware and software purchases, broadcast-quality audio and video equipment, and significant hearing room renovations easily totaling in the tens of thousands of dollars. As internal House-wide funding and support of this technology has not been available, the purchase, installation, control, and maintenance of this equipment has been done on an *ad hoc* basis by each individual committee resulting in a significant variance across committees in equipment and procedures for its use. This process has resulted in a number of questions and problems that have forced the House to more closely examine the impact of this technology and to consider more formal and standard procedures for its implementation across House committees.

A related concern raised over the use of Internet broadcast technology by committees was in the procedures by which the transmission and its content was controlled. Simply put, while the chairman and committee majority has traditionally controlled the agenda and proceedings of the committee, the minority has always had the ability to have its views published and portrayed. Even on the Internet, committee Web pages include links to the Web site representing the views of the minority members. Such procedures are not always directly relevant where the broadcasting of hearings over the Internet, or any medium for that matter, is concerned. What is relevant, however, is the ability and rights of the minority to ensure representational coverage of their views during committee hearings and how that coverage is broadcast using committee equipment. In many cases, the control of the camera and other equipment during these transmissions is in the hands of the majority staff. Does this result in unfavorable broadcast coverage of the views of the minority? Are more formal procedures and standards required to cover the control of audio and video broadcast equipment by committee staff? Should such equipment even be controlled by committee staff or should the House itself assume control and maintenance of its use?

After examining these issues and their long-term impact on the ability of the House to adequately meet the increasing demands for increased public access to committee hearings and other congressional proceedings, including those concerns raised above, the Committee on House Administration recently determined to standardize the procedures concerning the upgrade of committee hearing rooms, including that equipment necessary for the Internet broadcasting of hearings. Specifically:

> The House Administration Committee believes that a standardized approach is the most logical and efficient solution to dealing with committee room upgrades. It is also critical that minimum technical standards be implemented to ensure the efficient use of resources and the compatibility of equipment and infrastructure. . . .
>
> The Chief Administrative Officer is directed to provide support staff to operate the broadcasting functions for each committee room that is renovated under the Committee Room Renovation Program. Committee staff are not authorized to operate broadcasting functions for such renovated committee rooms. The Chief Administrative Officer is authorized, but not required, to provide staff to operate the broadcasting functions of committee rooms that have been renovated prior to implementation of the Committee Room Renovation Program. The Chief Administrative Officer at the request of any such committee shall operate the broadcasting functions in such committee rooms.[25]

Prior to these recommendations, such upgrades and their funding requests were made during the regular committee funding process. By removing and funding these upgrade requests through a separate process and adding certain restrictions, committees have raised some concerns over loss of decision-making and equipment-use control. For example, what impact will this have on the already significant investments made by a number of committees? How will these standards be grandfathered to take into account the equipment and procedures already in use? What impact will this have on the prerogative of the committee chair to control the proceedings of the committee? What resources will be necessary for those authorized House staff to adequately support Internet broadcasts of committee hearings? What impact will these recommendations have on third-party organizations, including accredited news media that are looking to broadcast committee hearings to the public? Clearly the need for a move towards standardization on this issue is necessary, as the House sees no need to repeat the problems of uninteroperability seen with the initial House e-mail system as indicated above, but these concerns serve to illustrate the difficulties facing an organization as large and decentralized as the House when it comes to the implementation of various technologies. These and related questions promise to be mirrored across other areas as the House continues to increase its use of the Internet and other related tools for both internal and public use.

STATE LEGISLATURES: A COMPARISON

As part of its *21st Century Congress Project*, the House Rules Committee held hearings to assess the implications of technology utilization on the legislative process by state legislatures, held meetings with the National Conference of State Legislatures (NCSL), and visited a number of state legislatures. These meetings have been informative in illustrating how these tools have been adopted and implemented in a similar but significantly different environment.

Most state legislative bodies, acting under constraints of time and staffing, have designed and implemented an extensive legislative information system that serves to provide representatives, staff, and the public with information on all aspects of the legislative process from bill drafting, through committee work, to final passage. In addition, state legislatures have taken notice of, and have begun to study quite seriously, the overall impact of technology on the legislative process including staffing requirements and the rules and procedural changes made necessary by technology.

The main forces driving the development and implementation of information technology in state legislatures includes term limits, short legislative sessions, limited staff resources, the small size of legislative bodies, and the demands of elected representatives, many of whom use sophisticated information technologies in their private professions.

Time and again, state legislators and their staffs have pointed out that the implementation of term limits has greatly increased the number of legislators that lack a strong understanding of the legislative process. This, along with the fact that most state legislatures are part-time bodies, has forced legislators to adapt to a very steep learning curve in a short period of time. With limited staff resources available, technologies such as laptops, the Internet, e-mail, and others are proving critical in assisting state legislators in "getting up to speed" and providing them with the training, information, and tools needed to understand the rules and procedures of the legislative process.

In addition, as more legislators demand the tools they use regularly in their private occupations, implementing uniform, standard technological tools has become necessary in order to prevent problems associated with compatibility, scalability, and security. Prior to the introduction of the Colorado legislature's legislative information system, for example, many legislators were using personal equipment to communicate with colleagues and constituents and to access various information available via e-mail and the Internet. As this number continued to rise, it was necessary to develop a system that provided legislators and staff with the infrastructure and equipment vital to ensuring that information could be easily shared, future technological needs and requirements could be met, and any legal or ethical questions raised by the use of personal equipment would be minimized.

Finally, the demands brought on by increasingly complex legislative matters that must be dealt with during limited legislative sessions, along with other restrictions such as single-subject provisions, bill introduction limits, and deadline rules, have increased the complexity of the legislative process for many states. Unable to lengthen the legislative session, technology has helped state legislators deal with the increasing workload without dramatic increases in staffing or budget levels.

The point to emphasize is that, in state legislatures, the process is driving the development and implementation of technology, not the other way around. Technology has not been adopted for technology's sake nor has technology been allowed to diminish the deliberative nature of the process. In some instances, state legislatures have been slow to adopt technology, such as the video streaming of floor sessions, over concerns of disrupting or pressuring the vital deliberative, consensus-building nature of the legislative process.

Perhaps one of the most widespread uses of technology in state legislatures that differs significantly from Congress is the use of personal computers or laptops in the chamber. Thirty-five states now permit the use of computers in the chamber and during committee hearings.[26] These allow legislators to read legislation and proposed amendments as they are offered on the floor, communicate with fellow members and staff, and even surf the Web. While there have been similar efforts in Congress to permit the use of such technology,[27] it is interesting and important to note a number of significant differences between the two situations, some of which were alluded to earlier.

In the overwhelming number of states, legislative action on the floor is extremely structured and regimented, often including strict rules on the offering of amendments and single-subject provisions, unlike Congress where debate on the floor is more freewheeling and open. Logistically, most state legislatures have assigned seating, and during floor debate, attendance is often mandatory, again, unlike Congress. This, too, contributes to an environment where the development and adoption of various legislative information systems, including the use of computers in the chamber, has been a necessity rather than a choice. Interestingly enough, California, one of the first states to use computers in its chambers for access to legislative material, is still constitutionally mandated to provide hard-copy prints of the same material at every member's desk. Given the provisions that these bodies must work with and their reluctance or inability to lengthen the legislative session or significantly increase the number of personal support staff, these tools have allowed them to meet their legislative responsibilities, and provide the public with a high level of access to their activities, making for a more *effective* system while maintaining a process that is meant to be *inefficient* by design.

As a side note, a number of states make use of processes that are much more open to direct democracy and therefore may be much less likely to see any threat to representative government arising from the expanding use of technology. Specifically, there are currently twenty-seven states that provide for some sort of Initiative and Referendum (I&R). Adopted by states ranging from South Dakota in 1898 to Mississippi in 1992, these procedures allow citizens to directly adopt laws or amend the state constitution (Initiative) or reject laws or amendments proposed by the state legislature (Referendum).[28] States that permit these processes may in fact more enthusiastically embrace the use of technology, especially where it can be used to enhance the I&R process; however, it also serves to illustrate another significant difference between the legislative processes and procedures of the state and federal governments. Pure, direct-democracy advocates aside, the call for advancing the use of technology by Congress comes from those who largely seek to promote and enhance public participation in and understanding of its activities, not implement processes in use by various states that are ill-fitting at the federal level.

Congress clearly works in a different environment. While the overall process is quite similar, the institutional environment varies widely. In a number of areas, the use of technology in Congress and in state legislatures is quite similar and serves convergent purposes, especially in the areas of communications and access to legislative information in electronic format. In other areas, however, where the institutions diverge in terms of process, including the length of the legislative session, term limits, staff resources, committee and chamber activities, and more, the tradition and the environment of Congress differs significantly from that of the state legislatures and makes comparing the use of technology across these bodies at times irrelevant. While Congress will continue to adopt technologies to improve the inner workings of the body and to provide wider public access, often at the urging of members of Congress who served in various state legislatures and successfully used similar tools there, it will also continue to do so in a manner that serves to strengthen and protect the deliberative, consensus-building process that has historically served the institution and the nation so well.

Conclusion

In a short time, the Internet's impact on Congress has been real and substantial, and it continues to grow. Internally, its research and communications applications have significantly improved on many of the labor intensive and cumbersome procedures of the recent past. Externally, it has provided the American public a clearer and more immediate view of the activities of the House, arguably bringing them closer to their government than ever before. In addition, and similar to the demands seen elsewhere, the application of these technologies has forced upon lawmakers the need for staff experienced and knowledgeable not of the legislative or policy process, but in supporting and maintaining these new tools. As the tools of the Internet and related technologies continue to expand throughout society, their application in Congress will continue to grow as well. And while the House will never be at the cutting edge, the improvements they allow in research, communications, and other areas will be appreciated and applied by both members of Congress and the public they serve.

While many continue to criticize Congress for limiting access to certain information or for not being open and responsive enough to the immediate demands of the public, it is unarguable that in a very short time, Congress has made itself more accessible and its activities more transparent than ever before. While it certainly has more to do in this area, it also has an important responsibility to help educate the public on the reasons it functions as it does. Congress is not meant to react to the public emotions and demands of the moment. By its very design, it serves to check the popular passions and develop legislation through a deliberative, consensus-building process. While this process may often frustrate those demanding immediate action on any number of issues, it is a time-tested method that has served our country admirably in good times and bad. While technology can serve to help Congress and the public communicate more effectively and to improve the internal efficiency of certain congressional operations, its impact on the deliberative nature of the legislative process *may* be detrimental. As Congress continues to use such tools as the Internet and other technologies, it remains crucial that it do so in a deliberative and thoughtful manner that serves the interests of both an often critical and frustrated public as well as the solemn responsibilities of the institution itself.

Notes

1. Subcommittee on Rules and Organization of the House, 1997.
2. <www.house.gov/cha/publications/cybercongress/body_cybercongress.html>, 2001.
3. "CyberCongress Accomplishments during the 104th Congress," Committee on House Oversight Computer and Information Services Working Group, 104th Congress, 2nd sess., February 11, 1997.

4. Committee numbers include standing House committees as well as Joint Committees in existence during the 104th Congress (1995–1997).
5. Transcripts available on-line: "Legislating in the 21st Century Congress," <http://www.house.gov/rules/21hear01.htm>; "Impact of New Information Technologies on Decision-Making in the House of Representatives," <http://www.house.gov/rules/tran02.htm>; and "Legislating in the Information Age," <http://www.house.gov/rules/rules_hear05.htm>.
6. See "Information Technology in the House of Representatives: Trends and Potential Impact on Legislative Process," <http://www.house.gov/rules/infotech99.htm>; and "Electronic Devices in the House Chamber," <http://www.house.gov/rules/e-devices.htm>.
7. House Information Resources, 2001.
8. Jeffrey W. Seifert, *Information Technology in the House of Representatives: Trends and Potential Impact on Legislative Practices for the 107th Congress*, Congressional Research Service (Washington, D.C., April 19, 2001).
9. House Information Resources, 2001.
10. Ibid.
11. Ibid.
12. Kathy Goldschmidt, et al., "E-Mail Overload in Congress: Managing a Communications Crisis." A report by the Congress Online Project, <www.congressonlineproject.org/email.html>.
13. Regardless of the format incoming constituent messages take, be they phone call, fax, public e-mail or Web mail, members of Congress overwhelmingly choose to respond via hard-copy "snail mail" for a number of reasons including security and tampering concerns, internal quality control issues, and basic resource limitations.
14. Goldschmidt, "E-Mail Overload in Congress: Managing a Communications Crisis."
15. During various meetings with state legislative staff and members, the House Rules Committee, as part of its *21st Century Congress Project*, heard widespread anecdotal evidence that many state legislators, especially in larger, full-time legislatures like California, have also moved away from public e-mail toward a Web-form system due to similar problems and concerns.
16. *Members' Congressional Handbook*, 2001. The *Members' Congressional Handbook* is available at <http://www.house.gov/cha/handbook>.
17. Ibid.
18. Tracy Westen, "Electronic Democracy: Ready or Not, Here It Comes," in *E-Government Briefing Book, Congressional Internet Caucus Advisory Committee*, <http://www.netcaucus.org/books.egov2001.pdf/edemoc.pff>.
19. Internal Congressional Research Service memorandum prepared by Jane Bortnick Griffith for the House Rules Committee, 2001.
20. Ibid.
21. R. 654 is available on-line at <http://THOMAS.loc.gov/cgi-bin/query/z?c106:h.r.654.ih> and S. Res. 21 available on-line at <http://THOMAS.loc.gov/cgi-bin/query/z?c107:s.res.21>.
22. Congressional Accountability Project's "Fact Sheet on Congress and the Internet," 2001. Available at <http://www.congressproject.org/infopolicy/factsheet.html>.
23. Internal Congressional Research Service memorandum prepared by Jane Bortnick Griffith for the House Rules Committee, 2001.
24. Even state legislatures, which have gone much further than Congress in allowing for the use of computers and other electronic devices, have so far refrained from permitting remote committee attendance for purposes of voting or quorum requirements.
25. U.S. Congress, House Committee on Administration, *Providing for the Expenses of Certain Committees of the House of Representatives in the One Hundred Seventh Congress*, 107th Cong., 1st sess., H. Rept. 107-25, 2001, p. 6
26. National Conference of State Legislatures, 2001.
27. See, for example, "Congress Mulls Laptops in Sessions" at <http://news.cnet.com/news/0,10000,0-1005-200-322160,00.html>.
28. The Initiative and Referendum Institute's "I&R Factsheet" is available at <http://www.iandrinstitute.org/factsheets/WhatisIR.pdf>.

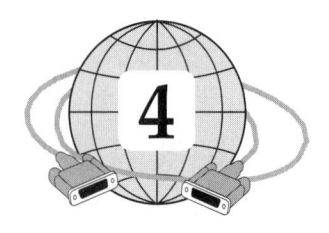

CAN CONGRESS COPE WITH IT?

DELIBERATION AND THE INTERNET

DONALD R. WOLFENSBERGER

> A popular Government, without popular information, or the means of acquiring it, is but a Prologue to a Farce or a Tragedy; or perhaps both. Knowledge will forever govern ignorance: And a people who mean to be their own Governors must arm themselves with the power which knowledge gives.[1]
> —James Madison (1822)

The Internet is just the latest development in a mass communications revolution that dates back to Gutenberg's invention of the movable-type printing press in the late fifteenth century. The Web's widespread popularity and expanding uses have inflated both hopes and fears about its potential impact on nearly everything.[2]

Not the least of these issues is how it will affect our system of government. If one were to combine both the most optimistic and pessimistic of projections, the Internet would appear as a two-edged sword hanging over representative democracy. One edge would enable citizens to cut through the smog that enshrouds our political system and obtain essential information about their government and its officials in a timely and useful manner. This, in turn, would produce a more active and informed citizenry, strengthen the bonds of understanding and trust between the people and their elected representatives, and restore public confidence in government.

The other edge of the sword, however, would cut to the quick of pending controversies so quickly that unformed, ill-formed, or misinformed public opinion would supplant considered public judgment as the new operational model of self-government and public policymaking. A passion-driven, populist-directed democracy would drive out the more ponderous, deliberative democracy that the Founders envisioned.[3]

Indeed, these competing scenarios for the impact of information-age globalism on governments and their ability to govern is captured in "Global Trends 2015," a report based on "A Dialogue about the Future with Nongovernment Experts," convened and published by the U.S. Central Intelligence Agency.[4]

The nongovernmental experts agree that the "state will remain the single most important organizing unit of political, economic, and security affairs through 2015." However, they predict that effective governance will confront two fundamental tests during this period: first, "how to benefit from while coping with several facets of globalization"; and second, how "to deal with increasingly vocal and organized publics."[5]

These experts also suggest that the authority of all governments will be challenged by several elements of globalization, including the "greater and freer flow of information, capital, goods, services, people, and the diffusion of power to nonstate actors." These nonstate actors, both profit-making and nonprofit, private-sector organizations, will gain increasing resources and power as a result of an expanding liberalization of global finance and trade, "as well as the opportunities afforded by information technology."[6]

The report goes on to predict that, "all states will confront popular demands for greater participation in politics and attention to civil rights—pressures that will encourage greater democratization and transparency." Successful states, say the experts, will be those who will "interact with nonstate actors to manage authority and share responsibility."[7]

Developed democracies will be best positioned for good governance "because they will tend to empower legitimate nonstate actors in both the for-profit and nonprofit sectors," and "favor institutions and processes that accommodate divergent communal groups." Moreover, they will press for transparency in government, the efficient delivery of public services, the regulation of legitimate nonstate actors, and the control of illegitimate groups.[8]

In those states that are unable to adapt to these new facets of globalization, say the experts, nonstate actors "will become more important than governments in providing services," and, "in the weakest of these countries, communal, criminal or terrorist groups will seek control of government institutions and/or territory."[9]

Certainly the United States is in a position to successfully adapt as a country to these new global trends because it has a longer and stronger democratic tradition than others. Nevertheless, the question remains as to just how successful our federalist system will be in sharing more power and authority with legitimate nonstate actors while at the same time retaining the fundamental attributes of its representative and deliberative character and its ability to regulate increasingly empowered and proliferating factions.

The purpose of this chapter is to explore the vast, unknown stretch of territory lying between the two poles of speculation described above with particular emphasis on how the Internet will affect deliberation in Congress. Obviously, with the Internet still in relative infancy, speculation at this early stage as to how and to what extent it will affect the way we govern ourselves is just that—speculation. Nevertheless, some possible trend lines are already appearing along with hints from various sources about the emerging shape of this latest stage of the mass communications revolution. Moreover, we already have the historical perspective of how other communications innovations were initially greeted, compared to their actual impact. Such a valuable perspective cannot be ignored in considering the latest innovations, nor should it be considered predictive of the future. If nothing else, though, this exploration demonstrates that it is still possible, and hopefully fruitful, to ponder the future of deliberation.

THE FOUNDERS' VISION

The Founders have sometimes been mistakenly portrayed as being disdainful of the masses and public opinion, or, even worse, of ignoring public opinion as a legitimate or significant political factor. One historian, for instance, argues that James Madison had "a surprisingly limited conception of the role of political information in public life." For example, this historian writes, "nowhere in his essays [*The Federalist*] did Madison imagine the possibility that printers might establish newspapers that would report continuously on the proceedings of Congress. . . . Indeed, at no point did Madison even go so far as to envision the emergence of public opinion as a political force."[10] According to this historian, Madison viewed the United States "as so geographically extended that its far-flung citizenry could not possibly secure access to the information necessary to monitor the government's ongoing affairs." The only opportunity citizens would have to catch up on such news was "when the representatives returned to their home districts to meet with their constituents face-to-face."[11]

Nothing could be further from the truth. Madison was acutely aware of the role public information and public opinion would play in the operation of the new government. Not only were the *Federalist* essays published in New York newspapers to influence public opinion in favor of ratifying the pending national Constitution at the state conventions of delegates *chosen by the people*, but the essays themselves are replete with references to public information and public opinion. In *Federalist No. 49*, Madison said it is "true that all governments rest on opinion," and that "in every nation," except those ruled by philosophers, "the most rational government will not find it a superfluous advantage to have the prejudices of the community on its side."[12]

In the same essay, however, Madison draws a careful distinction between two types of public opinion—those opinions that are the product of immediate passions, and those that are the product of reason. And he clearly comes down on the side of the latter, saying, "It is the reason alone that ought to control and regulate the government. The passions ought to be controlled and regulated by the government."[13]

Madison enlarges on this distinction in *Federalist No. 50* when he says, "When men exercise their reason coolly and freely on a variety of distinct questions, they inevitably fall into different opinion on some of them. When they are governed by a common passion, their opinions, if they are so to be called, will be the same."[14]

This leads to Madison's defense of representative government as a means both for controlling public passions and promoting public reason. It is best summed up in *Federalist No. 10* when he says the advantage of a Republic is its ability "to refine and enlarge the public views by passing them through the medium of a chosen body of citizens whose wisdom may best discern the true interest of their country" and whose public voice may well happen to be "more consonant to the public good than if pronounced by the people themselves, convened for that purpose."[15]

Alexander Hamilton, in *Federalist No. 84* dispels the notion that the Founders thought the people would only learn the news about their government from their representatives at election time. Hamilton poses the question of how people will get their information about the actions of government. He answers his own question by saying the people will "depend on the information of intelligent men, in whom they confide" who will obtain their information "from the public prints, from correspondence with their representatives, and with other persons who reside at the place of deliberations." Moreover, "the public papers will be expeditious messengers of intelligence to the most remote inhabitants of the Union."[16]

In December of 1791, as a member of the House of Representatives, Madison wrote a brief essay for the *National Gazette*, which he titled, "Public Opinion." In that essay Madison expands on the importance of public opinion: "Public opinion sets bounds to every government, and is the real sovereign in every free one." Sometimes "public opinion must be obeyed by the government," and sometimes, when it is not fixed, "it may be influenced by government."[17] He cites the Bill of Rights, the first ten amendments to the Constitution ratified that same month, as an example of how government was influenced by public opinion. He concludes his essay as follows:

> Whatever facilitates a general intercourse of sentiments, as good roads, domestic commerce, a free press, and particularly *a circulation of newspapers through the entire body of the people*, and *Representatives going from and returning among every part of them*, is equivalent to a contraction of territorial limits, and is favorable to liberty, where these may be too extensive [emphasis added].[18]

In summary, the Founders' vision of deliberative democracy rested on the ability of the people's representatives "to refine and enlarge the public views" until decisions were reached that were in the national interest or public good. This presupposes not only a representative's intimate knowledge of his congressional district, its inhabitants and their interests, but an ongoing exchange of views between the elected and the electors. This takes place not only during a representative's home visits, but also through an ongoing "intercourse of sentiments" between the representative and his constituents. It is conducted through correspondence and the public press. These communications help to shrink the geographic distance between citizens and their elected representatives—something considered not just desirable but essential to the success of a representative government in a large country.

Deliberation is dependent on information, and deliberative democracy depends on a two-way flow of information between the people and their representatives. The Framers understood this, even though they also understood the danger that public passion might sometimes overwhelm public reason and result in irrational and precipitous decisions. The system of bicameralism, separated powers, and checks and balances was thus designed specifically to cool such passions and arrest potential abuses.

Deliberation Today

Would the Founders even recognize our system of government today as being the one they erected over 212 years ago? How would they view what now passes for deliberation in the Congress? And, how would they regard the Internet and its potential impact on deliberative democracy?

Judging from their writings cited above, the Founders might not be as surprised as one might think about today's government. They did envision an evolving system of transportation and communication that would make such visits and exchanges of information and opinions more frequent and timely. Whether the Founders could ever imagine that a representative would one day be returning to his (let alone *her*) congressional district on a weekly basis, or that constituents could keep tabs on their representative's actions in Congress in real time on C-SPAN or the Internet, is highly doubtful. Nevertheless, they did foresee a developing system of communications and transportation that would shrink the time and distance between the governed and their government.

As the Founders made clear, they were well aware of the dangers that representative government, especially the House of Representatives, might become too close to the people and react too quickly to the popular passions of the day instead of taking the more dispassionate approach of cool and measured reason, that is, of acting in an informed and deliberative manner.

Smith defines deliberation as "reasoning together about the nature of a problem and solutions to it," and "a careful consideration of all the alternatives."[19] Bessette defines it as "a reasoning on the merits of public policy," the proximate aim of which is "the conferral of some public good or benefit."[20]

Bessette identifies the three essential elements of a deliberative process as being information, arguments, and persuasion. In the Congress formal deliberation takes place in committee hearings, during the debate on and amendment of legislation in committees and on the floor of the two chambers, and during the final House–Senate conference committee negotiations.[21]

The aforementioned types of formal deliberation share the common thread of a "reasoning *together*" about problems and alternative solutions. And "together" is meant to imply face-to-face, collective discussions. In his *Manual of Parliamentary Practice,* Thomas Jefferson stressed the importance of such face-to-face, collective discussions and decision making:

> A committee meets when and where they please, if the House has not ordered time and place for them, but *they can only act when together*, and not by separate consultation and consent—*nothing being the report of the committee but what has been agreed to in committee actually assembled* [emphasis added].[22]

In its infancy, the House of Representatives actually deliberated in the Committee of the Whole House about what the general thrust of a bill should be before appointing a select committee to draft the details. But, as the House grew in size and it became more difficult for such deliberations, standing committees were established. The role of the Committee of the Whole was reduced to debating the products of the committees through the offering of amendments. As early as 1885, future U.S. president and political scientist Woodrow Wilson observed that, "Congress in session is Congress on public exhibition, whilst Congress in its committee-rooms is Congress at work."[23] Serious debate and deliberation, Wilson complained, had shifted to the committees, which conducted their business in secret, far from public view, thus depriving the people of the benefit of the reasoning behind legislation.

In reaction to the institutional reforms of the 1970s that made the formal committee and floor processes more open and accountable, more and more of the actual deliberations and bargaining retreated behind closed doors once again—to party leadership meetings and party caucuses, to informal member organizations (or special-interest caucuses), to private meetings with lobbyists and constituents, and to negotiations with executive branch representatives (e.g., the eleven-day 1990 budget summit between White House representatives and congressional leaders at Andrews Air Force base). Moreover, with the more frequent visits of members to their districts, a type of deliberative process is often replicated in town hall meetings between members and their constituents. Nevertheless, these examples of informal deliberation have in common with their formal counterparts the element of face-to-face meetings and discussions, an actual convening to reason about problems and possible solutions.

So, how can something like the Internet, which by its nature involves a *virtual* accessing or exchange of views and information affect either the formal or informal deliberative processes in which members engage *directly* with each other or external actors? The answer, quite simply, is that the information or views requested and/or received (by a member or his staff) via the Internet can influence the representative's own thinking and decisions. They can do so to the extent they become part of the lawmaker's arsenal of information and arguments used during informal and formal deliberations. Or, they can do so to the extent that they bring pressure on the lawmaker to act in a certain way by virtue of the strength of the information or arguments, the numbers of constituents, or the importance of interest groups presenting views in support of or in opposition to a particular proposition. Such pressures may prevail regardless of whether the representative publicly embraces or expresses those views as his own.

While the latter type of influence may be considered antideliberative because it is a visceral response to popular or special-interest pressures rather than the product of a reasoning together about the nature of a problem and its solution, it cannot be dismissed for purposes of this discussion. It still affects the deliberative process and its outcomes, whether reasoned or not.

By the same token, such external pressures not only can affect the agenda setting stage of the policy process (what does or does not get considered by the legislature) but can also determine how alternatives get considered or rejected once a problem is on the agenda and is under deliberation. Again, the failure to consider a particular alternative (e.g., through a closed or restrictive amendment process), or the rejection of an alternative due to external pressures, may not be a rational or well-reasoned action, but it is still an integral part of the overall deliberative process. As one congressional observer puts it:

> In neither chamber of Congress does floor discussion achieve the ideal form of either debate or deliberation. . . . It is pointless to hope that the two chambers make such fundamental changes in how they conduct their business that they could achieve the ideal forms of debate and deliberation on their floors. Factors such as the important role of the president and other external agenda setters, the large congressional work load, and the size of the two bodies weigh against setting pure debate or deliberation as a standard for evaluating change and reform.[24]

The point here is not to assess the impact of the Internet on some ideal form of pure deliberation that never existed in the first place, but rather to determine how various aspects of the Internet may now, or in the future, affect deliberation in Congress as it exists at the turn of the century. To do so it must be recognized that there are already numerous other factors that have contributed to the decline of deliberation in the Congress long before the Internet was even a gleam in former Vice President Al Gore's eye. These include: the rise of party leadership powers and the corresponding decline in the authority and powers of committees; more frequent and longer congressional district visits, meaning shorter congressional work weeks (meaning less time for committee and floor deliberations); the proliferation of interest groups and their ability to tie up the process with special concerns and thereby discourage genuine deliberation over larger, national concerns;[25] and the effects of intensely partisan campaign strategies and tactics spilling over into the governing process, causing a shift in Congress from "a culture of governing through deliberation to one of perpetual campaigning through confrontation."[26]

In short, while the Internet may now be *connected* to all of the above reasons for the decline in deliberation, it can hardly be considered a causal connection. After all, the Internet only began to catch on in popular appeal and usage around 1995.[27] It is now just one more potentially accelerating force in these contradeliberative trends.

CONGRESSIONAL STAFF CONSIDER IT AND DELIBERATION

A bipartisan group of twenty-eight House and Senate staff members chosen as fellows in the Congressional Staff Fellowship Program of the John C. Stennis Center for Public Service in 1999–2000, organized their ten-month program around the following core theme questions: "How can Congress best fulfill its constitutional and deliberative role in a global information society?"; and, "How can or should the institution operate at a twenty-first-century tempo?"[28]

Their final report or "discussion paper," as they termed it, is titled, "Congress Meets the Information Age: Deliberation in the Twenty-First Century." The fellows present two possible scenarios as to how Congress will be affected by these rapidly changing technological developments over the next ten years. Under the "undesirable scenario," if Congress does not take steps to deal with the twenty-first-century tempo, it could "risk the eventual death of deliberative or representative constitutional democracy" because "the political system, including Congress, will move closer to direct democracy."[29]

The staffers cite a number of likely consequences of such a status quo scenario:

- Congress would become dependent on technology and fall into the role of delegate.
- It will continue to aggregate interests rather than foster compromise, and deliberation will degenerate into cut-throat competition and confrontation between the parties.
- People will come to expect immediate answers from Congress as they become accustomed to immediate answers from information technology; electronic communication will undermine personal contacts and Congress will be seen as less relevant and concerned.
- Congress will slip into a permanent campaign mode, more dependent on polling, focus groups, and campaign fund-raising, and thus be unable to deliberate effectively.[30]

The staff group depicted the desirable scenario as follows:

- Congress will harness technology and act on it in a broad context, and use it as part of its leadership strategy and to leverage policymaking.
- It will spend most of its time governing in a "deliberative and constructively partisan" manner, and be "visionary, educational, [and] instrumental in creating a sense of national purpose."
- Congressional oversight will serve as a national educational and deliberative device by using information technology in innovative ways to engage the public.
- Institutional leadership will be directed to increasing public respect for Congress.[31]

In short, Congress can remain relatively passive and allow itself to be overwhelmed by the information age revolution, or, it can become proactive by using the new technologies to achieve its core functions of lawmaking, oversight, and constituent service, all without sacrificing the essential deliberative nature of the institution.

The congressional report with its competing scenarios for Congress's future was given a broader audience on January 22, 2001. A group of nearly forty congressional staff, Wilson Center fellows, and Washington area political scientists heard a summary presentation of the report from three members of the 106th Congress's Class of Stennis Fellows and then further discussed the implications of their findings at some length.[32]

Several points were highlighted during the initial presentation that are important to keep in mind in considering what role, if any, the Internet is playing or will play in either enhancing or undermining congressional deliberation in the future. First, the group made clear that it was talking about how the totality of information age technologies, and not just the Internet, was affecting the Congress. This universe of technologies includes the exponential growth in e-mail messages over the Internet, blast faxes, phone trees, talk radio, proliferating cable television channels and 24-hour news cycles, and instant polling—all of which amplify the volume of new voices on all manner of emerging issues, great and small.

The e-mail burden alone, though, has proven especially frustrating for many congressional offices. Some Stennis fellows indicated that their offices received an average of 3,000 e-mail messages a week from their constituents. And yet, like many offices, they still attempt to answer them all with a signed letter from the lawmaker.

A recent survey conducted by the Congress Online Project confirms this trend. It found that the volume of e-mail to congressional offices has risen from 20 million messages in 1998 to 48 million in 2000, and that it continues to grow on average by one million messages per month. Much of this mail is attributable to grassroots lobbyists and e-businesses, which capitalize on the new technology to advance their causes. Unfortunately, the report concludes, "these advocacy groups are encouraging the public to engage in e-mail practices—like spamming congressional offices—that result in unmanageable demands on Congress."[33]

Second, the congressional staff group concluded that even though the ability of new technologies to empower individuals and new virtual communities is still in its formative stages, it is already affecting every walk of life in such a way that unless Congress "gets on the bandwagon," it risks being left behind as an obsolete institution. As one staff aide, perhaps hyperbolically, puts it, "adapt or die."[34]

But, third, say the staffers, the pace of technological change and its effects on society will always be much more rapid than political change can ever be. They add, though, that maybe that's not all that bad since speed for speed's sake is not an attribute best suited for national policymaking.

At the same time, the rapid rate of changes being wrought by information technologies presents Congress with an ever-expanding agenda of new issues about which it may be forced to deliberate. The Internet alone, for instance, poses vast new challenges in such areas as personal privacy, intellectual property rights, the "digital divide" (those who have access and those without access), on-line pornography, and taxation of e-commerce, to name just a few. How much of this new activity taking place on the Internet should be subject to government regulation? That question alone is the subject of extended deliberation both within the Congress and its committees, but also with the executive branch, and new and old types of businesses, educators, parents, state and local officials, and even (or especially) with international organizations.[35]

Thus the question for Congress becomes one of how it can retain its integrity and deliberative character while still being relevant to the new realities and tempo of an information-age world. The Stennis fellows concluded that Congress should embark on a proactive program of using the new technologies to carry out its core responsibilities of lawmaking, oversight, and constituent service.

Specifically, not only can these technologies be used to access information necessary to making policy more rapidly and efficiently, but to enable members to communicate more effectively with constituents and interest groups. Congress has a responsibility to become aware of and responsive to the concerns and needs of the citizenry. But it also has a responsibility to inform citizens about what their government is doing, including what issues currently are being debated in the Congress. In short, information technologies in general, and the Internet, in particular, can help to facilitate the larger, informal public deliberation that should be an important factor in Congress's more formal deliberations.

Moreover, Congress has a responsibility to explain to the people the processes of their government as much as it does the issues being dealt with through those processes. If the people do not "appreciate and revere the process of deliberation, debate and compromise" as much as they do the issues being debated, said one staff person, then they are likely to become impatient and frustrated with the pace of the process and look elsewhere for solutions.[36]

All of these things can be conveyed to the people through various avenues afforded by information technologies. But, as the staffer was quick to add, no technologies can replace the statesmanship that will be needed to advance certain issues in the process or to find and forge acceptable and effective national solutions. The appropriate technologies must be chosen for advancing Congress's decision-making process through deliberation—"an actual reasoning together"—and those that do not should be rejected.[37]

For instance, the group unanimously rejected such things as remote voting or deliberation through e-mail. Face-to-face contact among members is the best way to achieve deliberative results and to build relationships and trust. As one staff person said, "Congress needs to maintain or restore its collegial environment and its reputation for deliberation, even in the face of a twenty-first century society where everything instant is perceived to be good."[38]

A Virtual Reality Check

So, how is Congress doing so far in adapting to the new realities of the Information Age? Even though Congress was in on the popular take-off of the Internet in 1995 with former Speaker Newt Gingrich's (R-Ga.) initiative to establish the Library of Congress's THOMAS Web site, one gets the distinct impression from the group of congressional staff who considered the matter over a period of months that Congress has not begun to grasp what needs to be done to bring congressional deliberation into the twenty-first century.

Perhaps there is no better symbolic metaphor for this lag-time effect than the Congressional Internet Caucus, an informal, bipartisan group of House and Senate members joined together to learn more and inform their colleagues about Internet issues and legislation. If you tried to find the caucus using the House of Representatives' search engine, using the term "Internet," it would not come up on any of the first 100 (out of 9,291) entries, "ranked by relevance" in the 107th Congress (2001–2003). You would, however, turn up a large number of hearings and statements on Internet issues.

If one were fortunate enough to know that the two House cochairs of the Congressional Internet Caucus are Representative Rick Boucher (D-Va.) and Representative Robert W. Goodlatte (R-Va.), one might have more luck going directly to their House Web pages. Indeed, Representative Boucher's Web page does direct you to a page for the "Congressional Internet Caucus." However, when you click on that link, you end up on a page with the following message:

> This page is currently under construction. Please check back soon. Please visit the Internet Caucus Advisory Committee at http://www.net caucus.org.[39]

The latter referenced Internet Caucus Advisory Committee is an outside industry group that does have a working Web site and an up-to-date listing of coming forums and demonstrations. Moreover, the site explains its purpose (and that of the Congressional Internet Caucus) as follows:

> This site contains information about the program and activities of the Advisory Committee and the Congressional Internet Caucus—a bipartisan group of over 150 members of the House and Senate working to educate their colleagues about the promise and potential of the Internet.[40]

As it turns out, the Congressional Internet Caucus site has been "under construction" for most if not all of its existence, and has simply served as a front (or portal) for its outside advisory committee's more technically adept, current, and informative activities.

The point of all this is not to embarrass the Congressional Caucus (it has had plenty of time to get over any embarrassment caused by its inability to construct its own Web page), but rather to highlight just how behind the learning curve the "Internet leaders" in Congress seem to be about the Internet. As it turns out, a few members are quite active in their own right on Internet issues as is evident from the hearing testimony presented, legislation introduced, and Internet-related information posted on their individual Web pages. But, beyond this responsiveness to industry concerns, very few members are expressing any concern about how this is affecting the institution of Congress and its deliberations, and how Congress might proactively get back in the game of being relevant to the new age and the increasing number of people who are looking to the Internet not just for shopping and entertainment, but for a greater "connectedness" to public-policy issues, their government, and elected representatives.

A nonscientific survey of member Web sites, for instance, turns up only a smattering of representatives who provide links to plain-English information about how the legislative process works, or simple explanations of major pending policy issues and what the options are for addressing them. And yet, explaining or providing ready access to process and policy information should be two of the most important responsibilities of Congress in assisting the public in being a part of the national deliberative process.

A more detailed survey by this author of all House member Web pages taken a week after the March 8, 2001, House vote on the major piece of President Bush's $1.6 trillion tax cut revealed that only 28 percent of the members posted news on the vote and their position, as evident in Table 4.1 (on page 90).

While an increasing number of committee Web sites are putting more information about issues they are dealing with on their sites, most people do not get beyond their own representative's site if they get that far. Even then, committees quite often give succinct summaries of pending or reported bills without offering a broader explanation of the policy issue context. Members and committees could easily remedy this problem by making available on their

TABLE 4.1 THE POSTING OF TAX VOTE NEWS ON HOUSE MEMBERS' WEB PAGES*
(MARCH 8 VOTE ON H.R. 3, THE ECONOMIC GROWTH AND TAX RELIEF ACT OF 2001)

PARTY	MEMBERS WITH TAX VOTE NEWS ON THEIR WEB PAGES	MEMBERS WITHOUT TAX VOTE NEWS ON THEIR WEB PAGES	TOTALS
Democrats	36 (17%)	175 (83%)	211
Republicans	85 (39%)	135 (61%)	220
Independents	2		2
Totals	123 (28%)	308 (71%)	431**

*This survey was conducted on March 14, 2001, six days after the House passed the president's tax bill (H.R. 3), by a vote of 230–198. Members were credited for posted news releases, newsletters, or floor statements taking a position on the bill between March 1 and the date of the survey. The thirty members who did not have Web pages are counted as not posting tax news on a Web page.
**There were two vacancies in the House at the time of the survey, one from each party.

sites the "issue briefs" prepared by the Congressional Research Service (CRS) at the Library of Congress. But, because the CRS is prohibited by its authorizing statute from making their products available to anyone but members of Congress, few members have taken the initiative to release the materials themselves on their Web pages (though most members have no compunctions about responding to constituent requests for information by sending them the relevant CRS documents). One member who has made things easier for the public is freshman Representative Mark Green (R-Wis.). He has posted an index and link to all currently active CRS issue briefs and reports.[41]

Another notable exception to the inaccessibility of CRS reports is the Web site of the House Rules Committee which includes brief explanations of various aspects of the legislative process, plus a large number of CRS issue briefs and longer background papers on everything from committees and the budget process, to bicameral differences between the House and Senate, and relations between the president and the Congress.[42]

Moreover, Representative David Dreier (R-Calif.), beginning with his service as a Rules subcommittee chairman in the 104th Congress (1993–1995), inaugurated a *21st Century Congress Project* that posed the very questions and challenges this chapter and book are attempting to cover, that is, the impact of the Information Age on Congress, and its potential use of information technologies to improve the deliberative, legislative, oversight, and informing functions of the Congress.[43]

While the work of the Rules Committee in this area to date has not been groundbreaking, it has at least been toe-wetting. One of the early hearings, for instance, used, with mixed results, both teleconferencing and Webcasting with opportunity for the public to pose questions to committee members and witnesses by e-mail.

FUTURE POSSIBILITIES

In connection with its *21st Century Congress Project*, the Rules Committee commissioned a Congressional Research Service report, released in 1999 that expanded upon ways in which information technology might impact on the legislative process. It concluded that the application of technology "has the potential to significantly impact the legislative processes."[44]

One of the striking conclusions relevant here is the finding that moving toward an electronic document system in Congress (and its committees) will probably mean "reduced time for the deliberation process." As the report elaborates:

> The use of computers makes it possible to put draft material into a format that appears to be "final" very rapidly. Yet the appearance of a correctly formatted document may mask the fact that there has been little time to analyze or validate the content. . . . As legislative text moves more seamlessly from initial drafts through final publication, one loses the time between each stage of the process that historically has been available for further consideration of the wording and for performing quality control.[45]

This prospect of instant, electronic availability of evolving bill text and proposed amendments in committee or on the floor raises the larger question of whether the same materials should be made available simultaneously to the public over the Internet as some public interest groups have strongly urged.[46] As the CRS report notes on this point:

> The time gaps that traditionally have existed as drafts were revised, bills marked up and committee reports prepared—time which is often used to reach compromises, eliminate errors, and consider alternatives—may be lost if electronic versions of bills are rapidly composed and placed on Web sites. Conversely, increased public exposure to the process may permit citizen input to be more directly considered during committee deliberations.[47]

The report goes on to offer a veritable (or virtual) potpourri of electronic possibilities that Congress might utilize in its committees, from electronic briefing books for hearings and markups, to "virtual" markups and reporting of bills using networked systems, including remote, electronic voting.[48]

Likewise, the report revisits the issue of whether members should be allowed to bring their own laptop computers onto the floor of the House and Senate, something both the House and Senate rules committees informally rejected after commissioning CRS reports on the issue, on grounds they would detract from the dignity, decorum, and integrity of the deliberations in the two chambers.[49] Among the questions raised by the CRS reports, which provided both pros and cons on the floor use of laptops, were: whether members would be inundated with e-mail from lobbyists and constituents during actual floor debate; whether members would have better access to information that could make a positive contribution to the deliberations underway; and whether the presence of laptops might sacrifice collegiality to efficiency.[50]

As with the prospect of remote committee voting, the 1999 CRS report speculated on the possibility of remote floor voting using any number of options for ensuring security and authentication, from digital signatures to biometric verification (digital fingerprints or retinal scans). Putting all these possibilities together, the report concludes that, "In the future, one might be able to convene a 'virtual' House and conduct votes without members being physically present." The report adds, however, that, "there seems to be little support among Members . . . for the idea of voting remotely and strong sentiment in favor of coming together to debate and vote on legislation."[51]

Other issues raised by both internal and external electronic communications that affect deliberation include the ability of members to more easily form *ad hoc* groups to promote a cause, bill, or amendment; the effects such member-to-member communication have on the leadership's ability to hold party members together; the increasing use of information technologies by outside interest groups to mobilize their membership for legislative purposes; and the growing adeptness and frequency of constituents in using e-mail to contact members on pending legislation.[52]

Given all these converging factors, the report asks how these trends will affect members torn between conflicting constituent and national interests; how on-line polling of constituents by members will affect a member's position on an issue; whether the new communications possibilities will weaken allegiance to party leadership; and whether the ability of constituents and interest groups to observe members acting in real time will affect members' abilities to develop compromises and experiment with new approaches.[53]

The possibility cited above of members using their Web pages to conduct polling of their constituents on pending matters was raised in another and earlier committee report. In 1997, a subgroup of the House Oversight (now House Administration) Committee reported to the full committee on the "cyber" accomplishments of the 104th Congress.[54]

In its report, the working group noted that House Web sites were becoming "increasingly more attractive and innovative," and that members and committees were experimenting with the technology "to develop new ways to communicate with and empower the citizens of our nation." Such empowerment includes enabling citizens to "be better informed about legislative and legal issues," and facilitating communication between them and their elected officials. One of the examples cited in the report of how the twin aims of legislative information and communication could be joined through the Internet was, "Conducting electronic surveys using interactive sites," among other things, "to find out how constituents would vote on *pending* legislation" (emphasis added).[55]

Conclusion

Notwithstanding these pioneering efforts by the House Rules and House Oversight (now House Administration) Committees, the fact is, as with so many congressional initiatives, there has been little follow-up work done on the implications and options presented in the two reports. As of the beginning of the 107th Congress (2001–2003) in 2001, the *21st Century Congress Project* Web page had been removed from the Rules Committee's site (it has since reappeared on the Web page of the committee's recently renamed Subcommittee on Technology and the House). The House Oversight Committee's Computer and Information Services Working Group was not reconstituted in either the 106th (1999–2001) or the 107th Congresses (though many of its recommendations have been implemented by the Chief Administrative Officer through House Information Resources [HIR]). It is true, with each passing year, that the information capabilities of the House, Senate, and THOMAS Web sites continue to expand and improve.

But what is missing from this technological progress is some clear vision shared by members of the House and Senate of what the relationship should be between the new information technologies and the core lawmaking and representational functions of Congress. The Stennis Center congressional staff fellows in the 106th Congress are the first group of knowledgeable insiders to express concern publicly about the seeming indirection of Congress in this regard and what the implications might be if Congress continues to ignore the issue.

One should not be too surprised that Congress does not now see any of this as a possible problem for our representative democracy, let alone that it does not have a proactive approach to addressing it as the Stennis fellows have advocated. One thing that has remained relatively constant about the institution over the years is that it is a reactive rather than a proactive body, and usually does not act until a crisis is literally on top of it.

In the meantime, however, to the extent that anyone is paying attention to this problem within the institution, it is the "techies" who will likely set the course in the absence of direction from above or from the whole. This includes the management of HIR, the information technology–literate staff of the House and Senate Administration Committees, and the "systems administrators" in member, committee, and leadership offices. It may also include a few computer-literate members of Congress who are willing to take some time to attend to such internal housekeeping functions with little or no psychic reward from their colleagues. But their chances of involving their more technologically challenged colleagues in the larger questions of such an enterprise are negligible.

Does it really matter whether members actually confront the implications and options of the information age as long as there is a willing, committed, and competent staff to look after the technical details of keeping the systems up-to-date and state-of-the-art? Will things just naturally evolve, given capable staff guidance, to meet the needs of the new Information Age?

The Stennis fellows, at least, did not think that increased staff expertise alone was enough. As was brought out at the Wilson Center conference, they considered recommending a chief information officer for Congress to make decisions on which new systems and uses would be in the best interests of a deliberative institution. But the fellows decided against including that recommendation in its final "discussion paper"—perhaps because it sidesteps the need to engage members more in deciding what directions Congress should take.

Instead, the Stennis congressional staff fellows called for the creation of House and Senate short-term special committees on Information Technology and Congressional Deliberation, patterned after the recent Senate Special Committee on the Y2K Problem. The committees would "explore needed institutional changes (innovations) to strengthen congressional deliberation with information technology." As the staff fellows see it, this exercise would produce "some champions among members" for the cause of ensuring that information technology development is compatible with and promotes better deliberation—defining deliberation in the broader sense of greater involvement of the public in the policy process, without destroying the ultimate responsibility of Congress to make the final deliberative decisions.[56]

And therein lies the conundrum. How close is too close? Stated differently, is it possible for Congress to allow real-time public awareness of and participation in a process that requires sufficient time and space for Congress to develop the necessary compromises for a national policy consensus that is acceptable both internally and externally? Two congressional watchers captured the essence of this legislative conundrum before the Internet was even a factor in the deliberative process.[57] Their historic overview demonstrates how the decline of deliberation in Congress has been inversely proportional to the growth in the number and complexity of issues with which it has had to deal, meaning that there is less time available to deliberate on each.

The Computer and Information Services Working Group of the House Oversight Committee offered the following concluding comments on how the new computer technologies are the culmination of the Founders' intentions:

> Although the Founding Fathers could not have foreseen the technology that would give rise to the CyberCongress initiative, they would have readily understood the value of its implementation. Communication is the very essence of representative democracy. The empowerment of the citizen through computer-mediated communication technologies is the focus of [Speaker Gingrich's] vision. While it promises to usher in a new era of informed citizen participation in the business of the House, it is not a new idea, but rather the realization of the full potential for representative democracy envisioned by the Founding Fathers at the Constitutional Convention two centuries ago.[58]

Indeed, what the working group has written is not incompatible with the epigram from Madison at the beginning of this chapter on the need for a self-governing people to be armed with knowledge. But, how much citizen knowledge and participation is a logical extension of the Founders' intent? In advocating two-year terms for House members, according to one constitutional scholar, the Federalists recognized that "for the whole process to work, members must look forward and deliberate with each other—an impossibility if every moment is spent looking over the shoulder at the home constituency."[59] As Alexander Hamilton put it in arguing for longer terms during the constitutional convention's debates, "There ought to be neither too much nor too little dependence on the popular sentiments."[60]

Are we nearing the point at which internal deliberation may be made impossible in Congress because external participation is both continuous and overwhelming? There can be no question that the Information Super-Highway can further arm the people with the knowledge that will enable them to better govern themselves through their elected representatives. However, just because the Information Superhighway and deliberation are both two-way streets does not mean that they are perfectly integrated and compatible systems. The fact is they have drastically different maximum speed limits. If the Information Superhighway is not used to enhance both congressional deliberation and citizen involvement in a balanced manner, our system of deliberative democracy may well become a relic of the last century.

That is the challenge Congress will have to face or ignore at its peril in the next few years. Will it travel the path of least resistance, that is, go with the electronic flow that promotes the greatest convenience, efficiency, and self-preservation for members through constituent service and reelection efforts, while merely processing public opinion polls into public laws? Or, will it still make time for the much less efficient, more time-consuming, and politically perilous path of deliberative lawmaking? Put another way, will Congress recognize that e-liberation is not synonymous with deliberation, and that House and Senate committee and chamber debates cannot be replaced by cyber-polling and chat room exchanges?

Madison left no doubt as to where he would come down on this question. For him it would be the simple choice between a pure democracy driven by popular passions at the expense of minority and property rights (and thus doomed to a short life and violent death), and a republic in which public opinion is refined and enlarged through the medium of an elected body of citizens "whose wisdom may best discern the true interest of their country."[61]

NOTES

1. James Madison to William T. Barry, 4 August 1822, *James Madison: Writings*, ed. Jack N. Rakove (New York: Literary Classics of the United States, 1999), p. 790.
2. For the sake of convenience and variety, this chapter will use the terms Internet and Web interchangeably, even though they are technically not the same thing. The Web or the World Wide Web (www) is the Internet's hypertext system that allows you to travel around the world looking for information by using linked words.

3. In this chapter I intentionally avoid extended discussions of the prospect of the ultimate in direct democracy, a national Initiative and Referendum process that could be greatly facilitated through interactive debates and voting on national laws over the Internet. I avoid this discussion not because it is not a real possibility—indeed, many experts who both favor and oppose such a process consider it to be "inevitable"—but because of space limitations here and the fact that the prospect of a national Initiative and Referendum process has been dealt with amply in other works. See, for instance, Dick Morris, *VOTE.com* (Los Angeles: Renaissance Books, 1999); David S. Broder, *Democracy Derailed: Initiative Campaigns and the Power of Money* (New York: Harcourt, Inc., 2000); Donald R. Wolfensberger, *Congress and the People: Deliberative Democracy on Trial* (Baltimore, MD: Johns Hopkins University Press, 2000); and Brian Webert, "Instant Democracy for Everyone," *APSA Legislative Studies Section Newsletter* 24 (2001), pp. 9–11.
4. National Intelligence Council, "Global Trends 2015: A Dialogue about the Future with Non-Government Experts" (paper approved for publication by the National Foreign Intelligence Board under authority of the Director of the Central Intelligence Agency, NIC 2000-02, Washington, D.C., December 2000).
5. Ibid., p. 27.
6. Ibid.
7. Ibid.
8. Ibid., p. 30.
9. Ibid.
10. Richard R. John, *Spreading the News: The American Postal System from Franklin to Morse* (Cambridge, MA: Harvard University Press, 1995), p. 29.
11. Ibid.
12. James Madison, *Federalist 49*, in Alexander Hamilton, James Madison, and John Jay, *The Federalist Papers* (New York: New American Library of World Literature, Inc., 1961 [1962]), pp. 314–315.
13. Ibid., p. 317.
14. James Madison, *Federalist 50*, in Hamilton, Madison, and Jay, *The Federalist Papers*, p. 319.
15. James Madison, *Federalist 10*, in Hamilton, Madison, and Jay, *The Federalist Papers*, p. 82.
16. Alexander Hamilton, *Federalist 84*, in Hamilton, Madison, and Jay, *The Federalist Papers*, pp. 516–517.
17. Madison, *James Madison: Writings*, pp. 500–501.
18. Ibid., p. 501.
19. Steven S. Smith, *Call to Order: Floor Politics in the House and Senate* (Washington, D.C.: Brookings Institution, 1989), p. 239.
20. Joseph M. Bessette, *The Mild Voice of Reason: Deliberative Democracy and American National Government* (Chicago: University of Chicago Press, 1997), p. 46.
21. Ibid., pp. 49–55.
22. Thomas Jefferson, "Jefferson's Manual of Parliamentary Practice," in *House Rules and Manual, One Hundred Sixth Congress* (Washington, D.C.: U.S. Government Printing Office, 1999; House Document No. 105-358), sec. 407, p. 198.
23. Woodrow Wilson, *Congressional Government: A Study in American Politics* (Baltimore, MD: Johns Hopkins University Press, 1981 [1885]), p. 69.
24. Smith, *Call to Order*, p. 239.
25. See especially, Jonathan Rauch, *Government's End: Why Washington Stopped Working* (Washington, D.C.: Public Affairs, 1999), originally published as *Demosclerosis* (1994); and Burdett A. Loomis, "The Never Ending Story: Campaigns without Elections," in *The Permanent Campaign and Its Future*, ed. Norman J. Ornstein and Thomas A. Mann (Washington, D.C.: American Enterprise Institute and Brookings Institution, 2000).
26. Wolfensberger, *Congress and the People*, p. 270; see also Loomis, "The Never Ending Story."
27. For a discussion of the emergence of the Internet and issues related to its growing use, see, for instance, Leslie David Simon, *NetPolicy.com: Public Agenda for a Digital World* (Washington, D.C.: The Woodrow Wilson University Press and Baltimore, MD: Johns Hopkins University Press, 2000).
28. John S. Stennis Congressional Staff Fellows, 106th Congress, "Congress Meets the Information Age: Deliberation in the 21st Century, a Discussion Paper," Washington, D.C.: Typescript, September 2, 2000, p. 2.
29. Ibid., p. 13.
30. Ibid.

31. Ibid., p. 14.
32. The summary presentations of the group's discussion paper were delivered by Rochelle Dornant, chief of staff to Representative Sam Farr (D-Calif.); Robert Simon, Democratic staff director of the Senate Energy and Natural Resources Committee; and Kristine Iverson, Legislative Director to Senator Orrin G. Hatch (R-Utah). To encourage a frank discussion, the roundtable was off-the-record, so no quotes will be attributed here to any of the participants by name.
33. "E-Mail Overload in Congress: Managing a Communications Crisis," a report of the Congress Online Project, funded by the Pew Charitable Trusts, accessed at <http://www.congressonlineproject,or/email.html>, March 19, 2001. See also Amy Keller and Ben Pershing, "Study Faults Hill on E-Mail," *Roll Call*, 19 March 2001, p. 1; and Thomas B. Edsall, "In Congress, They've Got Mail—Far Too Much of It," *Washington Post*, 19 March 2001, p. A-5.
34. Pew Charitable Trusts, "E-Mail Overload in Congress."
35. See Simon, *NetPolicy.com: Public Agenda for a Digital World*.
36. Pew Charitable Trusts, "E-Mail Overload in Congress."
37. Ibid.
38. Ibid.
39. Accessed on February 13, 2001, at <http://www.house.gov/boucher/underconstruction.htm>.
40. Accessed on February 13, 2001, at <http://www.house.gov/boucher/underconstruction.htm>. In addition to listing past and future briefings and talks, the Advisory Group lists all the House and Senate members of the Congressional Internet Caucus (with links back to their home pages), all the supporters and members of the Advisory Group (with links to their home sites), and provides separate pages of statistics and data, briefing books, and issues. Moreover, it promises in the near future to provide links to relevant committee hearings, reports, and the legislative status of relevant bills.
41. The CRS index page on Representative Green's Web site can be accessed at <http://www.house.gov/markgreen/crs.htm>.
42. See the House Rules Committee's Web site at <http://www.house.gov/rules/welcome.htm>.
43. The *21st Century Congress Project* page of the Rules Committee's Web site was taken down at the beginning of the 107th Congress in 2001. It may be transferred in the future to the page of the newly renamed Subcommittee on Technology and the House at <http://www.house.gov/rules/sub_th.htm>.
44. Jane Bortnick Griffith, *Information Technology in the House of Representatives: Trends and Potential Impact on the Legislative Process*, CRS Report prepared for the House Committee on Rules, 1999, p.1. Formerly found at <http://www.house.gov:80rules/infotech99.htm> (see endnote 39 above).
45. Ibid, p. 9.
46. See, for instance, Gary Ruskin (director of the Congressional Accountability Project) and Kenneth R. Weinstein, "Congress Is Plugged-In; Now It Must Increase Access to Information," *Roll Call*, 9 December 1996. At the beginning of the 105th Congress, in 1997, the House did adopt a new rule that reads, "Each committee shall make its publications available in electronic form to the maximum extent feasible" (now House Rule XI, clause 2(e)(4)). This does not address the demand by some that committee amendments and chairmen's marks be posted on the Internet contemporaneously with their consideration in committee, since these are not considered committee publications, that is, printed documents available to the public. Under House Rules, a committee report is not an official document until it is filed with the Clerk. That is not to say, however, that prior publication of a substitute bill as a "committee print" is prohibited. Many committees already publish such documents for the use of members, staff, and the public during committee markups of bills.
47. Bortnick Griffith, *Information Technology in the House of Representatives*, p. 12.
48. Ibid.
49. Walter J. Oleszek and Jane Bortnick Griffith, *Electronic Devices in the House Chamber*, CRS Report, November 21, 1997. At the beginning of the 106th Congress in 1997, the House had adopted a rule that reads: "A person may not smoke or use any personal, electronic office equipment, including cellular phones and computers, on the floor of the House" (now House Rule XVII, clause 5). The rule was initially prompted by members' receiving and making cellular phone calls in the House, though the future prospect of requests to bring personal computers was also contemplated by the rule's prohibition. The Senate has no specific rule

banning personal computers on the floor, but it is prohibited under the general rules of decorum in the absence of a rule authorizing their use.
50. Bortnick Griffith, *Information Technology in the House of Representatives*, p. 13.
51. Ibid.
52. Ibid., pp. 14–15.
53. Ibid., p. 15.
54. U.S. Congress, Computer and Information Services Working Group, Committee on House Oversight, "CyberCongress Accomplishments during the 104th Congress," Washington, D.C., February 11, 1997 (accessed January 2000), at <http://www.house.gov:80/cha/publications/publications.html>.
55. Ibid., pp. 6–7.
56. Stennis Congressional Fellows, "Congress Meets the Information Age," pp. 16–17.
57. George E. Connor and Bruce I. Oppenheimer, "Deliberation: An Untimed Value in a Times Game," in *Congress Reconsidered*, 5th ed., ed. Lawrence C. Dodd and Bruce I. Oppenheimer (Washington, D.C.: CQ Press, 1993).
58. Computer and Information Services Working Group, "CyberCongress Accomplishments during the 104th Congress," p. 10.
59. Connor and Oppenheimer, "Deliberation: An Untimed Value in a Times Game," quoting from Michael J. Malbin, "Congress during the Convention and Ratification," in *The Framing and Ratification of the Constitution*, ed. Leonard W. Levy and Dennis J. Mahoney (New York: Macmillan; London: Collier Macmillan, 1987), (p. 193) p. 318.
60. "Debates in the Federal Convention of 1787 as Reported by James Madison," June 21, 1787, in *Documents Illustrative of the Formation of the Union of the American States*, House Document 398, 69th Cong., 1st sess. (Washington, D.C.: Government Printing Office, 1927), p. 256.
61. Madison, *Federalist 10*, p. 82.

THE "WIRED CONGRESS"

THE INTERNET, INSTITUTIONAL CHANGE, AND LEGISLATIVE WORK

C. LAWRENCE EVANS AND WALTER J. OLESZEK

The relationship between Congress and the Internet is multifaceted. The emergence of any major technological development (railroads, radio, automobiles, etc.) always gives rise to legislative debates about the need for new tax, regulatory, or management laws. The Internet is no exception. It has changed the character of the legislative agenda and expanded the lawmaking function. Congress is now grappling with a host of complex Internet-related issues heretofore not on its agenda, such as the extent to which copyright protections should be extended to material transmitted in cyberspace or whether state and local governments should collect sales taxes on goods and services traded on the Internet.[1] Scores of information technology bills (from a few dozen during the 104th Congress [1995–1997] to hundreds today) are introduced, influencing the work of nearly all congressional committees and members and spawning the growth of a new array of interest groups. Thus, the invention of the Internet as a new communications medium formed by the interconnection of numerous computers has led Congress into new frontiers of lawmaking and oversight.

The Internet's influence is evident within and between the chambers of Congress. Nearly every nook and cranny is filled with diverse technologies. For example, member and committee offices are "wired" to various electronic networks; numerous Internet databases provide lawmakers, committees, and staff aides with a wide range of information; legislative support units, such as the Congressional Research Service or the Government Printing Office, integrate the Internet into their work; committees and lawmakers maintain their own Web sites; and the exchange of legislative e-mail addresses is as common as trading telephone numbers. There is even a bicameral, bipartisan Internet Caucus which has as one of its prime goals moving Congress ever more quickly into the Information Age. The Congress Online Project, a partnership of the Congressional Management Foundation and The George Washington University funded by the Pew Charitable Trusts, provides relevant information and ideas to congressional offices on how they might enhance their use of online communications.

Despite widespread discussion about how the Internet will revolutionize politics and policymaking, Congress usually reacts cautiously to new complexities and innovations. "The Congress never moves as fast as the rest of the world does," said Senator Joseph Lieberman (D-Conn.).[2] Long-standing traditions, customs, and procedures exert a powerful influence in both the House and Senate and inhibit frequent changes in the way Congress conducts its day-to-day work. However, Congress also recognizes that, "ready or not," it must adopt certain new technologies both to enhance lawmakers' performance and to remain a relevant and effective branch of government.

Our main argument is that generalizations about how the Internet is fundamentally transforming the Congress are overdrawn. In our view, the Internet is an important technological tool that has become a routine part of congressional life without altering the fundamental character of the House or Senate. While the Internet is an important part of the legislative process, its introduction to the Congress followed a fairly predictable route, which tracked how other technologies came to Capitol Hill. We explore this pathway in the first part of this chapter. Broadly, it starts with development of the technology followed by advocates who believe the technology can be applied to Congress. Lawmakers view the technology negatively at first, but opposition to it is gradually overcome as members recognize its value and utility. Then the technology is adapted to the workways of Congress and woven into the routines of the legislative process. In the second part of the chapter, we examine several implications associated with the Internet and congressional decision making and suggest that the technology bolsters policy, procedural, and partisan trends already underway in the Congress. In the final part, we provide summary observations about the Internet and congressional governance.

TECHNOLOGICAL INVENTIONS COME TO CAPITOL HILL

Members of Congress often approach the application of new technology to legislative processes with a mix of caution, skepticism, and resistance. As one lawmaker put it: "Whatever the future holds, we can be sure of one thing: At first, Congress will always be very good at resisting it."[3] This general attitude among many lawmakers is understandable. Change often brings in its wake both pluses and minuses and has the potential to change the distribution of influence within Congress. Before lawmakers sign on to change, they want to know: Who stands to win or lose power with the new technology? Are there electoral risks associated with its use? What are its costs and benefits? Will members become too dependent on the technology? How long will it be before the technology becomes obsolete? What rules or customs are likely to change if the new technology is used by Congress? Is the new technology applicable to all the functions of Congress? What is the best way to integrate the technology into the legislative process? The list of questions can go on and on.

The point is that just because new technologies are constantly developed and marketed does not mean they will find ready acceptance in Congress or even among the general public. For example, a scholar pointed out that the video telephone was demonstrated at the 1964 World's Fair in New York City with home units available in the 1990s and inexpensive versions available for use on the Web. Still, there is little public interest in employing them. Why? The camera would add an unwelcome burden to the technique of conversation. You would need to look your best, be careful about facial expressions (you're being recorded), and perhaps be forced to tidy up the visible background.[4] A look at the lengthy process of installing electronic voting machines in the House, the televising of House and Senate floor sessions, and applying computers in Congress highlights the general congressional pattern of resistance followed by embracement.

Electronic Voting

On June 1, 1869, Thomas Edison was granted a patent by the U.S. Patent Office for his electric vote recorder. "Having observed the great loss of time attending roll calls for votes in Congress [when he used to report them on the press wire]," Edison conceived the idea for an electronic voting machine.[5] He explained that the places where lawmakers sat would be wired to a central receiving instrument:

> In front of each member of the House [would be] two buttons, one for aye and one for no. By the side of the Speaker's desk was erected a square frame, in the upper part of which were two dials, corresponding to the two classes of votes. Below the dials were spaces in which numbers appeared. When the vote was called for, each member pressed one or another of the buttons before him and . . . the number of votes appeared automatically on the record. All the Speaker had to do was to glance at the dial and announce the result.[6]

Edison believed that his voting machine would win wide acceptance by state legislatures and the U.S. Congress. He was wrong. For example, the Massachusetts Legislature rejected Edison's machine on the ground that it would infringe on the minority's right to delay action on legislation. Undeterred, Edison went to Washington, D.C., and demonstrated his apparatus to a committee chairman whose panel was authorized to purchase such equipment. The chairman told Edison:

> Young man, that is just what we do *not* want. Your invention would destroy the only hope that the minority would have of influencing legislation. . . . And as the ruling majority knows that at some day they may become a minority, they will be as much averse to change as their opponents.[7]

Still, there was support in the House for Edison's voting machine. On July 6, 1870, the chamber considered a report from the Committee on Rules recommending that the House experiment with a voting machine to expedite the counting of votes. "I believe a machine like this, which will facilitate the taking of the yeas and nays in this House," declared Representative Samuel Cox (D-N.Y.), "is consonant with the spirit of our progressive country and our progressive age."[8] Another member, Thomas Ferry (R-Mich.), stressed the large amount of time that would be saved by using the new voting apparatus. During a session of the 40th Congress (1867–1869), he said, "The roll was called three hundred and forty-six times, consuming one hundred and fifteen hours, which would be some twenty-three days, or a calendar month."[9] These arguments were unsuccessful, and the House tabled (or killed) the proposition by a roll call vote of 86 to 82.

One hundred years passed before the House authorized the use of electronic voting equipment for roll call votes or quorum calls. The relevant part of Section 121 of the Legislative Reorganization Act of 1970 (P.L. 91-510) stated: "[U]pon any roll call or quorum call, the names of such Members voting or present may be recorded through the use of appropriate electronic equipment." In the interim between Edison's time and 1970, there were periodic calls from lawmakers and others to install electronic voting equipment. In 1945, for instance, two House members testified before the Joint Committee on the Organization of Congress and recommended an automatic roll call device. Twenty years later, several lawmakers testified in favor of electronic voting in the House before another joint reorganization committee. Then, in the midst of large public concern about secrecy in Congress, especially the lack of recorded votes in the Committee of the Whole (the prime amending forum in the House), the 1970 LRA made provision for recording the names of lawmakers either by tally clerks or an electronic device. A bipartisan coalition of lawmakers deserves large credit for generating public support for recording these votes. They employed an antisecrecy strategy, which gathered support from editorial writers and public interest groups across the country. The electronic voting provision became effective on January 23, 1973.

Periodically, suggestions are made in the Senate to permit electronic voting. On January 6, 1987, for example, Majority Leader Robert C. Byrd (D-W.Va.) introduced a resolution (S. Res. 29) to permit electronic voting on measures or matters, subject to the joint approval of the Democratic and Republican leaders.[10] To date, the Senate has yet to emulate the House and install electronic voting. One reason for the Senate's reluctance to modernize its voting system is that many senators prefer the drama associated with calling the roll on highly controversial issues where the outcome is in doubt. Furthermore, during the period when the roll is called, senators welcome the opportunity to discuss legislative business with colleagues and to socialize with one another.

TELEVISING FLOOR PROCEEDINGS

Not until the 1970s did the House make a concerted effort to employ a technology—television—that had been in American homes a quarter century earlier. As with electronic voting, legislative resistance to television was strong.

Many lawmakers argued that if floor sessions were televised, it would promote grandstanding and distort floor proceedings, encourage broadcasters to portray Congress unfairly (focusing on members reading newspapers rather than paying attention to the discussion, for example), and either be too complicated or too boring for the average viewer. However, even as early as the 1920s, lawmakers began proposing radio coverage of the House and Senate and later, with the invention of television, they introduced legislation authorizing radio and television coverage of chamber and committee proceedings.

The year 1947 saw a television first on the opening day of the 80th Congress (1947–1949). Television coverage of the House was permitted for the first—and last—time until the 1970s. (Television was allowed in the chamber for the president's State of the Union message or for speeches by certain dignitaries, but key party leaders opposed its broader use.) House and Senate committees were sometimes televised—for example, the nationally televised hearings in the 1950s on the communist threat or the 1960s hearings on the Vietnam War—subject to the rules of the pertinent panels. For a time in the 1950s, Speaker Sam Rayburn (D-Tex.) even banned televised committee hearings arguing that they were not authorized by House rules. Not until enactment of the Legislative Reorganization Act of 1970 did the House and Senate formally authorize the televising of committee hearings subject to the committees' broadcasting rules.

Pressure to extend television coverage to floor proceedings, especially in the House, continued into the 1970s during a time of heightened public interest in "sunshine in government" and legislative–executive clashes over the Vietnam War. According to Don Wolfensberger, who served as a top staff aide to the House Rules Committee's 1975–1976 *ad hoc* subcommittee on broadcasting:

> What gave impetus to televising House floor debates was the recognition by the Democratic leadership in early 1970 that President Richard Nixon was dominating the airwaves with defenses of his Vietnam War policies, while congressional opponents were not being given equal access by the networks. Finally, after several closed-circuit tests were authorized by the Speaker, the House on March 19, 1979, went public for the first time with live floor coverage carried over the Cable Satellite Public Affairs Network (C-SPAN) whose founder, Brian Lamb, was instrumental in transforming the House floor into the "electronic gallery."[11]

If the House was slow to permit gavel-to-gavel broadcast coverage of its floor proceedings, the Senate was even slower. On May 2, 1924, the Senate did agree to a resolution sponsored by Senator Robert Howell (R-Neb.) whose background was in radio, to consider the radio broadcasting of the chamber's floor proceedings. Many senators opposed Howell's proposal, including Majority Leader Henry Cabot Lodge (R-Mass.) who stated: "I do not at all know whether or not the Senate desires to have everything which is said here broadcasted."[12] Nothing ever came of Howell's broadcast idea until July 29, 1986, when the Senate, after a six-week trail period, voted 78 to 21 to permit gavel-to-gavel coverage of its floor proceedings over C-SPAN II.

Institutional pride, competition, and self-image were among the prime factors that contributed to the Senate vote in favor of televised coverage. Senators, who were accustomed to receiving much more publicity than rank-and-file House members, were concerned about the heightened public visibility accorded the House and its lawmakers. A telling argument for television coverage heard over and over again in the Senate was made by Majority Leader Howard Baker (R-Tenn.): "My point is that the House of Representatives will become the dominant congressional branch of government of the United States, simply because the public has access to their proceedings, if we do not provide similar access here."[13] Added then–Minority Leader Robert C. Byrd (D-W.Va.), "Many people think Congress is only what they see on TV—Tip O'Neill and the House of Representatives—and it shouldn't be that way."[14] Or as Speaker Thomas "Tip" O'Neill (D-Mass.), phrased it: "They got a little tired of us grabbing the news."[15] Many senators, too, wanted their own electronic "bully pulpit" as a counterweight to the White House's.

COMPUTERS AND CONGRESS

The introduction of information technologies to the Congress was also a slow process. A lawmaker in the mid-1960s who opposed (perhaps feared) computers for Congress stated: "In my opinion, it will be a sorry day for the country when Congressmen have been replaced by computers."[16] Nonetheless, there were lawmakers during this period who recognized the importance and value of technology for congressional use. They proposed legislation to encourage use of automatic data processing systems to better manage, store, and retrieve information, making Congress less dependent on the executive branch or special interests for data and analysis.[17] Several House and Senate committees and other legislative entities also examined where to apply computer technology (member offices, committees, administrative units, and so on), for what purposes (payroll preparation, inventory control, mail preparation, and so forth) and how it could best be used to assist lawmakers in making informed judgments on a myriad of complex issues.[18] For instance, a proposal by a committee reform panel won Senate adoption on February 4, 1977, requiring establishment of a computerized scheduling system for all Senate committees. Still, by 1993, a report of the Joint Committee on the Organization of Congress noted:

> Congress is an institution that has not kept pace with the developments in technology widely used in society. The House and Senate spend more than $150 million per year on information and technology resources, yet critical information is often not readily available to the Members. There is little coordination between the entities that provide technological support to the Congress. Members require modern technological support to deal with the scope and variety of information on a huge span of issues. It is not being provided.[19]

Technological development on Capitol Hill accelerated in the mid-1990s because of the determined effort of many lawmakers to bring Information-Age technology to Capitol Hill. Former Speaker Newt Gingrich (R-Ga.) was a strong champion of employing diverse technologies to empower both individual lawmakers and individual citizens to acquire an expanded range of legislative information in a timely and cost-effective manner. Soon after he became Speaker in 1995, Gingrich inaugurated a computer system called THOMAS (after Thomas Jefferson) in the Library of Congress. It is an on-line legislative information resource—http://thomas.loc.gov—which provides anyone in the world who is interested with materials (bill summaries and status updates, committee reports, the *Congressional Record*, etc.) that were previously easily accessible only to Capitol Hill insiders and Washington lobbyists. This Internet-accessed system was a watershed event for it made the legislative process more transparent and promoted the wide and easy availability of materials about the Congress. Not everything of legislative significance is available on THOMAS, such as the "chairman's mark" (the document to be considered during the committee amendment, or markup, stage), but THOMAS provides a large amount of current and unfiltered information about Congress to the general public.

The Speaker in 1995 also directed a Computer and Information Services Working Group to upgrade and revamp the House's information system. Two years later, Gingrich supported adoption of a new House rule: "Each committee shall make its publications available in electronic form to the maximum extent feasible." Previously, committee publications were available only in printed form.

Gingrich believed, too, that improving the information technology available to Congress would make the institution more responsive to a public mood that, in his estimation, increasingly favored the Republican party. Also in January 1997, the Library of Congress and the Congressional Research Service, at the instigation of the Senate Committees on Appropriations and Rules and Administration, brought on-line a legislative information retrieval system (the LIS) which is "available only within the legislative branch."[20]

To summarize, a number of significant forces and factors commonly combine to trigger technological change on Capitol Hill. First, new innovations arrive in the House or Senate because determined lawmakers champion their cause, as do key congressional committees. Second, external challenges from the White House or other sources require the House and Senate to embrace technology as a way to modernize and strengthen their competency and effectiveness. Third, lawmakers recognize the "competitive advantage" of the technology and realize that it improves their ability to manage their workload and to better serve their constituents. Fourth, the application of the technology can be accommodated to suit the unique requirements, responsibilities, procedures, traditions, and operations of the legislative branch. Fifth, the broader political environment fosters support for the technology and lessens internal opposition to it. Finally, election results produce an influx of new members who support technological innovation.

THE NET'S STRATEGIC IMPACT ON CAPITOL HILL

Today, every lawmaker is an "electronic legislator" to one degree or another because the major functions of Congress—representation, lawmaking, and oversight—are all affected by information technology. Members' representational role has probably been affected the most by the array of new information technologies as witnessed by, for instance, the advent of e-mail. Constituents communicate their opinions around-the-clock to lawmakers. In turn, many members embrace the same technology to respond to voters' inquiries. (Lawmakers also use the Internet for e-campaigning purposes—raising money and enlisting volunteers.) The Internet also expands the concept of "representation" beyond a distinct geographical area (a district or state) to include people who share similar interests and electronically network to form a global community of interest. (Some lawmakers block e-mails from outside their constituency or, while maintaining a Web site, choose not to receive e-mails at all.)

Information technology affects lawmaking in numerous ways from the ready supply of data and analysis for policy formulation to the rise of e-lobbying to concerns that some form of electronic "direct democracy" might short-circuit our representative system of government. Both the House and Senate prohibit members from using electronic devices on the floor on the grounds that they would disrupt the deliberative process. As House Rules Chairman David Dreier (R-Calif.) stated: "There is a sanctity to the floor of Congress. There are no constituents there, no lobbyists, no interests other than your colleagues."[21] Representative Jesse Jackson, Jr. (D-Ill.) disagrees. "It's ridiculous that we can't have laptops on the floor," he said. "We could use laptops to get up-to-the-minute information while giving a speech or receive a message from a staffer about something we should mention in the speech. It would make things run that much more efficiently."[22]

As for Congress's oversight role—the monitoring of the executive branch—computer-based technologies appear to be underutilized for this purpose compared to representation or lawmaking. Nonetheless, lawmakers do rely upon information technology in tracking the fiscal expenditures of executive agencies and programs and in evaluating agency and program performance. Senators Lieberman and Fred Thompson (R-Tenn.) established a Web site "to collect ideas from citizens on how the government might offer more services and better on-line information."[23] There are also many governmental and private Web sites, which provide abundant information on "the anatomy of almost any [federal] rule" or regulation.[24] A relatively new private Web site also breaks down hard-to-get information on federal spending by program, agency, and function for each congressional district.[25]

To probe more specifically how changes in technology affect congressional decision making, the next section will discuss the Internet's influence on two major centers of institutional power: committees and parties. The new possibilities of information technology are transforming the strategic behavior and expectations of both committee and party leaders. At the committee level, there is a surge of jurisdictional rivalry; at the party level, there is an acceleration of "message politics."

COMMITTEES AND INTERNET POLITICS

The Internet's effect on committees occurs in numerous ways. For example, committees can make available to everyone important materials, such as reports and documents, on their home page. The House Education and Workforce Committee even became the first panel ever to create a Spanish-language Web site so Spanish-speakers could obtain President George W. Bush's "No Child Left Behind" educational initiative.[26] Many House and Senate committees broadcast hearings over the Internet or organize interactive hearings with witnesses located outside of Washington, D.C. and viewers able to e-mail their questions to committee members.[27] Committees sometimes distribute conference reports in cyberspace. Committee staff aides share information and analysis over the Internet. To be sure, outside groups can use the Internet to quickly mobilize support or opposition to legislation, nominations, or other matters being considered by a committee. High-tech lobbying groups also strive to win committee assignments for favorite lawmakers who will work on behalf of their issues.

Committee jurisdictions loom large with respect to the Internet, because they are central to congressional policymaking. Which committee has jurisdiction over a bill determines how, when, and by whom the legislation is considered and whether legislation will make it to the floor. Regular battles between or among committees over jurisdictional turf are a critical, although little publicized outside Capitol Hill, aspect of congressional politics and decision making. Even in an era characterized by the decline of committee autonomy, jurisdiction still translates into power on Capitol Hill. Ambitious and turf-conscious chairmen seek to expand (or protect) their policy domain, especially when new issues or technologies appear on Congress's agenda. As a colleague said of Representative John Dingell (D-Mich.) when he chaired (1981–1995) the Energy and Commerce Committee, he "thought that every bill that began with H.R. began in the Commerce Committee."[28] Committee leaders, in brief, seek to exploit ambiguous committee boundaries or referral rules and precedents to lay claim to emerging issues.

Take the case of energy, for instance. When it became the number-one issue in Congress with the Arab oil embargo of 1973, which triggered long gasoline lines around the country, members clamored to participate in the energy debate. Numerous House and Senate committees got involved in the issue by, for instance, incorporating energy-related topics into measures reported from their panels even if they had scant responsibility for energy (such as a committee whose jurisdiction encompasses education), or by holding hearings and issuing reports on the topic. "[M]ost [House] committees have attempted to engage in some energy-related activity," declared the House Select Committee on Committees in 1974. "The interest has been stimulated by the current crisis atmosphere."[29] Like any broad subject area, energy does not fit neatly into one committee's mandate and the multiple referral of legislation since 1975 in the House added to the jurisdictional layers and rivalries. To minimize jurisdictional disputes, the House in 1977 created a temporary *ad hoc* Energy Committee to coordinate and report out President Jimmy Carter's national energy program.[30]

A similar pattern of jurisdictional evolution is associated with the Internet because, in a knowledge-based society, it influences virtually every kind of social, legal, cultural, economic, or political activity. Understandably, lawmakers and committees want a hand in shaping its development and to obtain a "piece of the technology action." As a rough indicator of this trend, a search was made of the LEGIS database using the bucket term "Internet" to determine how many measures introduced in the 104th (1995–1997) and 106th (1999–2001) Congresses, respectively, referenced that word in legislation.

During the 104th Congress, 26 bills introduced in the House and Senate addressed the topic of the Internet. Eight House committees and three Senate committees received the legislation. By the end of the 106th Congress, 529 measures mentioned the Internet, and they were sent to 19 committees in the House and 14 committees in the Senate. Unsurprisingly, as in the case of energy, the Internet has spawned jurisdictional rivalries, the artful use of referral precedents, and even the formation of a few *ad hoc* panels.

Jurisdictional Rivalries

It is noteworthy that the term "Internet" is not mentioned in the formal jurisdictional rules of either chamber (House Rule X; Senate Rule XXV). As a result, committee entrepreneurs have leverage to win Internet referrals either by emphasizing the information technology's impact on matters within their formal purview, by using extant precedents, or by initiating actions, which bolster their jurisdictional claims, such as memorandums of understanding between or among committees. These primary jurisdictional sources—formal rules, referral precedents, and memorandums of understanding—are employed by committees to claim Internet-related measures.[31]

First, the formal jurisdictional rules of House and Senate committees run the gamut from being overly broad ("interstate and foreign commerce generally") to narrowly specific ("Gallaudet University and Howard University and Hospital"). Committee leaders are adept at developing plausible arguments at either extreme if they want to assert jurisdictional prerogatives. A recent Internet example illustrates how "turf" arouses the territorial instincts of committee chairmen.

When the 107th Congress (2001–2003) began, about a dozen House committees, including Energy and Commerce and Judiciary, had new chairmen because of the six-year term-limit rule adopted by the House in 1995. Energy and Commerce Chairman Billy Tauzin (R-La.) and Judiciary Chairman James Sensenbrenner (R-Wis.), are both known as strong-willed lawmakers who aggressively defend their panel's turf. Chairman Tauzin teamed with his ranking minority member and the former chair of the panel, John Dingell, to introduce a bill (H.R. 1542) with over one hundred cosponsors to amend the landmark Telecommunications Act of 1996. H.R. 1542 would permit the Baby Bells (the four regional telephone companies such as Verizon Communications) to provide high-speed, or broadband, Internet service over their telephone lines without opening their local telephone markets to competitive rivals (cable television companies or satellite companies, for example) as required by the 1996 Act.[32] A spokesman for Chairman Tauzin emphasized that, "the Energy and Commerce Committee has sole jurisdiction over telecom policy."[33]

Judiciary Chairman Sensenbrenner, concerned about the bill's antitrust implications, launched a public lobbying campaign to win a referral of the legislation. He "sent a highly detailed eleven-page letter to Speaker Dennis Hastert (R-Ill.)—and to the media—making the case for why Judiciary should receive sequential referral of the bill. Sensenbrenner also pressed his case with the House Parliamentarian."[34] (House rules state that the Speaker refers all measures, but in practice the function is performed by the parliamentarian. The Senate Parliamentarian also refers legislation on behalf of the presiding officer.)

Sensenbrenner's letter to the Speaker, which he posted on Judiciary's Web site, detailed the reasons why his committee wanted the Tauzin-Dingell bill referred to his panel. For example, he highlighted the long history of hearings (since the 1950s) the Judiciary Committee conducted on antitrust and the communications industry. He spotlighted the legislation referred to Judiciary, either on an exclusive basis or jointly with the Energy and Commerce Committee, that dealt with the topic. He cited committee reports accompanying telecommunications legislation prepared by Judiciary. And he made explicit reference to House rules, which, he argued, justified the sequential referral of the Tauzin-Dingell measure to his panel.

Rule X(1)(k)(5) of the Rules of the House of Representatives provides the Committee on the Judiciary with jurisdiction over the "[p]rotection of trade and commerce against unlawful restraints and monopolies." In addition, Rule X(l)(k)(2) of the Rules of the House provides that the Committee on Judiciary has jurisdiction over "[a]dministrative practice and procedure." Fundamentally, H.R. 1542 addresses a monopoly issue. It takes its place at the end of a long line of legislative efforts that confront the monopoly power of incumbent local exchange carriers in the telephone industry. For decades, such efforts have come under the jurisdiction of the Committee on the Judiciary.[35]

A Democratic member of the Judiciary Committee, Jerrold Nadler of New York, strongly supported Sensenbrenner's determination to protect the panel's jurisdiction. He said: "I . . . want to express my appreciation and fervent desire to cooperate with the chairman in a vigorous defense of the jurisdiction of this committee against any imperialist assaults by other committees."[36]

In mid-May 2001, Speaker Hastert granted a thirty-day sequential referral of H.R. 1542 to Judiciary but limited its review of the bill to provisions dealing with the Department of Justice. On June 13, 2001, the Judiciary Committee reported the broadband legislation unfavorably and with an amendment "tearing out the heart of the [Tauzin-Dingell] measure."[37] To avoid a nasty parliamentary fight on the floor between the two chairmen, Speaker Hastert directed Tauzin to negotiate differences with the opponents of his bill or he would not schedule the legislation for floor consideration.[38] Each side in the jurisdictional battle marshaled an array of outside interests to lobby in support of their position.

REFERRAL PRECEDENTS

Knowledge of referral precedents, combined with astute drafting, can shape which committee receives what legislation. One referral strategy is for members to introduce legislation that amends statutes over which their committees have sole jurisdiction. To lay claim to Internet legislation and avoid referral of their bill to the Commerce Committee, two House Judiciary Committee members drafted their measure to amend the Sherman Anti-Trust Act, which is within their panel's exclusive jurisdiction, and not the Telecommunications Act of 1996, which falls under the Commerce Committee. Lawmakers, too, may work to draft their bill during the introductory and committee markup stages to limit its chance of sequential referral to another panel.

Knowledge of specific precedents also influences the referral of legislation. For example, precedents dictate that reference to taxes or the internal revenue code means that bills will be sent to the tax-writing committees. There are exceptions, however. To avoid referral of his bill barring taxation of Internet commerce to the House Ways and Means Committee, Representative Christopher Cox (R-Calif.) took advantage of precedents stating that "so long as the bill is limited to the taxing powers of state and local governments, it is the domain of the Judiciary or Commerce Committees."[39]

Committees may also draft memorandums of understanding to deal with issues that overlap their responsibilities. These memorandums, which have precedential value, are usually printed in the *Congressional Record*, kept on file in the Parliamentarian's office, and guide the reference of legislation implicated by these bicommittee agreements. For instance, when the House reconfigured its committee system at the start of the 107th Congress by establishing a new Financial Services Committee and a renamed Energy and Commerce Committee, which saw some of its jurisdiction shifted to the new panel, both committees claimed authority for "the electronic communications networks that automatically match buy and sell orders for stock transactions."[40] To end the turf battle, Speaker Hastert brokered an agreement between the two panels, which was entered in the *Congressional Record*.[41]

AD HOC PANELS

The House and Senate create *ad hoc*, or temporary, committees for a variety of reasons, including the need to coordinate consideration of issues that overlap the jurisdiction of several standing committees. This approach is intended to reduce jurisdictional bickering and to expedite review of an issue. Another reason is to provide direction, visibility, and laser-light attention to an issue spread diffusely and unclearly among several standing committees. A good example concerned the Senate's unanimous establishment on April 2, 1998, of the Special Committee on the Year 2000 Technology Problem, chaired by Senator Robert F. Bennett (R-Utah), with Senator Christopher J. Dodd (D-Conn.) as vice chair. The Special Committee's function, as defined in its authorizing resolution (S. Res. 208), was "to study the impact of the year 2000 technology problem on the Executive and Judicial Branches of the Federal Government, State governments, and private sector operations in the United States and abroad" and to make recommendations to deal effectively with the dire warnings associated with a computer software flaw known as the "millennium" or "Y2K" bug. (Speaker Newt Gingrich created a House Year 2000 [Republican] Task Force and appointed GOP Representatives Steve Horn of California and Constance A. Morella of Maryland to oversee executive branch efforts to address the millennium bug.)[42]

The Y2K problem concerned the reprogramming of computer software programs so they could recognize "00" as 2000 rather than 1900. "If the appropriate adjustments are not made when New Year's 2000 rolls around," said former Representative Lee Hamilton (D-Ind.), "many of these [computer] systems will jump back to the year 1900, causing disruptions in government and private sector operations, here and abroad."[43] A combination of factors—the foreseeable nature of the problem and the efforts made by many public and private leaders, groups, and organizations worldwide, including the Special Senate Committee—resulted in few computer glitches on January 1, 2000. On the other hand, there were political, parliamentary, and jurisdictional issues which emanated from the Y2K problem.

Politically, for example, Republicans laid the groundwork to blame former Vice President Al Gore (widely acknowledged to be the leading Democratic presidential nominee for 2000) in case there were major computer problems. "I can't imagine anything more destructive for Gore's political future than to talk about the Information Superhighway and then to have the largest wreck in history on the 1st of January 2000," declared House Speaker Newt Gingrich.[44]

Parliamentarily, when the Senate took up a bill in 1999 that addressed the Y2K computer liability issue (limiting class action lawsuits and punitive damages against high-tech businesses in the event of computer breakdowns in 2000), it became enmeshed in bitter procedural battles that produced multiple cloture attempts and the rare tactic of filling the amendment tree by Majority Leader Trent Lott (R-Miss.), to block unwanted Democratic amendments.[45]

Jurisdictionally, a turf battle erupted between the Senate Commerce and Judiciary Committees as each panel rushed to be first in reporting out a bill to resolve the Y2K problem. The respective chairmen of the two panels—John McCain (R-Ariz.) and Orrin G. Hatch (R-Utah)—produced bills that were nearly identical. "There's not a lot of difference in the bills," remarked Chairman Hatch. "McCain took our bill and followed it." In response, Chairman McCain discounted any similarities in the two bills saying he "hasn't wasted the time" to look at Hatch's version.[46] Majority Leader Lott took up the Commerce Committee's bill on the floor.

CONGRESSIONAL PARTIES AND MESSAGE POLITICS

Congressional party leaders increasingly focus their time and resources on framing issues in a way that maximizes support among their core constituencies and swing voters. With the two parties at electoral and legislative parity, congressional leaders understand the importance of using communications and public relations strategies to promote legislative agendas, which resonate with voters and that party members solidly favor. Today, the parties in each chamber assemble partisans in "theme teams," "message groups," or "speaker's groups" to deliver coordinated and targeted statements on the House or Senate floor and in other forums. They use hearings, floor debates, amendments, votes, schedules, press conferences, and more to orchestrate agenda priorities and to differentiate their image and issues from the other party's.

The development of new technologies for research and publicity, such as the Internet, underscores the importance of political communications in (1) the passage, modification, or defeat of priority legislation (message politics); (2) the formulation of party platforms that have broad popular appeal (message agendas); and (3) the parliamentary and political maneuvers used to advance party goals (message strategies). A basic aim of these coordinated efforts is to frame the national debate in a way that fosters public support for partisan goals and that inoculates the party from attacks by opponents.

Coordination, consultation, and communication are important functions of party leaders. Much of this activity can be done via public Internet sites. In addition, the parties maintain Intranet sites, which only party members or their staff may access. For example, House GOP Conference Chairman J. C. Watts of Oklahoma developed a Web site for Republican lawmakers that provides them with "one-stop shopping" with respect to legislation before the House. The "committee central" site (www.gop.gov/committee) provides "bill summaries, issue briefings and sample op-eds. Parts are open to the public; some are for GOP members only."[47] Lobby groups post letters on this site indicating which bills will be scored as a "key vote" for their annual voting scorecards. (Interest groups use these scorecards to determine which candidates will win endorsements and receive campaign contributions.)

Suffice it to say that lawmakers can easily access information that will keep them appraised of their party's agenda priorities, the daily or weekly schedule, and updates of floor action throughout the legislative day. As House Majority Leader Richard Armey (R-Tex.) told colleagues about the timing of legislation: "Let me just say we will again remind [Members] through e-mail and Whip notices . . . at the time that the committee has prepared the bill for filing."[48] The Internet is used by parties for more than keeping colleagues up-to-date and informed about legislative business. On the message politics front, the Internet influences a confluence of overlapping party matters: agenda setting, partisan competition, and policy stagecraft.

AGENDA SETTING

In recognition of the Internet's contribution to technologically-fueled economic growth and the industry's ability to contribute large amounts of campaign funds, both parties in the House and Senate work continuously to win the political backing of the high-tech community. As part of the courtship, Democrats and Republicans advance Internet agendas with dual purposes: to appeal to the technology industry and to differentiate their plans from the other party's. For example, to contrast their approach with President George W. Bush's, the Democratic leaders of the House and Senate—Representative Richard A. Gephardt of Missouri and Senator Tom Daschle of South Dakota—proposed ten high-tech policy recommendations (closing the "digital divide," increasing federal research and development support, providing every American with high-speed Internet access, and so on) to spur technological growth. "President Bush has outlined one approach [to revive the high-tech economy]—cut taxes and slash regulations. We also support tax cuts and deregulation, where appropriate. But we don't think those things alone are enough," said Senator Daschle.[49]

Republicans, too, recognize the growing political clout of the Internet industry. House Majority Leader Armey, for instance, drafted the GOP's "E-Contract 2000"—a high-tech version of their famous mid-1990s "Contract with America." Although many of the topics on Armey's agenda (expanding high-speed Internet access or providing digital opportunities for the disadvantaged) enjoy Democratic support, both parties compete vigorously to push legislation favored by the information technology industry. As Senate Democrats and Republicans left Capitol Hill for the August 2001 recess, they traded barbs over which party is doing more to promote technology issues. "If Republicans were still in the leadership," remarked Senator George Allen (R-Va.) the Senate would already have acted on making permanent a research and development tax credit long sought by the Internet community. A top Daschle aide retorted that "it's better to do it right than [to] do it fast."[50]

Party task forces are also formed to woo the technology industry. Senator Allen, for example, chairs the Republican High-Tech Task Force appointed by GOP Leader Lott. When Lott established the group in 1999, he said: "This new task force will take a broader perspective, consulting with leaders in the field to identify and address the full range of legislative priorities for the high-tech industry."[51] Added Senator Allen when he became chairman two years later: "We want you all [in the tech community] to understand we are your portal to the Senate."[52] The other three parties on Capitol Hill also have partisan groups, which meet with technology executives, visit Silicon Valley and other high-tech facilities, and work diligently to attract the support of this important sector of the economy.

Partisan Competition

Recent Congresses have witnessed a sharp rise in political rancor and lack of trust between the two parties. One reason for today's hard-edged partisanship is that the parties are at virtual parity in Congress and the country. Both sides realize the high electoral stakes of their decisions, and each party calculates constantly how to enlarge their chances of either winning or expanding majority control of the House and Senate. Any slight advantage could tilt majority control in one partisan direction or the other. Unsurprisingly, the World Wide Web is among the technological tools that parties employ to advance their causes. Three examples make the point.

First, in the November 1996 elections, Democrat Loretta Sanchez of California was an upset victor over incumbent Robert Dornan (known in the media as "B-1 Bob" for his strong defense rhetoric). The GOP-controlled House launched a contested-election investigation to determine whether Sanchez won because of illegal voting by noncitizens. Democrats argued that the year-long GOP investigation had turned up no evidence that Sanchez had been elected illegally. Republicans countered that all the facts had not been uncovered and continued their investigation.

Much of the controversy over the Sanchez-Dornan case can be traced to a 1984 election, which Republicans said the Democrats stole from them. In a close House election in the 8th congressional district of Indiana, Democrat Frank McCloskey seemed to be the winner but the Indiana Secretary of State said some votes were counted twice and declared Republican Richard McIntyre the victor. However, the Democratically-controlled House refused to seat McIntyre and began an investigation of the election. Republicans waged parliamentary "guerrilla warfare" on McIntyre's behalf. In the end, the House voted along party lines to seat McCloskey. When the decision was announced, Republicans walked en masse from the House chamber. Thirteen years later the situation was reversed as Democrats tried parliamentary stalling tactics to shut down the GOP-run investigation and hold a newly won seat.

When Republicans blocked the dilatory tactics on behalf of Sanchez, House Democrats moved to cyberspace to continue their battle to seat their colleague. They created and publicized a "Stop Bob Dornan" Web site (www.house.gov/democrats/orange) to generate broad public support for their effort. "On the site, visitors can read the Democrats' version of the investigation's history, copy a 'Stop Bob Dornan' [logo] onto their own Web site, and sign an Internet petition to Speaker Newt Gingrich telling him to prove Dornan won or end the investigation."[53] In the end, Dornan's challenge was dismissed by the House in February 1998.

Second, Web sites are used to promote partisan agendas, to stake out positions, and to attract audiences different from that reached by floor speeches or constituent newsletters. In 1997, the GOP-controlled Congresses targeted the Internal Revenue Service (IRS) because of its overly aggressive approach to tax enforcement. House Republicans introduced a Web site to the public during Halloween to solicit "horror stories" about taxpayer abuse by the IRS. The Web page was titled "IRS Horror Stories" and urged citizens to recount stories of abuse by the IRS. "This Halloween, the Republican Congress is unmasking the IRS for what it really is: a bureaucratic monster stalking the American taxpayer," declared Representative John A. Boehner (R-Ohio). "Our Web page is a silver bullet for taxpayers fighting the . . . beast."[54] The House Republican initiative along with well-publicized hearings by the Senate Finance Committee led to enactment of the Internal Revenue Restructuring and Reform Act of 1998.

Third, "politics by other means" is waged on Capitol Hill, and it involves court cases, investigations, media disclosures, and bitter partisan conflicts.[55] Lawmakers lodge ethics charges against colleagues; interest groups and journalists look for dirt on lawmakers; and the Internet is used to spread unsubstantiated allegations against party members or entities. This form of harsh competition between the parties has also been called the "criminalization of politics."[56] The objectives of politics by other means are several, such as destroying political careers, immobilizing the opposition, and tarnishing a party's popular image.

For example, in the lead-up to the November 2000 elections, the Senate Democratic and Republican Campaign Committees each charged the other with breaking copyright and other laws. Democrats said the GOP's campaign committee's Web site (www.nrsc.org) violated copyright laws by posting newspaper articles without the media organization's permission and paying the required fee to use the material. Republicans said the allegation was baseless and lodged legal complaints of their own, such as charging that the Democratic campaign group's Web site (www.dscc.org) solicited contributions in violation of federal election and IRS laws and rules. The legal counsel to the GOP campaign committee declared: "I think the DSCC must have a case of Web envy because we have a great Web site and theirs is rather static, or Jurassic, in my opinion. They need to throw another hamster onto the wheel to keep it running."[57] Nothing came of these legal challenges, but they illustrate how the parties search for any reasonable "hook," including Web sites, to tarnish the credibility of the other.

Policy Stagecraft

The strategy for moving or blocking major legislation is often as much technological—television, radio, the Internet, and so on—as it is political or procedural. Congressional leaders understand the importance of the technological component in framing issues, molding public opinion, and generating grassroots support to achieve policy initiatives on Capitol Hill. The shrewd use of words and communications strategies is part of the competing stagecraft parties employ to target their message, advance their agenda, and attract popular support. Republicans, for instance, transformed the "estate tax," which highlighted wealth and privilege, to the "death tax" and won enactment of a tax cut "that at first appeared to be an easy target for Democrats."[58] As Representative Nancy Pelosi (D-Calif.) pointed out: "We can do all we can with our inside maneuvering, but without the outside mobilization we'll never achieve what is possible."[59]

The technology behind policy stagecraft is illustrated by these two cases. First, President Bush announced in May 2001 a comprehensive initiative to promote domestic energy production through more drilling for oil and gas, tax incentives to encourage energy production and conservation, and funds for nuclear energy research and clean coal technology. Democrats attacked Bush's plan for emphasizing energy production over energy conservation and environmental protection. Democrats set up a "war room" in the Capitol to coordinate radio and television interviews and opened a Web site (www.grandoldpetroleum.com) to bolster public opposition to Bush's plan. Republicans responded by creating their own Web site (www.bushenergy.com) to encourage supporters to call radio shows with the message that Bush "is doing everything he can—as soon as he can—to help Americans who are feeling the energy crunch at the gas pump and in their utility bills."[60] Both parties also make available on-line briefing materials, which lawmakers can download and use in their states or districts either to attack or promote the Bush energy plan, as the case may be. House Republicans developed a CD-ROM presentation tailored to the energy picture in different states, which members could use in their town-hall meetings with constituents.[61]

Second, public anger at health maintenance organizations (HMOs) escalated in the late 1990s and caused efforts by both congressional parties to draft legislation to deal with this issue. In general, Democrats supported more federal regulation of HMOs and Republicans supported a market-based approach to health care reform. One divisive issue involved the Democratic proposal, granting patients the right to sue HMOs for malpractice. Republicans said the proposal would raise the costs of health care and serve the interests of trial lawyers, a favorite Democratic support group. Democrats said that Republicans favored the insurance companies over patients. On popular issues like the patients' bill of rights, where Democrats enjoy a large public advantage as the party best able to deal with it, Republicans employ "defensive" messages to inoculate their members from attacks by the other side and to blur interparty differences. Thus, when the Senate addressed a patients' bill of rights measure in the 106th Congress, Republicans "offered amendments with similar titles to those sponsored by Democrats—but embodying more limited rights and applying to fewer people."[62]

When Democrats took over the Senate in June 2001 following Senator James M. Jeffords's (Vt.) switch from Republican to Independent, Majority Leader Daschle successfully made chamber enactment of a patients' bill of rights his top priority. As part of the strategy to widely broadcast the Democratic health care message, Daschle created an "intensive care unit" (ICU) in a leadership conference room "equipped for live broadcasts over television, radio and the Internet."[63] Senators, for instance, went on-line to discuss HMO reform, rebut opponent's charges, and advertise the Democratic plan. Not to be outdone, Senate Republicans established their own communications unit in the Capitol dubbed the "delivery room"—after their stated goal of delivering an HMO bill that President Bush would sign into law. The GOP's room was also equipped with various technological devices "from computers for interactive chats to cameras and microphones for senators to use for interviews."[64]

THE INTERNET AND CONGRESS: SUMMARY POINTS

The Internet's impact on legislative decision making presents a complex picture. It influences nearly everything that Congress does, and sometimes in significant ways. Although information technology shapes how Congress and its members do things, it has not changed their fundamental roles and functions. They still represent constituents, make laws, oversee the executive branch, educate the public, foster consensus for action, and so on. The Internet, some suggest, is qualitatively different from other technological developments in its potential to create a new paradigm of governance: direct democracy rather than representative government. Others wonder whether, by comparison, too much is claimed for the Internet's impact on Congress or society given the significance of other technological breakthroughs, such as electricity, the telephone, radio and television, or the jet plane. The point is that the importance of the Internet in and on Congress should neither be overestimated nor underestimated.

Congress operates more than 600 Web sites and the odds favor more extensive use of the technology as a new generation of technologically sophisticated lawmakers enter the House and Senate.[65] Today, young congressional staff aides are in the vanguard of using and exploring the Internet, in part because the Internet becomes a substitute for knowledge and experience. Inexperienced staff aides can "get smart quickly" on issues their members are interested in and even target and mobilize activists on behalf of those topics. One implication of the Internet is the increasing importance on Capitol Hill of combining legislative and technological skills. Several other implications also merit mention. They include the items discussed in the following sections.

TRANSPARENCY

The computer revolution has produced the ability to store huge amounts of information and to retrieve it quickly and efficiently. The large number of Web sites citizens can access to get reliable information and electronic documents about Congress is remarkable. These sites, whether public (e.g., the Library of Congress or the Government Printing Office) or commercial (e.g., Congressional Quarterly, Inc.), provide an abundance of trustworthy materials about the Congress to interested citizens. Internet access not only provides opportunities for citizens to be better informed about Congress; it also strengthens their ability to hold elected officials responsible and accountable for their actions and decisions. For example, citizens interested in the question: "Does Congress Delegate Too Much Power To Agencies and What Should Be Done About It?" can obtain the June 14, 2000, House committee hearing record by that title via <www.house.gov/reform>.

As more information becomes available on-line about Congress, there is also more demand that additional materials be distributed electronically to the public. For example, various groups such as Ralph Nader's Congressional

Accountability Project have urged Congress to post on-line drafts of committee "markup" documents, easily searchable voting records of lawmakers, or reports of the Congressional Research Service. There are many reasons why party or committee leaders do not want certain materials made easily available either to constituents or to other lawmakers. For example, after selected House and Senate members negotiate for days or weeks to hammer out a fragile compromise, which they must then "sell" to colleagues, there is an understandable reluctance to disseminate the product to the general public before it has been reviewed by the majority and minority leaders of Congress and the White House.

CONSTITUENT COMMUNICATIONS

The Internet has changed the way lawmakers and their staff aides communicate with constituents. Members can quickly keep constituents updated and informed about their activities. As Senator Bill Frist (R-Tenn.) explained:

> Our office ... uses a digital camera—which allows photographs to be downloaded, printed, and disseminated almost instantly. On a recent trip to Bosnia, for instance, I took pictures of our troops from Tennessee, downloaded them into my laptop, e-mailed them to local newspapers in Tennessee, as well as to my Washington office where they were posted on the Web for all to see. The whole process took only a few minutes.[66]

Cyber-savvy legislators interact regularly in "chat rooms" with constituents in their districts or states. Constituents, in turn, are able to quickly send e-mails to their members. The ease of sending e-mails to lawmakers has produced "e-mail overload" in Congress with many offices unable to be responsive to the increasing volume of e-mails flooding their offices (from 20 million sent to the House in 1998 to 48 million in 2000).[67]

Advocacy groups, too, are able to trigger constituent e-mails at Internet speed. When President Bush nominated the controversial John Ashcroft to be Attorney General, pro- and anti-Ashcroft "Web sites sprung up within hours of the nomination, and helped generate hundreds of thousands of messages to lawmakers."[68] While the Internet-generated activism enables lawmakers to hear from numerous people, it sometimes creates unmanageable burdens on Congress's e-mail system and inaction on legislative issues. On-line advocacy can mean that "some things are easier to stop," stated a top House Rules Committee staff aide. "You send an e-mail to all your friends and say Congress is about to do this horrible thing so write your congressman immediately."[69]

INFORMATION ACCESS/OVERLOAD

Members are inundated with information. There is so much information created and distributed worldwide that much of it can be characterized as "negative information." Neither legislators nor staff aides have the time to sift through the enormous amounts of available data to determine the useful from the useless. As former Senate Majority Leader George Mitchell (D-Maine) said: "What we do not lack is the means by which to learn about issues. There is no shortage of information. There is a shortage of time."[70] The Internet's prime virtue is the speed with which it can make unmediated information and data available to policymakers. What is often lacking on Capitol Hill is the time and human resources to make sense of it all and to find the policy-shaping "nuggets" in the information deluge. Significantly, lawmakers also need an array of information not found on the Internet and which is usually more difficult to obtain, such as the combination of political rewards or sanctions that would encourage wavering colleagues to vote their way.

Deliberation and Decision Making

The range of issues that every legislator must vote upon is truly immense. On any given day, lawmakers might be required to vote on measures involving defense, higher education, abortion, taxes, or public works. There is little question that the Internet can help members make informed decisions. As Representative Kevin Brady (R-Tex.) stated: "You know, we're in the Information Age and we're making decisions in so many different areas that it's a huge help. I mean, from a policy standpoint, [computer technology is] very productive for me and it's a very productive way to learn."[71]

On the other hand, numerous factors shape how legislators make choices, not just information. Constituency-based, party-based, or ideologically-based decisions are often more important than information-based judgments. In politics, an old saying goes, facts are negotiable. Members frequently want "objective" analyses that support their policy predispositions. Masses of reliable and timely data are of limited value to legislators making political determinations.

Paradoxically, although information and ideas can move with the speed of light, lawmaking usually requires time for reflection and reasoned deliberation to build the consensus to pass legislation. The legislative process is replete with political and procedural "speed bumps" to inhibit overly hasty action. A leader in the "cyber Congress" movement, Representative Vernon J. Ehlers (R-Mich.), put it this way: "The art of politics is the art of persuasion. When you're persuading, there's nothing more important than face-to-face contact."[72] "Virtual collegiality" through e-mails, laptops, or videoconferences is no substitute for the hard work of building personal and political relationships between or among lawmakers. "If I cannot eyeball you, I cannot see you, I cannot see your body language, I can't really listen to you," declared Representative Tony P. Hall (D-Ohio).[73]

The idea of a Congress means a "coming together" for the purpose of face-to-face deliberation and dialogue. The creative insights of lawmakers, their diverse and conflicting experiences, and all the things that make up their value systems are not found in Internet data banks. On-line information sources are invaluable for analyzing public policy, accessing and disseminating relevant information, and enhancing the technical quality of legislation. However, the Internet is no substitute for the many "off-line" qualities (for instance, bargaining and negotiating skills), which characterize the lawmaking process.

The Internet, in sum, has made it easy for technologically savvy lawmakers to acquire more and faster access to information and to disseminate materials to a huge audience. Many members do not have much familiarity with the Internet, however. For example, when Speaker Newt Gingrich conducted a GOP leadership meeting, he decided to place computer terminals in front of each member. "Instead of simply discussing ideas aloud, members typed in their responses to questions—which were then posted anonymously to a projection screen. The . . . tool is an attempt to increase honesty in discussions, reduce the influence of strong personalities in decision making and cut down on the repetition of arguments."[74] A GOP chairman confirmed that "[t]here were some Members who had never used a computer."[75] It is one thing to adapt state-of-the-art technology to the legislative process, but it is another to make sure that lawmakers have the requisite skills to make the best use of it. Nonetheless, the Internet is now a part of the broad information and communications context that affects congressional decision making. Although its evolution in Congress remains unclear, the Internet "redefines traditional tools of communication, consultation and decision making, forcing public servants to rethink their roles and the processes and structures" that guide their decision making.[76]

Notes

1. See, for example, Neil Munro and Drew Clark, "Digital Dilemma," *National Journal*, 28 July 2001, pp. 2386–2392.
2. Edward-Isaac Dovere, "Legislative Pace Appears to Be on Track," *The Hill*, 25 July 2001, p. 29.
3. Susan Crabtree, "Congress in the 21st Century," *Roll Call*, 24 January 2000, p. B-1. The member quoted is Representative J. D. Hayworth (R-Ariz).
4. Edward Tenner, "We the Innovators," *U.S. News & World Report*, 10 January 2000, p. 75.
5. Matthew Josephson, *Edison: A Biography* (New York: John Wiley & Sons, 1992), p. 65.
6. Ibid., p. 66.
7. Ibid.
8. *The Congressional Globe*, 41st Cong., 2nd sess., July 6, 1870, p. 5250.
9. Ibid.
10. *Congressional Record*, 100th Cong., 1st sess., January 6, 1987, p. S92.
11. Don Wolfensberger, "20 Years of House TV: A Bipartisan Reform for a Partisan Era?" *Roll Call*, 18 March 1999, p. 6. For more comprehensive treatments of Congress and television, see Stephen Frantzich and John Sullivan, *The C-Span Revolution* (Norman, OK: University of Oklahoma Press, 1996); and Ronald Garay, *Congressional Television: A Legislative History* (Westport, CT: Greenwood Press, 1984).
12. Quoted in Richard Baker [the Historian of the Senate], "Senate Historical Minute: May 2, 1924 Radio Days," *The Hill*, 2 May 2001, p. 6.
13. *Congressional Record*, 97th Cong., 2nd sess., April 14, 1982, p. S3476.
14. Steven Roberts, "Senators Ponder Value of Letting TV in the Door," *New York Times*, 16 September 1985, p. B-6.

15. Karen Tumulty, "Senate Decides to Live with TV," *Los Angeles Times*, 30 July 1986, p. 11.
16. Quoted in Representative Fred Schwengel, "Information Handling: 'For a Vast Future Also'," in *We Propose: A Modern Congress*, ed. Mary McInnis (New York: McGraw-Hill, 1966), p. 312.
17. For a summary overview of some of these developments, see Bruce Hopkins, "Congressional Reform: Toward a Modern Congress," *Notre Dame Lawyer*, February 1972, pp. 452–460.
18. For example, in 1969 the Special Subcommittee on Electrical and Mechanical Office Equipment of the Committee on House Administration established a Working Group on Automatic Data Processing to develop an automatic data processing system for the House. Prominent outside organizations, such as the Stanford Research Institute and The MITRE Corporation, and academics (political science professors Richard Fenno, Charles Jones, and Donald Matthews, among others) served as advisors and consultants to the Working Group. See *Second Progress Report of the Special Subcommittee on Electrical and Mechanical Office Equipment*, prepared by the Working Group on Automatic Data Processing for the House of Representatives, Committee on House Administration (October 1970).
19. Joint Committee on the Organization of Congress, *Background Materials: Supplemental Information Provided to Members of the Joint Committee on the Organization of Congress*, S. Prt. 103-25, 103rd Cong., 1st sess. (1993), p. 1624.
20. Jeffrey C. Griffith, "Congress's Legislative Information Systems: THOMAS and the LIS," *Government Information Quarterly* 18, no. 3 (2001), p. 45.
21. Kathy Kelly, "Capitol Hill at a Crossroads on Info Highway," *USA Today*, 3 November 1999, p. 24-A.
22. Crabtree, "Congress in the 21st Century," p. B-6.
23. Ben White, "Senators Go Looking for E-Ideas," *Washington Post*, 19 May 2000, p. A-29.
24. Cindy Skrzycki, "Web Sites Track Regulatory Changes," *Washington Post*, 24 April 2001, p. E-1.
25. Claudia Deane, "Federal Spending in Districts Tracked," *Washington Post*, 5 April 2001, p. A-25. At this juncture, this Web site (www.cnponline.org) has information for districts in Illinois, Michigan, and Ohio. The Web site was launched by the Center for National Policy, which is chaired by former Clinton White House chief of staff Leon Panetta.
26. National Journal's *CongressDaily/PM*, July 9, 2001, p. 7.
27. See, for example, Sean Piccoli, "Hill Samples 'Third Wave,'" *Washington Times*, 13 June 1995, p. A-8.
28. National Journal's *CongressDaily/PM*, March 30, 2000, p. 6.
29. House Select Committee on Committees, *Committee Reform Amendments of 1974*, 93rd Cong., 2nd sess., Rept. 93-916, Part II, March 21, 1974, p. 36.
30. See Bruce I. Oppenheimer, "Policy Effects of U.S. House Reform: Decentralization and the Capacity to Resolve Energy Issues," *Legislative Studies Quarterly* (February 1980), pp. 5–30.
31. For a discussion of jurisdictional politics, see David C. King, *Turf Politics: How Congressional Committees Claim Jurisdiction* (Chicago: University of Chicago Press, 1997).
32. See Neil Munro and Teri Rucker, "The Battle for Broadband," *National Journal*, 26 May 2001, pp. 1564–1568.
33. Peter Cobn, "House Judiciary Rings up Telecom Measure," *CQ Daily Monitor*, 13 June 2001, p. 13.
34. Ben Pershing, "Sensenbrenner Goes out of His Way to Defend Turf," *Roll Call*, 5 July 2001, p. 3.
35. <http://www.house.gov/judiciary/broadband>, p. 1.
36. Pershing, "Sensenbrenner Goes Out of His Way to Defend Turf," p. 3.
37. J. P. Cassidy, "Rep. Tauzin Needs Deal to Win," *The Hill*, 8 August 2001, p. 23.
38. Ibid.
39. National Journal's *CongressDaily/PM*, April 24, 1998, p. 6.
40. Alan Ota, "House Panels Vie for Upper Hand in Regulating the New Economy," *Congressional Quarterly Weekly Report*, 13 January 2001, p. 133.
41. *Congressional Record*, 107th Cong., 1st sess., January 30, 2001, p. H103. It is common for committees to waive their jurisdiction over measures in the interest of expediting floor consideration. However, an exchange of letters is usually inserted in the *Congressional Record* by the respective chairmen stating that the waiver does not constitute a precedent for any subsequent referral of legislation. In addition, the chairman of the panel that waives its jurisdictional right to a bill often states that he or she reserves the right to seek conferees in any subsequent conference with the Senate. See, for example, *Congressional Record*, 107th Cong., 1st sess., June 13, 2001, pp. H3105–H3106.

42. See *CQ Daily Monitor*, 23 June 1998, p. 9 and *Congressional Record*, 106th Cong., 2nd sess., May 2, 2000, pp. H2350–H2353.
43. *Congressional Record*, 105th Cong., 2nd sess., September 9, 1998, p. E1666.
44. Susan Page, "GOP Drops a Bug down Gore's Back," *USA Today*, 24 June 1998, p. 6-A.
45. See, for example, *Congressional Record*, 106th Cong., 1st sess., April 29, 1999, pp. S4405–S4417.
46. Philippe Shepnick, "McCain, Hatch Duel over Y2K Bills That Appear to Have Few Differences," *The Hill*, 10 March 1999, p. 3.
47. Juliet Eilperin and John Lancaster, "GOP Web Site Keeps Members Fully Briefed," *Washington Post*, 9 July 2001, p. A-15.
48. *Congressional Record*, 107th Cong., 1st sess., May 25, 2001, p. H2725.
49. Adam Marlin, "Democrats Outline Legislative Agenda for Technology Issues," *CQ Daily Monitor*, 6 April 2001, p. 6.
50. National Journal's *CongressDaily/PM*, 10 August 2001, p. 3.
51. Press Release, Senate Majority Leader Trent Lott, May 26, 1999.
52. National Journal's *CongressDaily/AM*, 2 March 2001, p. 4.
53. *Roll Call*, 13 November 1997, p. 3.
54. John Godrey, "GOP Sets Up Web Site to Attract IRS Horror Stories," *Washington Times*, 1 November 1997, p. A-4.
55. Benjamin Ginsberg and Martin Shefter, *Politics by Other Means: The Declining Importance of Elections in America* (New York: Basic Books, 1990).
56. Amitai Etzioni, "It's a Crime, the Way Politicians Go at It," *Washington Post*, 5 August 2001, p. B-1. Also see Ronald Brownstein, "New Appeals for a Return to Civility," *Los Angeles Times*, 15 February 1999, p. A-1.
57. John Mercurio, "Senate Committees War over the Web," *Roll Call*, 2 December 1999, p. 10.
58. Lizette Alvarez, "In 2 Parties' War of Words, Shibboleths Emerge as Clear Winner," *New York Times*, 27 April 2001, p. A-18.
59. John Nichols, "Is This the New Face of the Democratic Party?" *The Nation*, 6/13 August 2001, p. 13.
60. Mike Allen, "Democrats Turn Energy on Bush," *Washington Post*, 20 May 2001, p. A-9.
61. Mike Allen and Juliet Eilperin, "Bush, GOP Mount Effort to Sell Energy Plan," *Washington Post*, 28 June 2001, p. A-8.
62. Alissa Rubin, "Fine Lines Drawn in Senate Debate on Patients' Rights Bill," *Los Angeles Times*, 15 July 1999, p. A-6.
63. John Lancaster and Helen Dewar, "Daschle's 'Intensive Care Unit' to Attend to Patients' Rights," *Washington Post*, 18 June 2001, p. A-15.
64. Helen Dewar, "Dueling Rooms," *Washington Post*, 25 June 2001, p. A-13.
65. William Matthews, "Wiring Congress," *Federal Computer Week*, 19 February 2001, p. 20.
66. *Congressional Record*, 105th Cong., 2nd sess., May 22, 1998, p. S5466.
67. See the report of the Congress Online Project, "E-Mail Overload in Congress," March 19, 2001, p. 2.
68. Gail Russell Chaddock, "Behind Vote on Ashcroft, a Signal," *Christian Science Monitor*, 2 February 2001, p. 4.
69. *Creating a Digital Democracy: The Impact of the Internet on Public Policy-Making*, Foundation for Public Affairs, Washington, D.C., 1999, p. 11.
70. *Congressional Record*, 101st Cong., 1st sess., October 20, 1989, p. S13811.
71. George Archibald, "Technology Lets Lawmakers Remain Connected," *Washington Times*, 12 September 1999, p. C-10.
72. Kelly, "Capitol Hill at a Crossroads on Info Highway," p. 24-A.
73. *Creating a Digital Democracy: The Impact of the Internet on Public Policy-Making*, p. 14.
74. National Journal's *CongressDaily/PM*, 27 January 1997, p. 5.
75. Juliet Eilperin, "2001: A GOP Planning Odyssey," *Roll Call*, 27 January 1997, p. 18. Also see Susan Crabtree, "Members Score Poorly in New Tech Survey," *Roll Call*, 5 June 2000, p. 3.
76. Elisabeth Richard, "Tools of Governance," in *Digital Democracy: Discourse and Decision Making in the Information Age*, ed. Barry Hague and Brian Loader (New York: Routledge, 1999), p. 73.

COMMUNICATING WITH CONGRESS

CITIZENS, E-MAIL, AND WEB SITES

DENNIS W. JOHNSON[1]

Individual letters, postcards, and telephone messages to members of Congress have traditionally been the lifeblood of communications and remain for many legislators the most legitimate forms of communication. Thousands of pieces of mail pour into each lawmaker's offices annually. In fiscal year 1998, House offices received a total of 40 million pieces of mail, while the Senate received 35 million.[2] Communications are as varied as the national agenda and the responsibilities of a congressional office: everything from requests for tickets to a White House tour and a flag flown from the Capitol, to requests for U.S. military academy appointments, to individual problems and casework issues, to letters spontaneously sent on issues of the day, to sensitive "Dear _____:" letters (letters that require personal attention of the senator or representative and are addressed by first name back to the recipient). Most letters are in the form of postcards, not spontaneously written, and are generated by organized interest groups wanting to save Social Security, bring back the death penalty, halt stem cell research, or affect a myriad of other issues.

With good record keeping, coding, and data management, congressional offices can keep up with the normal flow of letters and telephone calls, and can generate responses that look as though they were given considerable thought and attention. A constituent may receive a response like this: "Dear Mr. Smith, Thanks again for writing to me. I want to thank you for your letter of last October 29 and your follow-up telephone call. Your ideas about the federal budget crisis and how it affects small business owners like yourself were very helpful to me. And I appreciate your letter of last week about the tax burdens that could be imposed if the House Democratic leadership has its way. Let me tell you in no uncertain terms that I oppose H.R. 212" . . . and so forth. This may be one of 10,000 letters on the subject of H.R. 212 that the representative's office received in two week's time. With good correspondence management, the policy paragraphs are preapproved, the writer's history has been acknowledged, and the letters bear the member's signature via auto-pen or a laser signature. Such letters are generated by the office's legislative correspondents and interns, with assistance from the legislative staff and chief of staff, with the ultimate approval (and responsibility) of the member.

Because of the heavy volume of mail, legislative staffs do not answer all correspondence, and responses are rationed. Members of Congress are often very parochial in responding, or even acknowledging, correspondence from the public. The most important correspondence comes from the district, then the state (especially if the member has ambitions for running for state-wide office), and then from interest groups that are of particular interest to the member. The rest, often, is detritus. Mass mailings, say, from California, sent to members of the Maryland delegation, will be routinely ignored—unanswered, most likely just tossed in the wastepaper basket. Some offices, especially in the Senate, will not even bother to answer organized postcard mailings, even if some of these mailings are sent from within their own state.

Always an important communication link, the telephone became much more important and more widely used with the lowering of long-distance rates, the publishing of legislators' telephone numbers, and especially with patch-through technology. In use for about a decade, patch-through technology is a highly effective way of directing many telephone calls toward selected members of Congress. An interest group, usually employing a phone-bank vendor, will call its own membership, explain why a certain issue needs their immediate attention, and ask if they would respond immediately to their legislators. Those "wired" members will be patched through directly to the phone line in their legislator's office. An interest group can target specific legislative offices and have their membership call directly, not risking the inertia that might set in if the member is left to place a call or write a letter at some later time. Get the interested party while they are still hot and immediately patch them through to their legislator's office.

This all sounds fine in theory, but there are definite risks. Congressional telephone lines become jammed, other constituents cannot get through, the office staff and the member get irritated. Further irritation comes from telephone calls generated by radio call-in shows, when the radio host gets listeners worked up over a certain policy issue and goads them to jam the telephones of legislators in Washington.

Faxes have become another vehicle for mass communication to lawmakers' offices. A vendor may rent telephone time to spew out hundreds of faxes to a congressional office each night. Faxes sent at night can be sent at lower transmission costs, so that in the morning, selected offices can have blast faxes from hundreds of constituents. However, fax transmissions are linear: only one can come in at a time to a particular office fax line, and thus there is a finite number that can appear over a period of time. Such fax campaigns also depend on the simplest of technologies not breaking down. The best laid broadcast fax campaigns can be defeated when the congressional fax machine runs out of paper, or jams, or an irritated staffer simply cuts off the machine at night, and deletes incoming faxes from the machine's memory in the morning.

Grassroots managers know that such advocacy techniques must be used wisely and sparingly. Employed too often, at the wrong time, with the wrong emphasis and they could backfire, waste money, and do nothing more than irritate or alienate members of Congress. This applies with equal force to e-mail messaging as a new lobbying weapon.

CONSTITUENTS AND E-MAIL

Nielsen NetRatings, a service that tracks Web use, in March 2001 showed that 163.4 million people in the United States had home Internet access—roughly 60 percent of the American population.[3] E-mail is the most used of Internet applications. Just as general use of the Internet and e-mail has grown dramatically, so, too, has electronic communications with Congress. With e-mail and congressional Web sites have come whole new levels of communications opportunities, issues, challenges, and frustrations.

To a great extent, e-mail communications to Congress reached its stride in reaction to the impeachment of President Bill Clinton in 1998. Much of the e-mail sent to Congress was spontaneous yet another 500,000 electronic signatures were forwarded to Congress by Moveon.org, an organization that sprung up out of nowhere to rally opposition to Congress wasting its time on impeachment. Over the years, Congress had seen its share of scandals and episodes of high public interest, such as Watergate, the Iran-Contra affair, the Clarence Thomas–Anita Hill hearings, and the House banking scandal. In each of these cases, House and Senate offices were in some form of nuclear meltdown, deluged with letters and postcards, swamped with angry telephone calls. Yet after each of those episodes, mail and telephone calls returned to normal traffic levels. Following the Clinton impeachment trials, however, e-mail did not drop off but, in fact, grew in volume each year.

Table 6.1 shows the growth of e-mails sent to the official member e-mail sites in the House of Representatives (e-mails@mail.house.gov).

TABLE 6.1 E-MAILS SENT TO <E-MAILS@MAIL.HOUSE.GOV>

YEAR	E-MAILS
1998	23,300,000
1999	30,688,570
2000	47,991,851

Source: U.S. Congress, House of Representatives, House Information Resources, April 2001.

In 2000, Congress received nearly 80 million e-mail messages, with the House receiving 48 million, and that number growing each month by a million messages.[4] E-mail continued to grow, and by May 2001, Congress was receiving a million e-mails a day—roughly twelve messages every second. Comparably, the official House Web site (http://www.house.gov) in mid 2001 received more than 20 million hits a month.

Grassroots Activism

Much of the e-mail during this time period came from organized efforts by interest groups and through electronic junk mail. As part of their grassroots lobbying arsenal, most trade associations, labor unions, corporations, nonprofits, and single-issue interest groups have developed interactive Web sites that can send electronic messages to Congress. There is a small industry of Web site designers who serve this niche market. Over 800 such organizations use the Web design of just one firm, Capitol Advantage, a fifteen-year-old firm that began by selling congressional directories to client organizations. The company has transformed from a low-tech business into a firm that provides powerful, interactive grassroots and membership Web sites designed for citizen activism. A look at a typical client shows the kinds of information that are now readily available in effective grassroots advocacy.

The Retired Officers Association (TROA), with some 400,000 members, represents about 60 percent of all the retired military officers. Through its Web site (www.troa.org), TROA provides a free e-mail account to its members together with legislative and policy information deemed important to TROA members. Members receive updates on key legislative issues, information about TROA's position on legislation and policy as well as tips on telephoning or writing to their representative. To make e-mail correspondence simple, all a TROA member has to do is enter his or her zip code; links then pop up to the two senators, representative, and the president (organizations that monitor state legislative activity can easily have the governor and state representatives added to their Web site search). On the MegaVote section of the Web site, TROA members are able to find out how their legislators voted, which political action committee gave them money for their federal elections, and who their key staff members are. Moreover, the Web site can be directly linked to House or Senate committee e-mail addresses, and to a legislator's official Web site and e-mail address. By typing in the zip code, a TROA member may send an e-mail letter to the editor of all the media outlets in his or her home community. At its annual conference in Washington, TROA even provides assistance for its members on how to navigate their Web site and send e-mail messages.

The Web site and grassroots activism model of The Retired Officers Association is typical of the thousands of member-based organizations that have an interest in affecting Washington. Not only do these organizations make it easy to connect to Congress, they also have ushered in a revolution in grassroots advocacy, targeting not only federal and state legislators and executives, but also private corporations. Douglas G. Pinkham, president of the Washington-based Foundation for Public Affairs, observed "The Internet is the most effective tool ever created for organizing people. Through e-mail, Web sites and listservs, like-minded people can find each other and have a major impact on public or corporate policy. Even small and poorly funded groups can speak with a much louder voice because of the Net."[5] The AFL-CIO, with 13 million members, urges its members to join the Working Families e-Activist Network through its Web site. To get blood pressures cooking, union members can click on to the Pay Watch database and find out how much the CEO of their company made and how their own salaries compared. Rainforest Action Network provides a preprinted letter to the CEO of Boise Cascade Corporation, the large timber company, blasting him for permitting the destruction of old growth forests. Rainforest activists who click on to this Web site need only put in their e-mail address, and if they like, their name and address, and the letter will be sent to Boise Cascade.[6]

In just a handful of years, e-mail has become a standard tool in the arsenal of activist organizations. Organizations have quickly appreciated the benefits of e-mail correspondence: It is far less expensive than faxes, organized telephone efforts, and preprinted postcards or paper action alerts. Further, e-mail campaigns can be far better timed and coordinated than older means of communication. In the fast-paced business of legislative policymaking, an organization overnight can change its message to its members via its Web site, broadcast an e-mail action alert to its members, and expect that the members will turn right around and e-mail their legislators. In the modern age of instant electronic communications, all it takes is a click of an Internet button to send messages. New voices are being heard, by the thousands, even the millions.

Organizations know that, like traditional forms of communication, an e-mail campaign must be used sparingly. There must be deft use of a combination of communication tools—at the right time, to the right audience, from the right audience. Organizations soon learned, for instance, that spammed e-mail messages to Congress were simply ignored, that sending an e-mail to a senator might be a good idea, but sending it to 100 senators and 435 representatives for good measure is wasted effort. Every congressional office filters out spammed messages and avoids answering those e-mails coming from outside their district or state.

Electronic Junk Mail

Another reason for the extraordinary rise in e-mail is due to electronic junk mail. Internet entrepreneurs have sprung up in the past few years, following the unexpected successes of MoveOn.org. One such entrepreneur is Dick Morris, a former political consultant to President Bill Clinton, and Morris's wife, Eileen McGann. Morris created a Web site, vote.com, and published a book (frequently seen in banner ads on his Web site) with the same title, *Vote.com*. Morris's Web site is designed to ask a series of topical policy questions, then asks visitors to cast a vote; the vote is then sent to the appropriate elected officials—national legislators, the president, governors, or local officials. In mid July 2001, the lead question was, "Should Congress grant legal residency to 3 million illegal Mexican immigrants?" Web site visitors were given a yes or no choice, with a short explanation of the issue, both pro and con. Vote.com covers other topics as well, including family, travel, movies, showbiz, sports, and it claims to have over 31 million persons voting on the site. The Web site promises to send the vote to "where it counts," to the president and Congress. It even quotes President George W. Bush, with an accompanying audiotape saying, "I believe that when you e-mail a congressman or a senator, it will make a difference."

In the House of Representatives, however, it does not seem to make any difference. In fact, of the three dozen House systems administrators and legislative correspondents interviewed, this kind of unsolicited e-mail is the first to be trashed or deleted. Below is what an actual vote.com e-mail petition looks like, the results of an electronic poll on the issue of whether or not to support a national missile defense system. The e-mail was sent to the office of the late Representative Norman Sisisky (D-Va.):

DATE: July 14, 2000 07:12 AM
NAME: A registered Vote.com voter
STATE: Virginia
ZIP: 23054
Dear Honorable Norman Sisisky:
On the question A National Missile Defense System: Worthwhile or Worthless?, I voted WORTHWHILE, SINCE IT WOULD DEFEND THE U.S. FROM ONE OF OUR BIGGEST THREATS.
Please consider my vote when making your decision on the issue.
Signed, 7 voters listed below:
[e-mail address], a resident of ZIP Code 23434
[e-mail address], a resident of ZIP Code 23833
[e-mail address], a resident of ZIP Code 23487
[e-mail address], a resident of ZIP Code 23860
[e-mail address], a resident of ZIP Code 23320
[e-mail address], a resident of ZIP Code 23703
[e-mail address], a resident of ZIP Code 23325

MANAGING THE E-MAIL BEAST

A difficulty for many congressional offices is to separate spammed e-mails and electronic junk mail from legitimate e-mail communications as well as respond to such legitimate e-mail communications in a timely, efficient manner, without exhausting staff resources.

One organization, the Congress Online Project, has looked critically at the overload of e-mail messages to Capitol Hill and how congressional offices cope with this communication crisis. Many congressional offices, and Congress as an institution, have failed to keep up with technology and modern communications. While there have been some increases lately, Congress has been unable to adequately fund technology improvements, hardware and software purchases, vendor support, and staff training. There is also a mind-set in many offices that e-mail is simply another form of postal mail, and that the member's reply should come in letter form rather than an electronic communication.

Congress can meet the avalanche of electronic mail, but must approach the problem more as a managerial problem than a technological one,[7] but in order to accomplish this, congressional offices must be aware of four important principles.

First, congressional offices need to establish e-mail policies and make sure they are communicated throughout the office staff. For example, there should be clear policies covering the following: the priority given to e-mail messages from constituents and the tone and content of e-mail responses; the expected turnaround times for e-mail messages; the degree to which e-mail should be automated; procedures for reviewing e-mail traffic flow; the role played by the Web site and outreach e-mail in reducing e-mail inquiries; the ethical and legal considerations, such as the franking rules, privacy policies, spam policies; and the record-keeping and filing procedures. All these policies are critical for getting a handle on the enormous flow of e-mail, and these policies need to be established at the chief-of-staff level.

Second, congressional offices should anticipate and reduce the amount of e-mail coming into their offices. Rather than simply react to e-mail, offices should provide information, both through their e-mail systems and through their Web sites. This can be accomplished in a variety of ways: sending e-mail issue updates; providing direct links from the member's Web site home page to information about critical issues; providing overviews of other important issues on the Web site; establishing and continually updating an FAQ (frequently asked questions) page on the Web site; conducting on-line issue surveys (with appropriate disclaimers that the results only reflect those who responded, not the public at large); and providing on-line comment forms and guest books so that constituents can convey their comments without expecting a reply.

Third, e-mail correspondence should be automated as much as possible. This depends heavily on the use of sophisticated e-mail sorting software. Congressional offices have two choices in how constituents can send them e-mail: They can provide a Web-based form, such as Write Your Representative or other vendor-provided software, which requires visitors to send messages through a form on the Congressional Web site or through an independent Web site; or they can use a public e-mail address (e.g., <contact@mail.house.gov>), which permits constituents to send messages using their own e-mail software. Software filters and rules become critical for automating e-mail. A congressional office will define key words—issue topics, zip codes, towns, and cities—for which their software will search filters for zip codes and rules that place e-mail with in-state zip codes in one folder and e-mail with out-of-state zip codes in another.[8] Available only in Senate offices is EchoMail, a new sophisticated Web-based service, now in a pilot phase that uses artificial intelligence to filter, sort, and respond to e-mail. Two other software packages, Intranet Quorum (IQ) and Capitol Correspond can automate and sort e-mail before it is viewed by congressional staff: They can automatically download e-mail at regular intervals, separate constituent from nonconstituent messages, sort the messages by topic, create or add to existing constituent contact records in the office database, assign form letters, and route the e-mail to appropriate staff members.

The fourth principle is to respond to e-mail, like all other correspondence, in a timely manner. The e-mail public expects two things: a response by e-mail and a response quickly.

Constituents who communicate to members of Congress through e-mail want their mail answered by e-mail, but 90 percent of the offices on the Hill do not reply to e-mail with e-mail. Instead, they reply by the most traditional of means, on letterhead stationery from the member, with the member's signature. But while all congressional offices have the technology to respond through e-mail, even though some may have older versions of hardware and software, responding to e-mail with e-mail can prove difficult for some. Interviews with Hill staffers reveal that many members prefer responding to constituents by using letterhead stationery, primarily on the belief that letters have a greater feel of legitimacy on letterhead. There also is some concern that e-mails sent from a House or Senate office may be modified indiscriminately, duplicated, and sent off to cyberspace.

Grassroots activists could assist Capitol Hill in processing its communication overload by targeting only their own members of Congress, sending meaningful messages (in citizens' own words) rather than sending "electronic postcards," avoiding duplicate messages from the same person, and providing complete identification (name, address, zip code) together with e-mail.

CONGRESSIONAL WEB SITES AND COMMUNICATIONS

During the past several years, members of Congress have created Web sites to assist them in communicating with their constituents and the public at large. Altogether, there are 591 congressional Web sites: All of the personal offices have them as well as standing committees and leadership offices. Not surprisingly, one finds considerable variation in the quality, content, and usability of congressional Web sites; some are elaborate, filled with rich graphics, audio and video links, and loaded with content; others are bare bones and static.

In a series of interviews with House system administrators and chiefs of staff, respondents were asked how they decided what went into their congressional Web site and how offices were sure such material reflected what the public wished to see.[9] The answer to the first question was that Web site content is decided predominately by staff (principally the press secretary, chief of staff, systems administrator, and legislative assistants) and only occasionally by members. In some instances, members have shown very little interest, in other offices, members are highly engaged. What goes into Web sites is content that promotes the legislator's career and record: a personal photo and biography, recent press releases, sponsored or cosponsored bills, and ways to contact the Washington and district offices. Basically, what goes into Congressional Web sites is a matter of guesswork, with considerable variation from office to office. In response to the second question, what was clearly evident is that the public, the principal clientele for the Web sites, is rarely consulted. Rarely are there any outside quality controls or plans for systematic review of electronic communications. And at times there is little coordination with other communications coming out of the member offices.[10]

To uncover what the public really thinks, the Congress Online Project assembled eight focus groups in four cities, Phoenix, Richmond, Philadelphia, and Washington, D.C. Individuals chosen for these focus groups were people comfortable with the Internet and e-mail. Half of the participants were "engaged" citizens—persons who had at some time written to their legislators, attended town hall meetings, or kept up with politics and public affairs. The other half of participants were "not engaged"—they were relatively savvy in using Internet and e-mail, but were generally not interested in politics and policy. Four of the focus groups consisted of "engaged" citizens, and the other four had "nonengaged" participants.

In the focus groups,[11] participants were given time to review the look, feel, and content of four downloaded congressional Web sites—a Republican Senate site and a Democratic Senate site, and a Republican House site and a Democratic House site—and asked to evaluate them.[12] Altogether, there were four key findings from our focus-group study.

First, while not always critical of their own representatives, citizens expressed frustration with Congress as an institution, feeling a growing disconnection between themselves and their lawmakers in Washington. Respondents were particularly frustrated with what they see as extreme partisanship, policy gridlock, backbiting, inefficiency, and too much time spent on campaigning. Many of their complaints echoed those found in earlier studies.[13] There was an overwhelming feeling that members of Congress simply do not communicate with constituents except at election time. Further, respondents felt that their own communications were not heeded. One participant in Richmond summed up many others' feelings: "Once the campaigns and elections are over, and they're [lawmakers] in Washington, they are very distant from us."

The second finding was that participants wanted their voices heard. They wanted assurances that their views are being acknowledged and taken into account; they appreciate it when legislators write back even saying they disagree, but at least have the courtesy, nonetheless, to tell the participants so. A very fundamental problem was that participants did not know the Web addresses of their legislators, nor did they feel they could readily find them on their own. While it takes little effort to use one of many search engines to instantaneously provide such information, it nevertheless can be an extra step that dissuades people from taking the next step. The executive branch provides an easily remembered new master site, Firstgov.gov, which links to many of the agencies and departments within the federal government as well as to state governments and others. There is no comparable master Web site on Capitol Hill. Citizens also wanted to see interactive polls on congressional Web sites, where policy questions could be asked, and they would have a chance to respond. When reminded that such on-line polling is in no way an accurate reflection of what the public thinks, focus-group participants did not seem to mind. What seems more important than the scientific accuracy is the chance for individuals to click on a yes or no response to a policy question, and have their vote recorded. A number of congressional Web sites have such interactive polls, but without a disclaimer that the results of these polls do not accurately reflect public opinion.

A third finding was that the public was basically unimpressed with congressional Web sites. Focus-group participants were used to seeing glitzy, interactive commercial Web sites; they did not expect the same kind of sites from their legislators. In fact, participants were decidedly opposed to glitz and self-promotion, criticizing Web sites with legislators surrounded by balloons and babies or even holding press conferences on the steps of the Capitol. All that smacked too much of self-promotion. Participants were also unimpressed by blinking icons, clever graphics, or folksy material. As one participant in Phoenix said, "I don't want a Web site where they send his wife's favorite recipe for bean dip or something like that." Citizens want a serious, sober feel to a Web site, filled with solid, useful information. In other words, Web site content matters to constituents, and a plain Web site, rich in content, will be preferred to a graphically slick site that is weak in content. One of the four sites shown to focus group participants was, on its surface, very plain, with few graphics, no interactivity, no audio or video streaming. It looked very amateurish, but it was loaded with content. The three other Web sites were far more sophisticated in design, but in one way or another they were deficient in content. In each of the eight focus groups, a clear preference for the plain, understated, but content-rich site was noted.

The fourth finding was that participants wanted to see accountability. They had only a vague idea of what their members of Congress did all day. Apart from seeing glimpses of them on C-SPAN or the nightly news, participants did not understand what goes on during a busy legislative week or, more importantly, during a congressional recess. In many peoples' minds, when Congress is on recess, their legislators must be off at some exotic tropical location goofing off at taxpayer expense or on a trip funded by a powerful interest group. As a focus-group participant said, "I'd like to know where they are. Making sure they're sticking to business. Where are they? What are they doing?" One of the member sites we showed to the focus groups unwittingly reinforced that misconception. When we clicked on to the schedule for the week, up came a link to the House official calendar, which simply said, "House in Recess." Had the member used his or her own schedule, it would have shown that he or she was back in the district with a busy schedule of constituent meetings each day.

Focus-group participants were most interested in seeing how legislators voted and not just seeing a listing of bills that they had sponsored or cosponsored. They wanted to know, in clear, understandable language, what the vote was and how the member voted, including an explanation of why the legislator voted a certain way.

Above all, focus-group participants wanted solid content, without the hype and fanfare, and answers to simple questions: Where do I go when I have a problem with a federal agency? Who can I write to? Where will the senator or representative be during the next two weeks? What committees does he or she serve on? What is the telephone number of the Washington or district office?

These findings ran consistently throughout each focus group, with no clear distinction between those participants who can be described as "engaged" or "not engaged" or among sections of the country. Congressional Web sites have enormous potential to benefit the flow of communications and understanding between legislators, their staffs, and the public. There is a great deal of public skepticism, and citizens have fairly low expectations of how lawmakers should communicate with them. Certainly, as more citizens use the Internet, congressional Web sites can help. But much more needs to be done.

Conclusion

There are many ways that citizens, on their own and organized, can communicate with members of Congress. There is no one right way, and the oldest vehicles of communication, writing letters and calling on the telephone, still prevail. In some congressional districts, particularly those with urban and tech-savvy populations, e-mail is reaching a critical mass as a preferred form of communications. In other districts, often rural and with fairly large concentrations of elderly constituents, electronic mail is important, but lags behind other forms of communication.

Yet there seems a certain inevitability about e-mail and the use of the Internet. It may never reach saturation as found with the telephone or television, but now more than half of the population uses it, and the percentage of users will undoubtedly increase. A novelty just a few years ago, e-mail and the Internet are becoming preferred means of reaching elected officials. Members of Congress, their staffs, and Congress as an institution will need to make even further changes to accommodate constituent demands for timely electronic communication. It will be a matter of adjusting budget and staff priorities, changing attitudes, and accepting this new medium as a legitimate communications vehicle. In this increasingly electronic age, Congress needs to squarely meet these communication challenges and opportunities.

NOTES

1. Research for this chapter was supported by a grant from the Pew Charitable Trusts. Thanks to my partners at the Congressional Management Foundation, Richard Shapiro, Kathy Goldschmidt, Michael Callahan, Nicole Folk, and Brad Fitch; to Rosita Thomas of Thomas Opinion Research; and graduate student Lisa Butenhoff of the George Washington University.
2. Roger H. Davidson and Walter J. Oleszek, *Congress and Its Members*, 7th ed. (Washington, D.C.: CQ Press, 2000), p. 152.
3. Nielsen NetRatings, March 2001.
4. Congress Online Project, "E-Mail Overload in Congress: Managing a Communications Crisis" (March 2001). Principal author, Kathy Goldschmidt, Congressional Management Foundation, <www.congressonlineproject.org>. The sections in this chapter on e-mail management rely heavily on the summary and analysis of this report.
5. "Activist Groups Use the Net to Gain Power and Influence," Public Affairs Council press release, December 12, 2000, accompanying the publication of Foundation for Public Affairs report, "Cyber Activism: Advocacy Groups and the Internet," December 2000, <www.pac.org/pubs/cyberactivism.htm>.
6. The AFL-CIO Web site is <www.aflcio.org>, and the Rainforest Action Network's Web site is <www.ran.org>.
7. Congress Online Project, "E-Mail Overload in Congress."
8. In Congress, the e-mail management software packages generally used are Exchange, Outlook and cc:Mail; there are also special filtering features available in ACS's Intranet Quorum (IQ) and InterAmerica's Capitol Correspond CMS packages.
9. Interviews conducted with approximately thirty House staffers, January–March, 2001. Interviews conducted by Dennis W. Johnson and Lisa Butenhoff, research assistant.
10. Congress Online Project, "Constituents and Your Web Site: What Citizens Want to See on Congressional Web Sites" (August 2001). Principal author, Dennis W. Johnson, George Washington University, <www.congressonlineproject.org>.
11. Eight focus groups were held altogether, with two each in Washington, D.C., Richmond, Virginia, Phoenix, Arizona, and Philadelphia, Pennsylvania, during January–March, 2001. Focus group interviews and analysis provided by Dr. Rosita Thomas and Thomas Opinion Research.
12. None of the congressional Web sites came from legislators in Virginia, Maryland, Arizona, or Pennsylvania, states where focus groups were held. The Congress Online Project did this to assure that no other factors (such as knowledge of the legislator or partisan biases) might creep into the discussion.
13. See, for example, John R. Hibbing and Elizabeth Theiss-Morse, *Congress as Public Enemy: Public Attitudes toward American Political Institutions* (New York: Cambridge University Press, 1995); Glenn R. Parker and Roger H. Davidson, "Why Do Americans Love Their Congressmen So Much More Than Their Congress?" *Legislative Studies Quarterly* 4 (February 1979), pp. 53–61; Randall B. Ripley, et al., "Constituents' Evaluations of U.S. House Members," *American Politics Quarterly* 20 (October 1992), pp. 442–456; Eric M. Uslaner, *The Decline of Comity in Congress* (Ann Arbor, MI: University of Michigan Press, 1994); and more generally, Joseph S. Nye, Jr., Philip D. Zelikow, and David C. King, eds., *Why People Don't Trust Government* (Cambridge, MA: Harvard University Press, 1997).

CONGRESS, THE PRESIDENCY, INFORMATION TECHNOLOGY, AND THE INTERNET

POLICY ENTREPRENEURSHIP AT BOTH ENDS OF PENNSYLVANIA AVENUE

RICHARD S. CONLEY

The 1990s ushered in a veritable information revolution made possible by digital technology and the convergence of telecommunications, television, video, and computer applications. American national institutions have struggled to keep pace with the rapid advances in information technology (IT) and the growth of the Internet that have far-reaching implications for politics and the policy process. Shaping the commercial development and regulation of cyberspace proved a complex and often daunting task for the president and Congress in the last decade.

A number of vexing subjects remain on the national agenda at the turn of the new millennium. From censorship to taxation of electronic commerce in the "new economy," these issues promise lengthy and continued debate. A central question, then, is what can we learn about the future direction of national policies on the Internet by examining presidential and congressional efforts in the 1990s? Surprisingly, few have given much attention to how the president and Congress have jointly and independently sought to cope with the mounting policy challenges of the Information Age.

The objective of this chapter is to explore the respective roles of the White House and Capitol Hill in the development and regulation of the Internet from 1993–2000. No single paradigm adequately explicates executive and legislative actions on Internet policy. The concept of "policy entrepreneurship" does, however, cast light on the distinguishable roles played at the opposite ends of Pennsylvania Avenue. This analytical perspective aids in reconciling charges of "policy chaos" with the reality that the 1990s witnessed significant progress toward a delicate balance between governmental promotion of IT development and regulation of the Internet.

Policy Entrepreneurship and the Internet: The White House and Capitol Hill

Responsibility for the Internet and information technology is shared and fragmented between the president and Congress. Attempts to fashion a national policy on the Internet fit very well within the framework of the "tandem institutions" perspective.[1] This perspective emphasizes interdependence between the two branches; policymaking cannot be understood "with reference to only one branch of government."[2] The American system of "separated institutions sharing powers" yields the probability that at various points in time, and on various policies, Congress or the president will be more or less dominant in setting the agenda and steering policy outcomes.[3]

The president and Congress played complementary, if dissimilar roles, on Internet policy in the 1990s. Policy innovation and issue foci differed within each branch. The Clinton administration concentrated both on spurring private sector development of information technologies and applying IT to federal agencies. Much of the president's agenda was accomplished through independent actions under a preexisting legislative framework when the administration failed to procure a new and expansive one from 1993–1994. Congress, by contrast, struggled far more with regulating unforeseen consequences of the Internet's mercurial ascent as a tool for everything from "e-commerce" to the distribution of pornographic material. Capitol Hill suffered from the lack of a unifying policy history on Internet-related issues capable of bridging institutional capacity with accelerated technological change. The multidimensional quality of Internet issues confounded lawmaking efforts and yielded an incremental and cautious approach to regulation.

Adding the concept of "policy entrepreneurship" to the tandem institutions perspective offers a useful lens through which to assess the basis for independent and joint presidential and congressional policy action on Internet issues. Policy entrepreneurs are concerned with *policy change*.[4] They are best defined as those political actors—in the executive or legislative branch—who seize the initiative to identify policy problems and offer substantive alternatives and solutions.[5] They seek to mold the public agenda, steer the debate, and are willing and able to invest the time, energy, and resources to engage networks of decision makers in "policy communities" and "policy networks" to coordinate vital support for new initiatives.[6] Policy success and status may constitute the central motivation for political entrepreneurs.[7] As one observer notes: "Policy entrepreneurs can be thought of as being to the policymaking process what economic entrepreneurs are to the marketplace. Policy entrepreneurs are able to spot problems, they are prepared to take risks to promote innovative approaches to problem solving, and they have the ability to organize others to help turn policy ideas into government policies."[8] Thus by navigating new initiatives through the policy process—from the definition of problems and agenda setting to coalition building—policy entrepreneurs may be a source of significant and punctuated advances in policymaking, or "serial policy shifts."[9]

The president and members of Congress have similar incentives, though different resources, to engage in policy entrepreneurship. Each branch faces different constraints and opportunities. Presidents, for example, have strong incentives to provide policy entrepreneurship because they are innately concerned with their historical legacies, and because they are well positioned in the American political system to take advantage of the media's intense focus on their actions and reach an extensive public audience. In addition, they may be able to employ the formal trappings and informal perquisites of the office to lure congressional interest in, and action on, their initiatives. Yet, presidents cannot control the internal dynamics of Congress. Legislative success is contingent largely on congressional-centered factors, including party, ideology, and constituency—factors that place the president "at the margins" of influence.[10] Presidents can, however, take independent actions including executive orders and administrative policies that do not require congressional assent. And they can utilize the expansive resources in the White House and executive branch to network within the federal establishment and link to private-sector interests to promote their agenda, through both formal and informal venues.

Presidents' interest in policy entrepreneurship is likely to converge around issues like IT and the Internet for which alternatives have not been adequately defined or debated. Presidents' ability to identify and shepherd such "promising issues" is a key component of presidential skill.[11] Bryan Jones notes that:

> Presidents at the national level (or governors and mayors at the state and local levels) are frequently the primary entrepreneurs seeking to redefine an issue in order to achieve maximum support for it. While political chief executives may act as brokers for the policy ideas of others, in the modern world they must also define a policy agenda themselves in order to be viewed as successful. That agenda must also be "packaged and sold" to Congress, the media, and to the public.[12]

On emerging issues such as new technology, presidents can stimulate public dialogue, lend their own perspective to the best course of action, and devote the vast resources of the White House to leave a lasting imprint on policy, whether through congressional liaison and legislative endeavors or through independent executive actions.

Members of Congress may be driven to engage in policy activism by electoral incentives[13] as well as by their desire to enact good public policy.[14] Their ability to play a prominent policy role, shape the contours of debate, and offer substantive alternatives to solve emergent problems may depend significantly on the policy niche that they are able to cultivate through their committee assignments.[15] Lawmakers who are well situated to engage in policy entrepreneurship include those party leaders in authoritative decision-making positions, including committee and subcommittee chairs with specialized policy expertise. These leaders are most likely to enjoy the status and access to the requisite human and financial resources to steer initiatives through the legislative process.

Opportunity structures in Congress—the distribution of authority and resources—shape the potential for policy entrepreneurship. Members can face considerable constraints in their bid to assume an assertive policy leadership role. The centralization of decision-making authority in party leaders beginning in the 1980s may limit members' ability to stray too far from leaders' policy objectives.[16] Jurisdictional lines between committees are often blurred. Committee leaders may attempt to encroach on each other's turf.[17] Party leaders' referral of legislation to multiple committees may additionally complicate policy innovation.[18] The successful congressional policy entrepreneur must therefore maneuver around numerous institutional hurdles and reach out to party leaders, other committee and subcommittee chairs, as well as rank-and-file members and organized interests, to build the requisite coalitional support.

The very nature of Internet issues complicates policy entrepreneurship in Congress. One basic problem is that the pace of legislative efforts can lag behind rapid technological advances. By the time that policy entrepreneurs have reconciled conflicting interests and brokered necessary support, the window of opportunity for legislative action may have closed with new technology that renders regulation ineffectual or unnecessary. Another problem is that the Internet represents a "computer-generated public domain, which has no territorial boundaries or physical attributes and is in perpetual use."[19] No single entity "owns" or is responsible for the Internet. Consequently, the intractable issues with which members of Congress must grapple often blur distinctions between the private and public spheres and transcend regulatory, distributive, and redistributive policy typologies.[20] Crosscutting committee jurisdictions over information technology, members' short-term electoral incentives, budget politics, and bicameralism frustrate bids to overlay a comprehensive, long-term national structure for Internet development and regulation.

In light of the divergent policymaking settings within which the president and members of Congress operate, policy entrepreneurship on Internet issues followed distinctive tracks in the White House and on Capitol Hill in the 1990s. Each branch grappled with different facets of IT and Internet development and regulation and assumed a different entrepreneurial role. President Bill Clinton and Vice President Al Gore sought to develop a National Information Infrastructure (NII) and streamline governmental information procedures and public access. When priority legislation for the NII stalled in the 103rd Congress (1993–1995), Clinton used a statutory framework that predated his administration—the High Performance Computing Act (HPCA) of 1991—to foster public–private partnerships toward IT development across the remainder of his term. Clinton also used his executive authority to assemble a task force of public and private sector concerns to facilitate problem solving. In addition, Congress was successful in passing several bills with broad bipartisan support that targeted IT in government agencies and the Administration incorporated provisions of the bills into Vice President Gore's National Performance Review (NPR) initiative. The White House, then, pursued policy entrepreneurship for IT development and usage on a variety of fronts—through an admixture of executive orders and independent actions, the expansion of research and development grant programs by "creative" budgeting, and congressional legislation that complemented Gore's focus on "reinventing government."

Congress, on the other hand, was (and continues to be) constrained by the enormously difficult task of updating existing laws and crafting *new* legislation to address the fresh issues raised by the very development and commercialization of the Internet championed by Clinton and Gore. Cross-cutting and seemingly contradictory issues that emerged on the public agenda were among the most difficult for Congress to reconcile. Capitol Hill sought to promote "privatization" of information technology while ensuring "privacy" rights for consumers. Legislators recognized the need to protect the most vulnerable segment of the population—children—from sexual predators on the Internet but found that striking a balance with First Amendment protections was an onerous task. And while physical borders are insignificant for the Internet, geography remains central for political choices in a federal system on such issues as the taxation of e-commerce. What legislation emerged in the 1990s frequently resulted from the steadfast efforts of a handful of enterprising leaders in Congress who devoted themselves to Internet issues on Capitol Hill and were able to broker legislative support for a tempered approach to regulation.

Major legislative efforts to weave together a coherent national Internet policy proceeded largely under the tutelage of select policy entrepreneurs in both chambers. In the House of Representatives, Bob W. Goodlatte (R-Va.), Rick Boucher (D-Va.), Thomas J. Bliley, Jr. (R-Va.), and Christopher Cox (R-Calif.) used their positions on key committees to innovate on issues of competitiveness, taxation, and business-related Internet policies and regulation. In the Senate Orrin Hatch (R-Utah), Ron Wyden (D-Ore.), and Ernest F. (Fritz) Hollings (D-S.C.) took the lead on bringing several laws current with Internet applications. The efforts of these policy entrepreneurs were complemented and supported by members of the bipartisan Congressional Internet Caucus, whose mission is to "educate their colleagues about the promise and potential of the Internet."[21]

A closer examination of executive and congressional policy entrepreneurship on Internet issues distinguishes the variable opportunities and constraints the White House and Capitol Hill faced in cobbling together development and regulatory policies for IT in the 1990s. The next section explores the White House's varied approach to Internet development and application to government agencies.

CLINTON, GORE, AND THE NATIONAL INFORMATION INFRASTRUCTURE (NII)

Although the search for national coordination of information technology policy dates to the 1970s in the Ford administration, President Clinton and Vice President Gore made IT central to the 1992 election campaign.[22] The new administration swiftly laid bare a comprehensive vision of a National Information Infrastructure (NII) in a document entitled "Agenda for Action" in February 1993. The document outlined the ultimate goal of constructing "a seamless web of communications networks, computers, databases, and consumer electronics that will put vast amounts of information at users' fingertips."[23]

The NII was established to bridge the public and private spheres. The plan involved a delicate "balancing act" by the administration by inviting public participation in the information policy debate while simultaneously developing incentives for private-sector development of the Information Superhighway.[24] The federal government's primary role was to promote private-sector development and reform regulatory impediments to development; to ensure "universal service" and accessibility; to increase government grants for information technology; to emphasize user-driven, interactive applications; to ensure information security and network reliability; to protect intellectual property rights; to coordinate the NII with state, local, and international governments; and to provide greater access to government information and improve government procurement practices.

Vice President Al Gore's efforts were central to the NII initiative. Gore had long championed IT issues during his tenure in both the House of Representatives and Senate.[25] In early 1993—now as vice president—he announced a legislative package the administration sought to move in earnest on Capitol Hill to transform the Agenda for Action from idea to practice.[26] The five principles accentuated by Gore—private investment, competition, open access, avoiding an information society of "haves" and "have nots," and flexible government action—were detailed in a widely distributed administration "white paper" (NII White Papers). The legislative initiative aimed to update the High Performance Computing Act of 1991 (S. 272, PL 102-194), which Gore had helped steer to completion while in the Senate. Gore had been unsuccessful in later attempts to amend the Act in 1992 to include a coordinated approach to IT development (S. 2947, Information Infrastructure and Technology Act of 1992). From his new vantage point in the executive branch, however, Gore was now free of the binding committee jurisdictions in the Senate that foiled his earlier proposal and was "able to design the initiative as a general blueprint for the challenges of the information revolution."[27]

Yet many of the same dynamics that dashed Senator Gore's 1992 proposal also thwarted passage of the administration's Information-Superhighway initiatives in the 103rd Congress. Jurisdictional jealousies and competing claims to IT issues by congressional committees and bicameral politics—much more than the partisan divides that would prove so tumultuous for other elements of the administration's agenda in the 103rd Congress—proved insurmountable. The Senate's failure to pass the National Competitiveness Act of 1993 (S. 4) was pivotal in impeding the White House's legislative agenda on IT issues and forcing Clinton and Gore to find more creative means to accomplish their policy objectives.

The S. 4 bill was sponsored by Commerce, Science and Transportation Committee Chairman Ernest Hollings. The bill would have authorized $380 billion for loans and research grants for computing and communications programs. The Department of Commerce's National Institute of Standards and Technology (NIST) was to be the locus of coordination of the funds. However, a provision for the Department of Commerce to develop a pilot program for investment in technology-based companies stirred controversy with former Senator Dale Bumpers (D-Ark.), then chair of the Senate Small Business Committee who was adamant that the Small Business Administration administer the program. The Energy and Natural Resources Committee also sought to influence elements of the high-performance computing provisions in the bill.[28] The inability of Senator Hollings and Democratic leaders to reconcile these programmatic conflicts precluded reporting the bill out of committee. The S. 4 bill never reached the floor for a vote by the full chamber.

Most importantly, the untimely failure of S. 4 left key House legislation dead in its tracks. The House had already approved two companion bills that represented the core of the administration's agenda. The H.R. 820 bill passed after enduring Republicans' skepticism on both principle and substance. The bill authorized just over $2 billion for the development of new IT programs through research grants and loans to the private sector. Many GOP legislators argued that the bill represented "too much government interference in the marketplace."[29] The bill was subject to a barrage of amendments. The Democratic leadership permitted an open rule on floor consideration of the legislation—the first time an open rule had been allowed since 1992—and thereby provided an opportunity for unlimited debate and change. The Democratic majority turned back the lion's share of the Republican amendments to curtail spending on the bill and several compromises on funding were eventually reached. Yet passage of the bill 267–167 was moot without Senate action.

The National Information Infrastructure Act (H.R. 1757), a House bill to coordinate a national network of Information Superhighways, was to be appended to S. 4 and therefore also fell victim to Senate inertia. The initiative was a central component of the administration's objective of linking government, schools, libraries, and medical facilities together through the Internet, though the bill did not take up Gore's controversial call for "universal access" to the Internet for consumers.[30] The bill's sponsor, Representative Boucher, drew a sharp distinction between public- and private-sector responsibility for IT development: The governmental role was to assist the private sector in structuring computer standards, protocols, and interoperability, but the federal government itself was in no way taking on the task of constructing or managing information networks.[31] The H.R. 1757 bill won strong bipartisan backing and passed 326–61.

In the absence of enabling legislation for the NII, the Clinton administration was now compelled to search for alternative means to pursue its IT agenda. Clinton and Gore did so through a number of independent actions. One of the most important components of that agenda was achieved by executive "extension" of provisions in the High Performance Computing Act (HPCA) of 1991. The main thrust of the HPCA was to advance high-speed computing applications through a multiagency effort.[32] The Clinton administration used the "central clearance" process in the Office of Management and Budget (OMB), through which all agencies must formally route (or clear) programmatic budget requests, to expand the contours of the HPCA. The result was a new Information Infrastructure Technology and Applications (IITA) Program beginning in FY 1994. Through executive maneuvers Clinton had accomplished what Congress could not. The expansion of the HPCA achieved to a large degree the objectives outlined in H.R. 1757.

The IITA dovetailed, with calls by the Computer Systems Policy Project (CSPP), an amalgam of the largest computer companies in the United States, to expand the High Performance Computing and Communications Program (HPCC). The IT industry supported development of a national information network to insure competitiveness in the global market. As Kahin notes, "The new component merely enlarged the scope of the HPCC budget crosscut rather than added a new funded program, but it answered CSPP's calls for broadening the focus of the HPCC."[33] Twenty-five percent of the HPCC FY 1995 budget was accorded to the IITA, which focused on awarding research and development grants to the private sector and private–public partnerships for NII development.[34] This policy represented the Clinton administration's broad emphasis in the NII on user communities, research, education, scientific community, and private-sector development, with the federal government playing a central role primarily in funding new initiatives.[35]

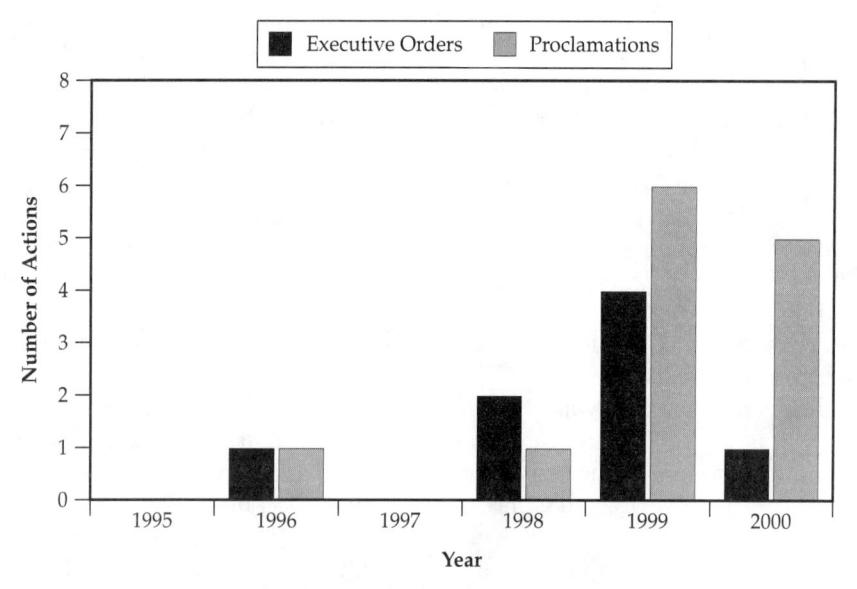

FIGURE 7.1 SUBSTANTIVE AND SYMBOLIC PRESIDENTIAL ACTIONS REGARDING THE INTERNET

Source: Federal Register.

Over the course of his two terms President Clinton took a host of other independent actions—executive orders and proclamations—that pertained to the Internet and information technology. Many of these actions were symbolic, such as the declaration of "World Trade Weeks" and "National Back to School Weeks," with explicit references to the role of IT. Other actions fit within the NII framework and were far more substantive, including executive orders on the formation of a Global Disaster Information Network (2000), a working group on unlawful conduct on the Internet (1999), and a presidential advisory commission on Next Generation Internet Issues (1997). The cumulative effect of these independent actions was twofold: to increase public awareness of IT issues and to streamline government information procedures. Two executive actions were particularly notable in these domains and merit closer examination: Executive Order (E.O.) 12864, which established an informal, public–private task force on the NII, and E.O. 13011, which addressed federal information technology practices.

Executive Order 12864, issued September 15, 1993, created the "United States Advisory Council on the National Information Infrastructure," chaired by the late Department of Commerce Secretary Ron Brown. Brown initially appointed twenty-five members from government agencies and the IT industry. The objective of the *ad hoc* task force was to foster a climate for the "coproduction" of policies by bridging various policy networks in the public and private sectors and spurring cooperation between government agencies, interest groups, and public institutions. The goal of the Council was to stimulate a collaborative exchange between the federal government and private-industry leaders toward a national strategy, including delineating the proper roles of the public and private sectors in NII development; enhancing public and commercial applications of IT; evaluating proposed regulation; optimizing the potential for economic growth; and evaluating interoperability of networks and protocols, access, privacy, copyright, and international issues.

The NII task force represented a central element in the Clinton administration's long-term objective to adapt the public-policy dialogue to new technology. The work of the task force focused on reorganizing government approaches to "informatisation"[36]—the development and administration of IT issues that cross the fields of service delivery, policymaking, policy debate, and deliberation. With respect to the multiple agencies and government entities responsible for elements of IT issues and development, the NII task force "helped to coordinate their often disparate, even contradictory, policies, while at the same time bringing them more into line with the Administration's focus on managing competition in the information marketplace, assessing regulatory flexibility, and guaranteeing universal service."[37]

The central function of the task force was to hold public meetings, draft position papers, and solicit comments.[38] Although the task force did issue a number of widely disseminated reports (NII Virtual Library), the impact of the group's efforts was negligible in terms of tangible policy outcomes. The public–private task force was never fully developed or institutionalized because it had no formal budget authority. Participation by members was voluntary, and the work of the task force largely ground to a halt with the tragic airplane death of Commerce Secretary Ron Brown in the former Yugoslavia in 1996.

The greatest effect of the NII task force was to coopt technology interests in the bid to define the appropriate private- and public-sector roles and scope of a national information policy. The administration used the task force as a "bully pulpit" through which to publicize technology issues, draw public attention to policy development, and build consensus about the need to guard the public interest, all the while emphasizing private-sector innovation.[39] This focus on public–private cooperation, rather than confrontation, may not have completely altered corporate uneasiness about government regulation of the Internet.[40] But the work of the task force acted as a confidence-building mechanism that gave Clinton and Gore more opportunities to credibly prompt the IT industry to self-regulate while accepting some government intervention.[41]

Another of Clinton's major independent actions took aim at IT in federal agencies. Executive Order 13011, signed July 16, 1996, addressed broad issues in information resources management at the federal level. The executive action entitled "Federal Information Technology" synthesized elements of three legislative statutes targeting government efficiency: the Government Performance and Results Act of 1993, the Paperwork Reduction Act of 1995, and the Clinger-Cohen Act of 1996. The Clinton administration took advantage of the congressional legislation to emphasize IT issues at the federal level as part of Gore's NPR or "reinventing government" campaign.[42] The order provided comprehensive guidelines for federal agencies to manage information resources as a "strategic asset," increase the efficacy of acquisitions, and integrate IT into agency investment and performance planning.[43] Above all, the administration's objective was to ensure greater public access to government information on the Internet, including data and forms. The executive order was supplemented by revisions to OMB Circular No. A-130, which emphasized information planning processes as well as service delivery to achieve agencies' missions.[44]

A review of the Clinton administration's independent actions and executive orders demonstrates the centrality of discretionary authority for presidential policy entrepreneurship on the Internet and IT issues. The White House was successful in promoting a research and development agenda by retooling an existing statutory framework when Congress failed to furnish a new one. The administration also provided instrumental guidance to federal agencies by unifying the provisions of several congressional bills to promote a strategic approach to governmental management of information resources. White House efforts on Internet and IT policy, like those in Congress, surely lagged behind soaring advances in technology. Divided party control of the national government also led to some interbranch tension over levels of research and development funding for IT and telecommunications reform after Republicans captured Congress in the 1994 elections.[45] Yet the administration's emphasis on industry self-regulation and general (and likely purposive) avoidance of hot-button regulatory issues averted considerable partisan confrontation with Congress over the Internet. Congressional policy innovation and attempts to come to grips with these issues, and the Clinton administration's variable role therein, is the subject of the next section.

THE INTERNET CHALLENGE, MAJOR LEGISLATION, AND POLICY ENTREPRENEURSHIP ON CAPITOL HILL

In the 103rd Congress (1993–1995), Representative Edward J. Markey (D-Mass.), then–Chairman of the House Telecommunications Subcommittee, expressed the dilemma that emerging Internet issues posed for Capitol Hill this way: "The good news from Washington is that every single person in Congress supports the concept of an information superhighway, the bad news is that no one has any idea what that means."[46] Such a lack of conceptual consensus in Congress did not, however, preclude legislators from gradually attempting to bring laws up to speed with the Information Age. The House of Representatives, in particular, took a steadily increasing interest in Internet development and regulation beginning in the mid-1990s.

Between the 103rd Congress (1993–1995) and the 106th Congress (1999–2001), the number of proposed House bills directly concerning IT and the Internet mushroomed from less than five to fifty. The pace of Senate legislation similarly quickened. Momentum for action ostensibly built between 1993–1996, peaked with the passage of a half-dozen major bills in the 105th Congress (1997–1999), and declined in the following biennial period. Growing congressional attention to Internet-related issues by the end of the decade did not, however, yield passage of a great deal of major legislation. The curvilinear relationship between the consideration and passage of major bills and time suggests a type of "surge and decline" or "life cycle" to regulatory efforts on the Internet, with only a few bills successfully coming to fruition.

Representative Markey's prescient observation about congressional uncertainty over IT issues, and the data trends in Figure 7.2 (on page 146), beg several important questions about efforts on Capitol Hill to regulate the Internet and how congressional activity differed from White House policy steps. First, what type of special obstacles did potential legislative entrepreneurs face vis-à-vis Internet regulation? Second, how did policy entrepreneurs contribute to the passage of major bills?

Several key problems inhere in congressional attempts to regulate the Internet-based "new economy." As James Boyle notes, "Although many other policy areas have distinct sides, issues concerning the Internet do not break down along easily defined lines."[47] The lack of a public-policy history surrounding Internet issues—and the broad and occasionally nontraditional coalescence of interests involved—complicates policy innovation. Legislators must maneuver through a veritable minefield of conflicting views in the bid to define whom the federal government should protect and whom it should regulate—consumers, Internet providers, or the nascent e-commerce industry—while addressing other vexing questions such as content and access.

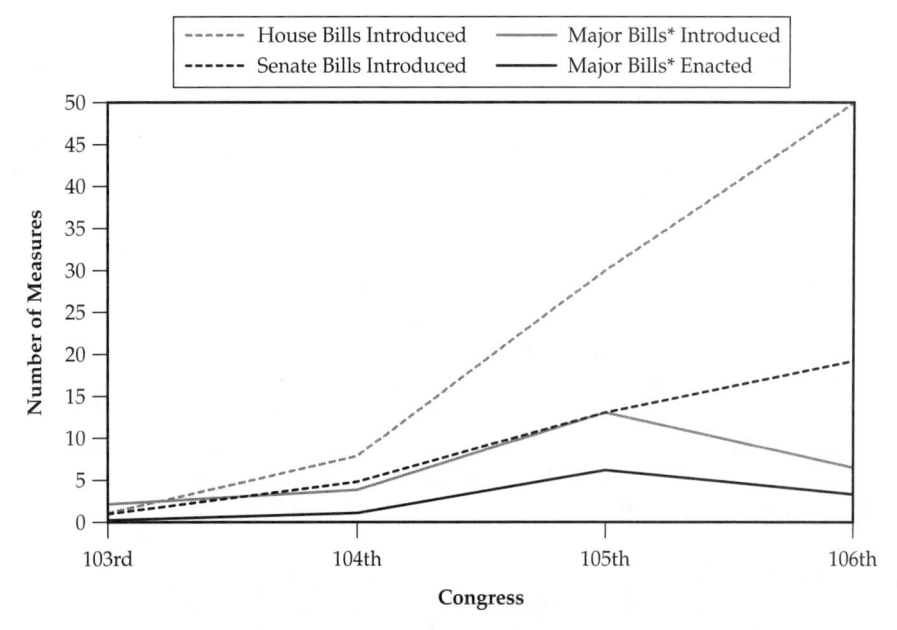

FIGURE 7.2 CONGRESSIONAL LEGISLATION ON INTERNET REGULATION, 103RD–106TH CONGRESSES (1993–2001)

*Major bills are those bills receiving coverage in *Congressional Quarterly Almanacs*.
Source: Library of Congress; <http://thomas.loc.gov>; *Congressional Quarterly Almanacs*.

Updating existing legislation and forging new laws in the Information Age has been further complicated by many legislators' unfamiliarity with Internet technology. A type of "digital divide" exists on Capitol Hill. David McClure, executive director of the Association of Online Professionals, described the situation in this manner: "We still have members of Congress who don't understand how the Internet works."[48] Representative Zoe Lofgren (D-Calif.) of San Jose's Silicone Valley noted that many members do not recognize "the potential it [the Internet] has for changing economic and human behavior."[49] The divide in Congress is exemplified by the differing characteristics of members of the Internet Caucus, like Lofgren, and nonmembers. The 103 members of the Internet Caucus in the House, for example, are more junior compared to nonmembers by nearly a full term. They also tend to be more ideologically moderate within their own party. And the constituencies represented by members of the Internet Caucus are highly urban, with strong IT industry ties and fewer blue-collar workers than nonmembers. A plurality of members are from technology-rich states including California, New York, and Massachusetts with vested interests in Internet development.[50]

The task of brokering the necessary support within Congress and among competing interests to steer complex legislation to passage frequently fell to select policy entrepreneurs, often drawn from the Internet Caucus. Members on technology- and commerce-related subcommittees, like Representatives Goodlatte and Boucher of Virginia, cochairmen of the Internet Caucus, were pivotal in defining the congressional Internet agenda and policy options. Such policy entrepreneurs placed a premium on rounding up bipartisan support, and for those bills that passed into law, they were successful in reconciling not only conflicting committee jurisdictions in Congress but also the crosspressures of interest group claims and IT industry demands.

A brief examination of the legislative history of three primary domains of Internet regulation—commerce, privacy, and antipornography legislation—emphasizes an incremental congressional response with a central role for policy entrepreneurs. Any rush to regulate the Internet was suppressed by the unique crosscutting conflicts that the medium generated. The tie that binds many of the successful legislative initiatives, consistent with the basic tenets of the sweeping Telecommunications Act of 1996 and executive actions, is the promotion of an environment of IT competition and development. In some cases, such as children's access to adult-oriented Web sites, technological innovation bolstered industry calls to self-regulate and was successful in ways that congressional intervention was not. In other cases, like the tax moratorium on electronic commerce, Congress came to the tenuous decision to put off definitive action and settled on an uneasy, if only temporary, compromise with competing interests. In still other cases, such as the export of encryption technology abroad, presidential action preempted the need for legislation. Congress was least successful in providing legislative "fixes" for gambling and privacy issues.

The Internet and Commerce, Taxation, and Intellectual Property Regulation

A synopsis of legislative efforts to enact taxation, copyright, and gambling legislation places into sharp relief policy entrepreneurs' difficulties in reconciling a web of tangled interests nearly as complicated as the negotiation of data transmission protocols on the Internet. These issues brought to the fore an amalgam of unique and competing interests, including governors and traditional retailers, the entertainment industry and librarians. Never far from the surface were nettling questions of regulatory enforceability in cyberspace with which legislators wrestled.

Congressional attempts to stave off state and local governments' taxation of electronic commercial transactions and Internet access involved issues of federalism and states' rights in addition to conflicts between traditional retailers and "e-tailers." The stakes for the IT industry, "bricks-and-mortar" retailers, and the nation's governors were high. Government and private sector studies of e-commerce transactions unveiled an astronomical growth in just four short years, with estimates of $5.6 billion in 1997, tripling to $16 billion in 1998, quadrupling to $66 billion in 1999, and more than doubling again to $132 billion in 2000.[51]

The question of state and local taxation of Internet purchases pitted numerous interests against one another in the context of little policy history available to Congress for guidance. The IT industry understandably championed swift congressional action on a tax moratorium, fearing state and local taxation would stifle the growth of Web-based commerce. But on the other side of the coin, the nation's governors contended that a moratorium deprives states of a lucrative tax base. Governors argued that it is unfair that Internet businesses be allowed to conduct transactions with residents of a state and be exempted from collecting that state's sales taxes simply because those businesses are not physically located in the state. States rely on sales taxes for roughly half of all revenues, and in 1997 governors estimated that Internet transactions cost states a total of $4 billion in lost taxes.[52] Finally, the growth in e-commerce also troubled traditional retailers who worried that consumers' ability to avoid taxes through the Internet would damage their sales.

The effort to enact a tax moratorium can be traced to two key policy entrepreneurs in the Senate and in the House. In 1997 Senator Wyden, a member of the Senate Commerce Committee, first introduced a measure (S. 442) to impose a "time-out" period for Congress to study the issue of Internet taxation. The proposed "Internet Tax Freedom" bill prohibited state and local governments from taxing interactive services and electronic commerce until the year 2004. The legislation was immediately opposed by the National Governors Association (NGA), which questioned Congress's assertion of control over Internet commerce. The governors contended that the legislation preempted states' taxing authority.[53] Governors also worried that in addition to the loss of revenue from Internet sales, some states which already imposed taxes on access to the Internet to the tune of $53 million in 1997 would lose this important source of revenue.[54] Some in the Senate also expressed reservations about the legislation's impact on traditional retailers. Former Senator Slade Gorton (R-Wash.), Wyden's colleague on the Commerce Committee, lambasted the bill for the potential effect on "Main Street" retailers by treating Internet sales "the way we treat mail-order catalogue sales."[55]

On the House side, Commerce Committee member Christopher Cox sponsored similar legislation, noting that the "Net's decentralized, packet-switched architecture makes every transmission vulnerable to multiple taxation. Thirty thousand state and local tax authorities could potentially tax the Internet to death."[56] Cox played a central role in nearly a year of negotiations with the NGA that produced a compromise bill in 1998 (H.R. 4105). The moratorium time frame was reduced to three years, and steadfast lobbying by the NGA won several key concessions. A "grandfather clause" enabled states already collecting taxes on Internet access before October 1, 1998, to continue doing so during the initial moratorium period. The legislation charged a commission, comprised of government and industry officials, to study the tax implications of e-commerce during the "time-out" period and fashion a uniform framework should states be allowed to levy taxes on Internet transactions.[57]

The drawback to passage of S. 442 was that the temporary measure only postponed the conflicts over Internet commerce and taxation that were bound to surface again as the sunset of the tax moratorium approached. As of early spring 2001, legislators have been unable to forge a compromise between states' rights concerns and the high-technology industry. Republican House Majority Leader Richard (Dick) Armey (Texas) pushed a five-year continuation of the moratorium to a successful vote in May 2000 over many objectors.[58] The moratorium question arrived at an impasse in the Senate, however, as a divided Commerce Committee was unable to reach consensus on any length of a moratorium extension. Senator Byron Dorgan (D-N.Dak.) has emerged as a key figure in the debate by sponsoring legislation that would allow states to conditionally levy taxes on Internet transactions. Dorgan's plan, supported by the NGA, would enable states to enter into a compact with other states and develop a unified tax rate on remote e-commerce sales.[59] Whether Dorgan's or a similar plan is ultimately enacted, the stakes for states, companies engaged in e-commerce, and traditional retailers have only increased. With estimates of Web-based sales approaching $454 billion by 2004, the congressional search for a resolution between the competing needs of states and e-commerce development will remain precarious.[60]

Congress also faced an uphill battle as legislators took steps to restructure copyright laws to meet the challenges of the Information Age. In similar fashion to the tax moratorium effort, legislators encountered a panoply of unique, rival interests that complicated the search for a balanced outcome. Initial attempts to modify copyright laws in 1996 never emerged from committee in the House. Complex issues of assigning liability for Internet copyright infringement and dissensus over circumvention technology stifled legislative progress. Representative Goodlatte described the process as being like "nailing Jell-O to the wall. The problem is that there were just too many contingencies to build the necessary support to pass the underlying legislation."[61] Goodlatte did spearhead a separate and more modest effort a year later to criminalize the theft of copyrighted works on the Internet. H.R. 2265, signed into law in December 1997, focused on thievery of copyrighted material by computer. The bill provided for stiff penalties for the piracy of music, movies, and software on the Internet.[62]

A much larger bid to bring U.S. copyright laws consistent with international treaties followed the next year and culminated in the passage of H.R. 2281, but not without considerable wrangling. Congress was prompted to action by two World Intellectual Property Organization treaties to which the United States had become a signatory in 1996. The treaties established international recognition of copyrights of music and software.[63] Hollywood, anxious to gain protection from copyright infringement on the Internet, furnished further incentive to key policy innovators on Capitol Hill. Representative Howard Coble (R-N.C.), Chairman of the House Subcommittee on the Courts and Intellectual Property, along with Senate Judiciary Committee Chairman Orrin Hatch (R-Utah) and Senator

Patrick Leahy (D-Vt.), were recipients of combined campaign contributions from the entertainment industry totaling $2.5 million.[64]

The final adoption of H.R. 2281 by voice vote in the House and by a 99–0 margin in the Senate belied the arduous path to success the legislation followed. The central controversy over the bill centered on fundamental questions about how best to protect copyrights and assign liability for infringement. On the one hand, the IT industry worried that a ban of all devices that could be used to circumvent the theft of copyrighted material on the Internet could retard technological innovation. The chief fear was that the regulatory effort could prove unworkable if products had to be designed around anticopying technology.[65] On the other hand, librarians and educators were troubled that individuals who use circumvention technology for personal use and without intent to violate copyrights would be subject to criminal prosecution. Such a scenario, they argued, might undermine the Internet's utility for library and academic research.[66] A final point of contention concerned whether Internet providers could be held liable for copyright infringements by individuals who utilize their access service.

Representative Coble and Senator Hatch steered efforts to find an acceptable compromise. Months of lengthy negotiation between House and Senate Judiciary and Commerce Committee members, interest groups, and advocates for the IT industry yielded a middle ground on many of the most contentious provisions. These changes did not necessarily dispel the high-technology industry's concerns about the effect of encryption devices on product innovation, but they did quell major opposition. The final legislation specified exceptions to the ban on circumvention devices and clarified that computer products did not have to be designed to be compatible with antitheft or anticopying technology. The legislation also provided a "fair use" provision championed by educators and librarians to allow individuals to use circumvention devices for personal use of the copyrighted material. To be sure, questions of liability for copyright infringements and the practicality of enforcement lingered after passage of the bill, signed by President Clinton in October 1998. But as Representative Barney Frank (D-Mass.) put it, "No one thinks this will be the last thing we do" on digital copyrights.[67]

Protracted congressional efforts to ban Internet-based digital gambling did *not* meet with success in the 1990s despite the best efforts of policy entrepreneurs. The several attempts to proscribe on-line gaming brought to the fore questions of federalism, Native-American rights, and feasibility of enforcement that ultimately proved impossible to reconcile. In 1997 Senator John Kyl (R-Ariz.) sponsored legislation (S. 474) to update current laws, which banned gambling only over telephone lines in the United States. Kyl's bill was expansive in scope. Apart from prohibiting all domestic Internet-based gambling operations and imposing stiff penalties on violators, the legislation also targeted off-shore gambling sites. Kyl's proposal would have enabled federal and state law enforcement entities to force Internet service providers to block access to gaming sites located outside the United States. Critics of the legislation, including gaming operators, contended that the legislation was simply unworkable and would impose "undue if not impossible burdens" on Internet service providers.[68] Senator Kyl's bill did receive voice vote approval in committee, but only after an amendment, which would have permitted states to allow Internet-based gambling within their own borders. The full Senate did not take subsequent action on the measure in 1997.

Both the House and the Senate took up the measure again in 1998, but controversies over pari-mutuel betting over the Internet stifled progress. The Senate folded the provisions of S. 474 into a Commerce, Justice, and State appropriations bill (S. 2260), which was passed with strong bipartisan support in midsummer. But the companion bill later approved by the House included provisions allowing pari-mutuel betting over the Internet in states or on Indian reservations where such gambling was legal, rather than just "closed-loop" betting not accessible to the general population. The House exceptions drew objections from Kyl, who argued that the bill would fail to prevent individuals in other states from gambling.[69] Critics charged that compelling Internet providers to enforce the ban with the pari-mutuel loopholes could prove unworkable.[70] In the absence of consensus and in the end-of-session rush to pass the appropriations bill, the antigambling provisions were dropped in entirety.

Representative Goodlatte took up the cause of an Internet gambling ban again in 2000, but similar issues surfaced to cast a pall over progress. Goodlatte and House colleague Billy Tauzin (R-La.) attempted to broker a compromise between legal gambling interests and social conservatives in Congress. The H.R. 3125 bill ultimately fell victim to an "ends against the middle" effect. Goodlatte brought the bill up under a suspension of House rules in order to stave off amendments that would have weakened the bill's antigambling provisions. Although the bill was backed by a strong majority (245–159), the vote fell short of the two-thirds majority required. Anticipated amendments allowing on-line dog, horse, and jai alai betting were subsequently opposed by conservative Republicans in Congress and a number of conservative advocacy groups.[71] The Clinton administration worried that the bill was unenforceable and would drive gambling interests off shore and out of the reach of U.S. jurisdiction.[72] Governors then contended that allowing these forms of gambling, but not the sale of lottery tickets, was unacceptable and violated states' rights.[73] And yet other members opposed stepped-up regulation of the Internet on principle. Representative Goodlatte pulled the bill from consideration but vowed to resuscitate the issue in the future. The failure of the gambling bill clearly accentuated the difficulties involved in reconciling Internet issues that traverse social concerns, states' rights, international borders, and questions of the practicality of enforcement.

THE INTERNET, CONSUMER AND PRIVACY RIGHTS, AND PORNOGRAPHY ISSUES

Consumer and privacy rights and the protection of minors from pornographic material were among the most difficult Internet issues for policy entrepreneurs to manage. From the export of encryption technology abroad and electronic signatures to the protection of Social Security numbers and children's access to adult-oriented Web sites, this subset of issues comprised contradictory calls for government action. On the one hand, the IT industry appealed to Congress to *remove* regulatory barriers for the export of encryption technology used to secure Internet transactions. On the other hand, consumer advocates called on Congress to *intervene* more forcefully to protect sensitive personal information. In this volatile mix of issues, states' rights, individual rights, First Amendment rights, and national security concerns erected considerable obstacles to legislative success.

At first glance the export of encryption technology for Internet transactions might seem noncontroversial. Encryption technology scrambles the coding of information sent over the Internet. Encryption software is a vital tool in the development of e-commerce as it insures individuals' privacy and prevents third-party access to sensitive personal, business, or classified information. Yet it can also be used for more sinister activity by "hackers" to steal credit card numbers, Social Security numbers, or even national security information. Governmental controls limiting encryption technology exports consequently pitted IT-industry interests and privacy advocates against law enforcement concerns. The IT industry contended that export restrictions placed American businesses at a competitive disadvantage with foreign firms already marketing such technology abroad, and privacy advocates argued that broader distribution of the technology would help to secure transactions over the Internet. Law enforcement and national security agencies opposed easing of restrictions for fear that the extensive use of encryption technology would hamper evidence gathering and enable criminal activity to go undetected.[74]

Representatives Goodlatte and Lofgren introduced legislation in 1997 (H.R. 695), backed by privacy advocates and the IT industry, that provided for the export of encryption technology generally already available abroad. A year later H.R. 695 had been approved by five separate committees in the House, but former Rules Committee Chairman Gerald Solomon (R-N.Y.), who represented legislators concerned with the law enforcement ramifications of the legislation, refused to accord a rule to bring the bill to floor for a vote by the entire House. Goodlatte spearheaded another effort in 1999 to ease export restrictions. He and fellow members of the Subcommittee on the Judiciary, Courts, and Intellectual Property attempted to broker a compromise between the IT industry and law enforcement by including a penalty of five years of imprisonment for individuals using encryption technology to conceal criminal activity. The bill won subcommittee and full committee approval but became bottlenecked in the House Select Intelligence Committee, which shared jurisdiction over the bill. At the same time, Senate Commerce Committee Chairman John McCain (R-Ariz.) attempted to shepherd a separate bill through the Senate (S. 798), which would have allowed firms to petition for exemptions to export encryption technology. But McCain's bill also encountered significant obstacles, including a filibuster threat from fellow Senator Ted Stevens (R-Alaska) who opposed the bill on national security grounds.[75]

The impasse was broken by President Clinton's intervention in early fall 1999. Under pressure from Congress, Clinton relaxed restrictions to allow licensed businesses to export encryption technology abroad after a review by the Commerce Department. An embargo remained for countries the United States suspected of terrorist activities, including Cuba, Iraq, North Korea, and three other nations.[76] The net effect of the president's actions was to accomplish the basic contours of H.R. 850 independently. Goodlatte suggested that "the administration's policy would give high-tech companies most of what they wanted."[77] But while Clinton's action marked a clear victory for Silicon Valley software developers, defense experts remained fearful of national security implications and law enforcement officials posited that without the source code of the encryption software, tracking Internet criminal activity would prove more difficult.

In 1999 the issue of "e-signatures" brought to the fore conflicts over consumer and states' rights. The primary goal of the "Electronic Signatures in Global and National Commerce Act" was to make paperless, electronic transactions and record keeping subject to a uniform set of national standards. By early 2000, eleven states had adopted laws giving legal status to "digital contracts" signed over the Internet.[78] Yet businesses championed the legislation to avoid compliance with a hodgepodge of separate state laws governing the retention of paper and electronic documents.[79]

Leading separate legislative efforts in the House and Senate, respectively, Representative Bliley and then Senator Spencer Abraham (R-Mich.) sought to standardize e-commerce practices across all fifty states with federal legislation that would supersede state laws. After bipartisan passage of bills in both chambers, the controversy over S. 761 centered around the conference committee, chaired by Bliley. Consumer groups and state agencies were concerned that the legislation did not provide adequate antifraud protection. States argued that federal legislation preempted their traditional role in the regulation of business activity.[80] Moreover Democrats argued for a provision that individuals acknowledge that they were capable of receiving on-line documentation before waiving rights to paper copies of such transactions including property, licenses, banking, and insurance. The provision was opposed by Senator Phil Gramm (R-Tex.), a primary spokesman for the financial services industry.

The compromise struck by House and Senate conferees included language that consumers must "reasonably demonstrate" that they can open electronic documents and that businesses must obtain their consent for electronic documentation. Gramm feared that this language would lead to interminable lawsuits over the definition of "reasonable" and jeopardize the financial services industry, but acceded. In addition Bliley addressed the states' rights issue by easing requirements on paper and electronic record keeping. The bill established federal standards but enabled states to develop their own rules and imposed a uniform time frame for implementation. President Clinton signed the bill on June 30, 2000. The legislation was widely hailed by the financial services industry as a boon for quickening transactions and opening new accounts, though worries about liability for security breaches in Internet transactions have prompted the banking industry to cover potential risks.[81]

The e-signatures bill prompted legislators like Senator McCain to begin contemplating more forcefully the hot-button issue of on-line privacy and companies' collection and resale of personal information. The IT industry's position has been, and remains, that Congress should allow time for the development of new technology and encourage self-regulation. The Clinton administration—and most Americans—seemed to agree in the late 1990s. In a Harris Poll completed in April 1998, 80 percent of Americans favored allowing the private sector to develop rules before Congress intervened with legislation.[82] However, widespread theft of individuals' Social Security numbers, Web site operators' ability to collect personal information and track browsing habits of Internet users through "cookies," and the general onus placed on Internet users to "opt out" of the collection of personal information hastened legislators' search for greater privacy protection.[83]

By the 106th Congress, the number of bills and amendments concerning on-line privacy exploded, though no major legislation passed. Senators McCain and Judd Gregg (R-N.H.) introduced measures bolstering on-line privacy alongside a number of bills banning private- and public-sector disclosure of Social Security numbers and other personal information without individuals' permission. McCain's bill, S. 2928, dubbed the "Consumer Internet Privacy Enhancement Act," was unique in that it received the backing of key players in the IT industry, including America Online and Hewlett-Packard.[84] The bill would have compelled Web site operators to conspicuously post privacy policies and facilitate Internet users' ability to "opt out" of sharing personal information, but stopped short of further regulation and oversight. Other legislation introduced by Senators Hollings and Conrad Burns (R-Mont.) was far more sweeping and sought to empower the Federal Trade Commission (FTC) to enforce strict regulation of on-line business transactions, an expanded authority the FTC urged after several reports.[85] Finally, President Clinton weighed in on the debate by crafting a privacy proposal targeted to financial transactions. The proposal, strongly opposed by proponents of the financial services industry like Senator Gramm, would have compelled companies to allow individuals to choose to "opt out" of sharing any and all personal information.[86]

The issue of on-line privacy remains a grand, unresolved issue with which Congress and the Bush administration will certainly grapple. The slow and cautious approach to the issue in the 1990s, however, fits comfortably with the general model of congressional action on Internet issues and the preferred course of action supported by the Clinton administration. The IT industry was accorded additional time to sort out the technical issues and self-regulate in the bid to promote the Internet as a tool of commerce. As Representative Rick White (R-Wash.) noted, "I think it will make a lot of sense to take our time. . . . We've been guilty in the past of rushing to judgment and getting it wrong."[87] It is also important to recognize that the lack of swift action on privacy issues on Capitol Hill did not occur in a vacuum. The IT industry increased its presence and visibility in the nation's capital, purposefully sought to cultivate ties to members of Congress, and dramatically increased financial contributions to members of Congress in the wake of interest-group pressures for greater regulation.

The issue on which Congress did not follow Representative White's warning about a rush to judgment concerned pornography and child protection. Congress *was*, in fact, successful in passing two major laws restricting content and access on the Internet, yet neither law was able to survive judicial scrutiny. Ironically, industry self-regulation may have accomplished what congressional legislation ultimately could not. The first effort to address pornography came in 1996 and yielded the Communications Decency Act, which was appended to the sweeping telecommunications overhaul. The law banned the transmission of "patently offensive" material to minors and charged Internet sites with the obligation to prevent minors from gaining access to adult-oriented material. The Supreme Court agreed to take the case in 1996 and later ruled in *Reno v. ACLU* (1997) that the law was unconstitutional because it violated free speech and was too vague. The second effort, led by former Senator Daniel R. Coats (R-Ind.) in 1998, culminated in the Child Online Protection Act (COPA). The bill was specifically tailored to address the High Court's earlier concerns. The provisions were narrowed to compel Web site operators to require a credit card or password for Internet material deemed "harmful to minors."[88] Yet a federal court in California ruled in June 2000 that the COPA imposed "an impermissible burden on constitutionally protected speech."[89] Part of the problem for legislators is that while the courts have ruled that communities can regulate pornography and children's access to adult theaters within specific geographical "zones," the Internet's lack of geography precludes the "real space" communities in which content and access can be easily regulated without violating First Amendment guarantees.[90]

While the debate over the constitutionality of legislation moved to the courts, the Clinton administration promoted several initiatives to insure greater parental control over minors' access to Internet content. In December 1997 leaders of the high-tech industry, including America Online, sponsored a three-day summit to unveil a "ratings system" of Web sites used in conjunction with filtering software that enables parents to better block children's access to pornographic material.[91] In 1999 Vice President Al Gore announced that fifteen of the nation's largest Internet providers were providing parents with "one-click access" to a Web page with over eighty different tools for blocking children's access to pornographic content and instructions on how to employ filtering software.[92] Although such efforts by Internet providers are voluntary—and indeed the ratings system of Web sites is also contingent upon voluntary efforts of Web site operators—the administration supported, and many Web site operators have chosen, compliance with parental controls to forestall burdensome regulation that could inhibit the growth of the Internet. Despite legal challenges to the COPA, many adult Web sites, to avoid liability, have instituted credit card access to prevent child access to pornographic material.

Conclusion

This review of presidential and congressional action on IT and Internet issues has shed light on the different types of policy emphasis and forms of entrepreneurship in which American national institutions engaged at the dawn of the Information Age from 1993–2000. The Clinton administration championed developmental issues and accomplished much of its agenda through independent actions. The Clinton-Gore team's formal and informal actions—from executive orders to the formation of task forces and forging of public–private partnerships—demonstrates the flexibility of presidential policymaking as well as the autonomous means by which presidents can shape the public debate by adapting preexisting legislative frameworks to their goals. Congress, by contrast, was saddled with the enormously complex task of updating laws to match rapid technological change and fashioning an initial and adaptable regulatory framework for e-commerce. The sheer technical complexity of emergent Internet issues, the diversity of organized interests that mobilized around those issues, and the competing committee jurisdictions within Congress with claims to these issues are the central features that distinguish the unique task facing policy entrepreneurs compared to other policy realms.

Several additional observations are noteworthy as scholars begin to examine governmental responses to technological change in the next decade. First, this analysis demonstrates that while there may be an *ad hoc* feature to Internet and IT development and regulation, "policy chaos" is *not* an accurate description of policymaking at the national level. Our "separated institutions" did indeed take separate tracks on Internet issues. Yet the tie that binds presidential and congressional action has been a common philosophy of selective intervention, caution, and support for Internet development. On Capitol Hill, it is true that the "legislative impulse" has increased with the growing ubiquity of the Internet.[93] However, unlike telecommunications policy in the 1980s for which "virtually every attempt at legislation bogged down somewhere in the legislative labyrinth,"[94] most successful legislative efforts on the Internet have occurred under the tutelage of those policy entrepreneurs who have steered the debate in broader terms. These leaders have had the *savoir-faire*, resources, and commitment to reconcile competing claims to, and visions of, the Internet's development and regulation.

Second, presidential and congressional Internet policymaking in the last decade is remarkable for what did *not* occur. The budget, abortion issues, and welfare reform yielded intense policy conflict and gridlock between the Democratic president and the Republican Congress during divided government from 1995–2000. This was *not* the norm on Internet issues. It is also the case that the careful regulatory steps taken by policy entrepreneurs in Congress typically yielded bipartisan consensus *within* Congress as well. This accomplishment must not be underestimated in light of overlapping committee jurisdictions in Congress and the multiplicity of competing interests that Internet issues galvanized—the high-tech industry on one side, and governors, retailers, consumer advocates, librarians, law enforcement officials, and the financial services industry on the other. And never far from the surface were the thorny questions of enforceability and practicality of regulating a medium that operates beyond geographical borders. Many scholars are correct to emphasize the rise in partisan conflict between the branches and within Congress in the last decade.[95] Yet an emphasis on discord misses key dynamics of policymaking on Internet issues, and most importantly the role of policy innovators in the resolution of conflicts that had highly divisive potential.

In the past decade the Clinton administration and Democratic- and Republican-led congresses began to forge a much-needed public policy history for Internet issues. The tempered approach of the 1990s may serve as an instrumental model for President Bush and members of the 107th Congress (2001–2003). To the chagrin of the high-tech industry, George W. Bush did not provide a clear blueprint for Internet and IT issues in the 2000 election campaign.[96] But much of the agenda has already been defined for him. The new president and Congress face a smorgasbord of issues both old and new on the legislative agenda, including privacy rights, taxation, information security, and the implications of e-commerce for the labor market. The type of policy entrepreneurship in which Bush, a thin Republican majority in the House of Representatives, and a Democratic-controlled Senate can engage, independently and jointly, may play a critically important role in determining the landscape of national politics as the 2002 and 2004 elections approach.

NOTES

1. Mark A. Peterson, *Legislating Together: The White House and Capitol Hill from Eisenhower to Reagan* (Cambridge, MA: Harvard University Press, 1990); and Charles O. Jones, *The Presidency in a Separated System* (Washington, D.C.: Brookings Institution, 1994).
2. Peterson, *Legislating Together*, p. 7.
3. Richard Neustadt, *Presidential Power and the Modern Presidents* (New York: Free Press, 1960).
4. David E. Price, "Professionals and 'Entrepreneurs': Staff Orientations and Policy Making on Three Senate Committees," *Journal of Politics* 33 (1971), pp. 316–336.
5. Frank R. Baumgartner and Bryan D. Jones, *Agendas and Instability in American Politics* (Chicago: University of Chicago Press, 1993); and John W. Kingdon, *Agendas, Alternatives, and Public Policies* (New York: Harper Collins, 1995).
6. Kingdon, *Agendas, Alternatives, and Public Policies*; William H. Riker, *The Art of Political Manipulation* (New Haven, CT: Yale University Press, 1986); and Hugh Heclo, "Issue Networks in the Executive Establishment," in *The New American Political System*, ed. Anthony King (Washington, D.C.: American Enterprise Institute, 1978).
7. Mark Schneider and Paul Teske, "Toward a Theory of the Political Entrepreneur: Evidence from Local Government," *American Political Science Review* 86 (1992), pp. 737–747; and Dennis C. Chong, *Collective Action and the Civil Rights Movement* (Chicago: University of Chicago Press, 1991).

8. Michael Mintrom, "Policy Entrepreneurs and the Diffusion of Innovation," *American Journal of Political Science* 41 (1997), p. 740.
9. Bryan D. Jones, *Reconceiving Decision-Making in Democratic Politics: Attention, Choice, and Public Policy* (Chicago: University of Chicago Press, 1994), pp. 25–26.
10. George C. Edwards, III, *At the Margins: Presidential Leadership of Congress* (New Haven, CT: Yale University Press, 1989); George C. Edwards, III, *Presidential Influence in Congress* (San Francisco: W. H. Freeman and Company, 1980); and Jon R. Bond and Richard Fleisher, *The President in the Legislative Arena* (Chicago: University of Chicago Press, 1990).
11. William W. Lammers and Michael Genovese, *The Presidency and Domestic Policy: Comparing Leadership Styles, FDR to Clinton* (Washington, D.C.: CQ Press, 2000).
12. Jones, *Reconceiving Decision-Making in Democratic Politics*, p. 197.
13. David R. Mayhew, *Congress: The Electoral Connection* (New Haven, CT: Yale University Press, 1974).
14. Richard F. Fenno, Jr., *Congressmen in Committees* (Boston: Little, Brown, 1973).
15. David E. Price, *The Congressional Experience*, 2nd ed. (Boulder, CO: Westview Press, 2000).
16. See David W. Rohde, *Parties and Leaders in the Postreform House* (Chicago: University of Chicago Press, 1991); and Barbara Sinclair, *Legislators, Leaders, and Lawmaking: The U.S. House of Representatives in the Postreform Era* (Baltimore, MD: Johns Hopkins University Press, 1995).
17. Baumgartner and Jones, *Agendas and Instability in American Politics*, pp. 198–199.
18. See Roger H. Davidson, Walter J. Oleszek, and Thomas Kephart, "One Bill, Many Committees: Multiple Referrals in the U.S. House of Representatives," *Legislative Studies Quarterly* 13 (1988), pp. 3–28.
19. Brian D. Loader, "The Governance of Cyberspace: Politics, Technology, and Global Restructuring," in *The Governance of Cyberspace*, ed. Brian D. Loader (London: Routledge, 1997), p. 1.
20. Theodore J. Lowi, "American Business, Public Policy, Case Studies, and Political Theory," *World Politics* 16 (1964), pp. 677–693.
21. Quoted in "Internet Caucus," *Congressional Quarterly Weekly Report*, 4 September 1999, p. 2071.
22. Steven E. Miller, *Civilizing Cyberspace: Policy, Power, and the Information Superhighway* (New York: ACM Press, 1996), p. 73; and Robert E. Dugan, Joan F. Cheverie, and Jennifer L. Souza, "The NII: For the Public Good," *Journal of Academic Librarianship* 22 (1996), pp. 133–141.
23. "Agenda for Action," Executive Summary (Washington, D.C.: Executive Office of the President, 1993).
24. Dugan, Cheverie, and Souza, "The NII: For the Public Good," p. 133.
25. Fred H. Cate, "The National Information Infrastructure: Policymaking and Policymakers," in *The Information Revolution*, ed. Donald Altschiller (New York: H. W. Wilson, 1995), p. 147.
26. Albert Gore, Jr., "The National Information Infrastructure," *Vital Speeches of the Day* 60 (1994), pp. 229–233.
27. Brian Kahin, "The U.S. National Information Infrastructure Initiative: The Market, the Web, and the Virtual Project," in *National Information Infrastructure Initiatives: Vision and Policy Design*, ed. Brian Kahin and Ernest J. Wilson, III (Cambridge, MA: MIT Press, 1997), p. 151.
28. *Congressional Quarterly Almanac* 49 (Washington, D.C.: Congressional Quarterly, Inc., 1993), pp. 241–245
29. Ibid., p. 243.
30. Susan Dentzer, "Bypass on the Information Superhighway," *U.S. News and World Report* 116 (24 January 1994), p. 63; and James K. Glassman, "A Right to an Internet Connection," *The American Enterprise* 11 (2000), p. 13.
31. *Congressional Quarterly Almanac* (1993), p. 246.
32. The primary agencies constituted the National Science Foundation, the National Aeronautics and Space Administration, and the Departments of Defense, Commerce, and Energy.
33. Kahin, "The U.S. National Information Infrastructure Initiative," p. 172.
34. Dugan, Cheverie, and Souza, "The NII: For the Public Good." The Technology Opportunities Program (TOP) is administered by the National Telecommunications and Information Administration (NTIA) in the Department of Commerce.
35. John Carlo Bertot and Charles R. McClure, "The Clinton Administration and the National Information Infrastructure (NII)," in *Federal Information Policies in the 1990s: Views and Perspectives*, ed. Peter Hernon, Charles R. McClure, and Harold C. Relyea (Norwood, NJ: Ablex Publishing Corp., 1996), p. 33.
36. Paul Frissen, "The Virtual State: Postmodernisation, Information, and Public Administration," in *The Governance of Cyberspace*, ed. Brian D. Loader (London: Routledge, 1997).

37. Cate, "The National Information Infrastructure," p. 151.
38. Miller, *Civilizing Cyberspace*, p. 111.
39. Kahin, "The U.S. National Information Infrastructure Initiative," p. 172.
40. Jack Clarke, "Regulating the Internet: Assessing the Threat," *Telecommunications* 32 (1998), p. 24.
41. Joint public- and private-sector initiatives to screen out violence on the World Wide Web and protect minors from pornography are one such example (see McConnell 1999). These issues are covered in greater detail in the next section on Congress.
42. Stephen H. Holden and Peter Hernon, "An Executive Branch Perspective on Managing Information Resources," in *Federal Information Policies in the 1990s: Views and Perspectives*, ed. Peter Hernon, Charles R. McClure, and Harold C. Relyea (Norwood, NJ: Ablex Publishing Corp., 1996), p. 90.
43. Patricia D. Fletcher and Lisa K. Westerback, "Catching a Ride on the NII: The Federal Policy Vehicles Paving the Information Highway," *Journal of the American Society for Information Science* 50 (1999), pp. 299–304.
44. John Carlo Bertot, Charles R. McClure, Joe Ryan, and John C. Beachboard, "Federal Information Resources Management: Integrating Information Management and Technology," in *Federal Information Policies in the 1990s: Views and Perspectives*, ed. Peter Hernon, Charles R. McClure, and Harold C. Relyea (Norwood, NJ: Ablex Publishing Corp., 1996).
45. See Kahin, "The U.S. National Information Infrastructure Initiative," pp. 181–183; and Bertot and McClure, "The Clinton Administration and the National Information Infrastructure (NII)."
46. Quoted in D. Blake and L. Tiedrich, "The National Information Infrastructure and the Emergence of the Electronic Superhighway," *Federal Communications Law Journal* 46 (1994), p. 398.
47. Quoted in Juliana Gruenwald, "Congress Haltingly Begins Writing the Book on Internet Regulation," *Congressional Quarterly Weekly Report*, 17 October 1998, p. 2817.
48. Ibid.
49. Quoted in Juliana Gruenwald, "Congress Finds No Easy Answers to Internet Controversies," *Congressional Quarterly Weekly Report*, 31 January 1998, p. 238.
50. Data were gathered by the author. The mean difference in seniority between members of the Internet Caucus and nonmembers is significant at $p < .05$.
51. See Rita Tehan, Congressional Research Service Issue Brief for Congress, "RL30435: Internet and E-Commerce Statistics: What They Mean and Where to Find Them on the Web," <http://www.cnie.org/nle/st-36.html#_1_9>.
52. *Congressional Quarterly Almanac* 54 (Washington, D.C.: Congressional Quarterly, Inc., 1998), pp. 21–22.
53. *Congressional Quarterly Almanac* 53 (Washington, D.C.: Congressional Quarterly, Inc., 1997), pp. 3–40.
54. *Congressional Quarterly Almanac* (1998), pp. 21–22.
55. Quoted in Alan K. Ota, "Internet Gambling Restrictions Edge toward House Vote; States' Rights Remain a Concern," *Congressional Quarterly Weekly Report*, 6 December 1997, p. 2762.
56. *Journal of Accountancy*, "New Bill Would Freeze Internet Taxation," 183 (1997), p. 27.
57. *Congressional Quarterly Almanac* (1998), pp. 21–22.
58. Alan K. Ota, "FTC Asks Lawmakers for Expanded Authority to Protect Internet Privacy," *Congressional Quarterly Weekly Report*, 27 May 2000, p. 1273.
59. Alan K. Ota, "Governors and Lawmakers Seek Compromise on Length of Internet Tax Moratorium," *Congressional Quarterly Weekly Report*, 3 June 2000, p. 1338.
60. Mark Trager, "Estimates of Global E-Commerce Point to Hypergrowth," *Inter@active Week*, <www.inter@activeweek.com>, May 8, 2000.
61. *Congressional Quarterly Almanac* 52 (Washington, D.C.: Congressional Quarterly, Inc., 1996), pp. 3–12.
62. *Congressional Quarterly Almanac* (1997), pp. 3–15.
63. *Congressional Quarterly Almanac* (1998), pp. 22–23.
64. Gruenwald, "Congress Haltingly Begins Writing the Book on Internet Regulation," p. 2818.
65. Ibid.
66. *Congressional Quarterly Almanac* (1998), pp. 22–27.
67. Quoted in ibid., pp. 22–23.
68. *Congressional Quarterly Almanac* (1997), pp. 3–43.
69. *Congressional Quarterly Almanac* (1998), pp. 22–27.
70. Gruenwald, "Congress Haltingly Begins Writing the Book on Internet Regulation," p. 2819.

71. Alan K. Ota, "Online Gambling Curbs Approved," *Congressional Quarterly Weekly Report*, 1 July 2000, p. 1617.
72. Alan K. Ota, "Resistance from Three Sides Slows Internet Gambling Ban, but Goodlatte to Seek Another Vote," *Congressional Quarterly Weekly Report*, 22 July 2000, p. 1808.
73. Ota, "Internet Gambling Restrictions Edge toward House Vote; State's Rights Remain a Concern."
74. *Congressional Quarterly Almanac* (1998), pp. 19–22 and *Congressional Quarterly Almanac* 55 (Washington, D.C.: Congressional Quarterly, Inc., 1999), pp. 20–22.
75. *Congressional Quarterly Almanac* (1999), pp. 22–24.
76. David E. Sanger and Jeri Clausing, "U.S. Removes More Limits on Encryption," *New York Times*, 13 January 2000, p. C-1.
77. Quoted in ibid.
78. Adam Marilin, "Panel Moves Moratorium on Internet Taxes," *Congressional Quarterly Weekly Report*, 6 May 2000, p. 1029.
79. Alan K. Ota, "Senate Clears E-Signature Bill as Gramm Gives in on Consumer Protections," *Congressional Quarterly Weekly Report*, 17 June 2000, pp. 1463–1464.
80. Alan K. Ota, "E-Signature Bill Readied for Conferees," *Congressional Quarterly Weekly Report*, 6 May 2000, p. 841.
81. Lee Ann Gjertsen, "Insurers Develop Products to Cover Banks' Web Risks," *American Banker* 9 (2001), <www.americanbanker.com>.
82. Juliana Gruenwald, "Who's Minding Whose Business on the Internet," *Congressional Quarterly Weekly Report*, 25 July 1998, pp. 1986–1990.
83. Ibid.
84. Ariana Eunjung Cha, "Key Firms Back Bill on Web Privacy; Hewlett-Packard, AOL Go to Hill," *Washington Post*, 4 October 2001, p. E-1.
85. Ota, "FTC Asks Lawmakers for Expanded Authority to Protect Internet Privacy," p. 1273; and Ira Teinowitz, "FTC Study Gives Fuel for Backers of Internet Regs: Report Reveals Few Marketers Have Addressed Privacy Issue," *Advertising Age* 69 (1998), p. 61.
86. Quoted in Marilin, "Panel Moves Moratorium on Internet Taxes," p. 1051.
87. Quoted in Juliana Gruenwald, "Hoping to Fend Off Regulation, High-Tech Industry Steps Up Its Campaign Contributions," *Congressional Quarterly Weekly Report*, 31 October 1998, p. 2958.
88. Quoted in Gruenwald, "Congress Haltingly Begins Writing the Book on Internet Regulation," p. 2819.
89. Quoted in Greg Miller, "Court Rejects Child Online Protection Act," *Los Angeles Times*, 23 June 2000, p. C-2.
90. Timothy Zick, "Congress, the Internet, and the Intractable Pornography Problem: The Child Online Protection Act of 1998," *Creighton Law Review* 32 (1999), pp. 1147–1204.
91. Alan K. Ota, "Internet Industry Hopes Self-Policing Will Click," *Congressional Quarterly Weekly Report*, 6 December 1997, pp. 3028–3029.
92. Bill McConnell, "'Click' to Safety: Gore Offers Initiatives for Filtering Out Web Violence, Porn," *Broadcasting and Cable* 129 (1999), p. 12.
93. *Congressional Quarterly Weekly Report*, 1999, p. 2029.
94. John A. Ferejohn and Charles R. Shipan, "Congress and Telecommunications Policymaking," in *New Directions in Telecommunications Policy*, ed. Paula R. Newberg (Durham, NC: Duke University Press, 1989), p. 301.
95. Jon R. Bond and Richard Fleisher, eds., *Polarized Politics: Congress and the President in a Partisan Era* (Washington, D.C.: CQ Press, 2000).
96. Patrick Thibodeau, "CIOs: Bush's, Gore's IT Plans a Mystery," *Computerworld* 34 (28 August 2000), p. 4.

THE E-RATE PROGRAM

PAVING THE DIRT ROAD
TO THE INFORMATION SUPERHIGHWAY

JEFF GILL AND DAVID CONKLIN[1]

The Internet is the leading edge of a wave of interactive technologies that are transforming the phone lines and video cables of the nation into pipelines for commerce, education, civic functions, and medicine. As such, one of the most important pieces of legislation that Congress has passed in recent years was the 1996 Telecommunications Act. A contentious part of this federal overhaul of the telecommunications industry was the split over the E-rate program, implemented in 1998, a federally controlled fund that provides discounts, ranging from 20 to 90 percent, for bringing the Internet and other information services to communities that the market might otherwise ignore. Specifically, E-rate is a surcharge on long-distance residential telephone calls to help defray the costs of bringing the Internet to schools, libraries, and health centers in poor and rural areas across the country.

The E-rate program has generated a bipartisan chorus of criticism during its short life. Few oppose providing Internet equity to improve education, but many disagree over the specifics of who should pay the surcharge, what precisely the money should be used for, and how the fund should be administered. At the height of controversy, during the 105th Congress (1997–1999), the Clinton administration lauded the program for closing the expansive digital divide. Conservative lawmakers, however, criticized the program for being a bureaucratic boondoggle, a futuristic "New Democratic" agenda that reflects traditional Democratic concerns for the underprivileged. They further contended that the additional charges to monthly telephone bills constituted an illegal tax, thus overstepping the constitutional authority of Congress; the "e," they claimed, stood for "evasion" not "education." Leading Democratic lawmakers protested that the program was too broad in scope and complained about it raising constituents' phone bills.[2]

We investigate the details of the E-rate program, why it endures in a seemingly hostile political and partisan environment, and the obvious political importance of appearing to support programs for children, education in general, and new technology initiatives. Public education is the largest public-service-sector expenditure in the United States: In the 1996–1997 school year alone, there were 45.6 million—roughly 93 percent of all school-aged children—public school students with expenditures totaling close to $318 billion.[3] Not surprisingly, education is a salient issue for voters as well as a key policy distinction in any presidential election. But while the Internet is a remarkable and innovative new application of technology that transcends geographic lines, the structure of political support among members of Congress for the E-rate program has both traditional and familiar patterns. The program serves as an illustrative example of how constituency-based politics can degenerate an otherwise legitimate issue into a nasty squabble.

THE INTERNET AND PUBLIC SCHOOL EDUCATION

Within the past decade the Internet has gone from being almost completely unknown by the general public to a key component of general research and economic development. Unlike traditional forms of communication, however, the Internet requires users to operate technology. Rather than simply picking up a newspaper or magazine, or turning on a television or a radio, users of the Internet must have some understanding of computer hardware and software, albeit at a basic level. It is this extra level of knowledge that drives the need to include computer experience in children's schooling. The obvious ramification of ignoring this difference in required computer and technical expertise is the subsequent development of the so-called "skills gap" between children of wealthier parents and children from low-income families, a phenomenon that is fundamentally political in that the technical literacy of children is an increasingly important determinant of economic potential, thus commanding the attention of politicians and policymakers.

Such increasing need for technological competency and access among school-age children generates two different but important concerns: how to protect children, which focuses on content generally considered unacceptable for children to view; and how to teach children, which is the wider challenge that consumes the bulk of governmental resources. The primary technique for protecting students is manual or automatic "filtering," the process of denying access to specific Internet content. This practice raises important questions about censorship and judgment.[4] Some decisions are straightforward, like blatantly pornographic or racist Web sites, while others are unclear and subsequently controversial. These decisions can and do lead to contentious ramifications concerning civil liberties groups and first amendment advocates. Representative Jeffrey Pollack (R-Ore.), for example, advocated the widespread use of filtering software until his own campaign Web site was blocked by frequently used filtering software.[5] There is also the question about protection for children when the triggers for filtering software are absent or outdated,[6] or the potential for criminal exploitation, such as when an Israeli teenager who arranged to meet a Palestinian girl via Internet communication was found murdered, leaving many to believe he was lured into a trap by the ease of anonymity that electronic communication provides.[7]

Another primary concern is considerably more difficult to address. There is no universal agreement about teaching approaches using the Internet in the classroom, in which a key issue—the skill level of the teachers themselves—varies considerably. Several approaches have been used to curb this problem: training and certification programs, grants and awards for software and hardware, and explicit compensation criteria tied to computer knowledge.[8]

The positive side for including Internet-sourced materials in class curriculum is obvious and undeniable, in addition to the need to provide technological literacy, most notably, historical research, such as original document examination,[9] access to distant museum content,[10] or direct downloading of information about government and civics.[11] It is also possible for teachers to enhance their classroom presentations by using graphical aids, background information, and interactive displays downloaded from Internet sources.[12] Distance learning, where students can view lectures on specialized materials not taught at their physical location in "real time," provides educational use of the Internet that has yet to be fully exploited. Additionally, cooperative programs can be developed by teachers at different institutions to benefit both groups of students. This is a very topical issue at the collegiate level; MIT in Boston, for instance, has developed a program in which students can view classroom lectures entirely over the Internet without classroom attendance, thereby freeing up valuable classroom space.[13]

Other advantages of Internet integration in schools are less obvious. In some parts of the country, teachers use the Internet as a way of compensating for lost time during snow days, when the school was closed, by the creative use of e-mail.[14] Similar applications are used to overcome other weather-related school closings throughout the country, and the trend is likely to continue as home computer ownership increases.

Of course students need not adhere to the scripted lesson plan that a teacher maps out for classroom use, when instead they have access to a wealth of distracting material.[15] By its very nature on-line information is widely accessible and unrestricted. A surreptitious student can evade the intended program and view noneducational Web sites or communicate electronically with others without much hindrance from the instructor.[16]

HISTORICAL VIEW OF EDUCATION TECHNOLOGY

The emphasis on basic technical skills has filtered down from professional jobs to many entry-level clerical and administrative positions in the past twenty years, which has contributed to a rising need for advanced studies at the collegiate level. This demand for higher education and technical skills dwarfs the ability of states and local jurisdictions to build physical infrastructure, however. For many, such as former Senator Bob Kerrey (D-Neb.), one solution is to increase funding to commercial schools, like the University of Phoenix, that provide on-line professional education.[17]

One area where history has not repeated itself is with the level of computer access by differing race and income levels. Currently there are virtually no observed differences across income or urbaness.[18] In contrast, as recently as 1994 only 58 percent of the nation's public schools with 1,000 or more students and a disappointing 49 percent of secondary schools had an Internet connection on campus.[19] Unfortunately, when the percentage of students in the free or reduced-cost lunch programs exceeds 75 percent, indicating the poorest of school districts, the percent of schools having Internet access drops to 94 percent. Looking at this phenomenon another way, the number of students per computer in the poorest districts remains noticeably higher than in other districts. Tables 8.1 and 8.2 show those districts with the highest levels of participation in free or reduced-cost lunch programs have the greatest number of students per computer (wired or not). Notice, however, the dramatic improvement in the 50 percent to 70 percent category provided in just one single year.

TABLE 8.1 DISTRICT ACCESS TO COMPUTERS BY LUNCH PROGRAM PARTICIPATION

	STUDENTS PER COMPUTER	
PERCENTAGE IN LUNCH PROGRAMS	1998	1999
0–11	10	7
12–30	11	8
31–49	11	9
50–70	16	10
71+	17	16

Source: U.S. Department of Education, *E-Learning: Putting a World-Class Education at the Fingertips of All Children* (Washington, D.C.: Office of Educational Technology, U.S. Department of Education, 2000), <www.ed.gov/technology>.

TABLE 8.2 NATIONAL INTERNET CONNECTION RATES

LOCATION	1994	1995	1996	1997	1998	1999
Schools	35%	50%	65%	78%	89%	95%
Instructional Rooms	3	8	14	27	51	63

Source: U.S. Department of Education, *E-Learning: Putting a World-Class Education at the Fingertips of All Children* (Washington, D.C.: Office of Educational Technology, U.S. Department of Education, 2000), <www.ed.gov/technology>.

Connection Technology and the Role of the Teacher

The percentage of schools with some sort of Internet connection is just part of the story, however. It is important to observe where the connection terminates and what type of equipment is used.[20] In 2000 the national average was five students per school computer and seven students per school computer with direct access to the Internet. These numbers increase somewhat for very high poverty areas.[21] In addition to the absolute numbers of computers, an important factor is the location of these computers within the schools. There is a significant difference, for example, in having wired computers in a school library or a set-aside laboratory (both of which require teacher scheduling) compared to those directly linked in the classrooms.

The type of connection that a school implements makes a significant difference in the quality of the Internet experience as an educational tool. There still exist schools that are unable to use standard telephone lines to connect with the Internet, for instance. This occurs because of the distance between these schools and the nearest central office of the phone provider, a common occurrence on Indian reservations in the western part of the country. As an alternative, many of these schools connect to the Internet through either radio or cellular phone technology or via satellite links, provided they have the resources. Such "last mile" connections, however, leave even less latitude to buy computers or provide teacher training.

There are also schools with antiquated computers that cannot fully connect to the Internet. Wealthier schools able to routinely update their systems accrue the tremendous gains in functionality that poorer schools cannot. Newer machines use higher quality audio and visual displays and process much larger sets of data than those on the older machines. Students who use more advanced computers have the choice of running multiple programs simultaneously, such as a Web browser to find information and a word processor to write up the report, or of accessing more complex resources, such as three-dimensional Web sites instead of using the standard picture Web sites or text-only sites. Greater computer capabilities undeniably translate into greater Internet accessibility.

With a teacher's help, students can use the classroom Internet connection as a portal to libraries, archives, and cultural sources that geography and limited financial resources would otherwise deny.[22] There are a number of recognized educational advantages to direct Internet access in schools: developing research skills such as finding, recognizing, and evaluating scholarly information; improving communication skills across cultures and languages; acquiring information processing analytical abilities; increasing problem-solving abilities with regard to search criteria, collating results, ranking importance; and developing an appreciation for other cultures and customs. Considerable progress has been made toward this end. Where only 14 percent of public school teachers had more than eight hours of technology training and nearly 50 percent had little or no training at all in 1993–1994, about one-third of public school teachers surveyed feel prepared to teach computer skills and Internet tools in the classroom in 2000.[23]

THE DEVELOPMENT OF A FEDERAL POLICY

Historically, the federal government has played little role in developing technology in the classroom since public education is overwhelming funded at the state and local levels. A major change in this policy occurred after President Bill Clinton took office, when in 1993, he issued two executive orders establishing *ad hoc* panels to examine the impact of science and technology on public education, which were subsequently joined by a council and a task force on the national information infrastructure. A year later, then–Vice President Al Gore championed technology by proposing that every public school classroom in the nation be provided Internet access. Early support from Congress included the Educate America Act, creating the Office of Education Technology within the Department of Education, followed by the Technology for Education Act. The sum of this legislative and executive attention was a new federal level of responsibility for improving technology in public school classrooms. Following the initial studies by the administration, a CEO roundtable was created along with a series of targeted grants designed to experiment with and understand the capabilities and limitations of federal policies. Other supporting developments included the founding of the American Technology Honor Society (a recognition group for industries supporting the Clinton administration computer-education program), and the Clinton TechCorps (a program similar to Americorps).

Congress overwhelmingly passed the Telecommunications Act of 1996— 414–16 in the House, 91–5 in the Senate—which was intended broadly to deregulate telecommunications markets and facilitate competition for monopoly providers of local telephone and cable television. Section 254 of the Act mandates programs to provide "advanced telecommunication services" to every school in the country. To implement this provision the Federal Communications Commission (FCC) unanimously adopted the Universal Service Order. The resulting program, dubbed E-rate for "education rate pricing," which went into effect January 1, 1998, created two new administrations: the Schools and Library Corporation (SLC), a semigovernmental nonprofit agency, that administers the applications process by which eligible schools, libraries, and rural health clinics apply for subsidies for Internet access purchases, and the Universal Service Administrative Company (USAC), a subsidiary of the National Exchange Carrier Association (NECA) telecommunications industry group, which administers the collection of the Universal Service Fund.[24]

The scale of the E-rate program is substantial. Chartered to distribute close to $2.25 billion each year, the program distributed $4 billion in its first two years across 25,000 individual discounting awards, producing over 500,000 newly wired classrooms, but leaving $1.3 billion unspent. The scale of the program is indicative of both the cost of the activities funded and the vastness of the public system in the United States. About 85 percent of the distributions have gone to state public school recipients.

Upon approval by the SLC, the recipient contracts with the local service provider and pays only the nondiscounted component of the cost, with the remaining part of the cost absorbed by the E-rate program. Phone lines, e-mail services, installation and maintenance of purchased equipment, and wireless infrastructure are the kinds of services that are eligible for coverage. Excluded items include software, training, voice and fax equipment, cable modems, and asbestos removal, the last of which is a serious issue for many urban school districts since running new network wiring requires asbestos removal and, thus, additional costs must be borne by the district budget. Because of the services provided, the program is completely focused on access with an emphasis on routine, but high-cost, "last mile" infrastructure. The bulk of the demand for this wiring and access falls to the public schools, which are the largest governmental bureaucracy (in total) in the United States. Table 8.3 gives the breakdown of award recipients by organization type.

Eligibility is often skewed toward high-cost rural areas and the "most disadvantaged" districts (based on percentage participation in reduced-cost or free school lunches in which library applicants use the participation of the local school system). Table 8.4 (on page 168) gives the breakdown of discount level by poverty classification and urban versus rural status.[25] The discount levels are the same at the highest poverty-level categories.

FUNDING AND CONSTITUTIONALITY

The E-rate program is not funded directly through the congressional authorization and appropriations process. Rather, phone companies collect a fee from every consumer's telephone bill, which are then pooled by an industry

TABLE 8.3 DISTRIBUTION OF E-RATE AWARDS

RECIPIENT TYPE	PERCENTAGE
Public school districts	79.2
State and federal schools	5.6
Individual public schools	5.5
Libraries	3.9
Private schools	3.0
All other	2.8

Source: U.S. Department of Education, *E-Learning: Putting a World-Class Education at the Fingertips of All Children* (Washington, D.C.: Office of Educational Technology, U.S. Department of Education, 2000), <www.ed.gov/technology>.

TABLE 8.4   DISCOUNT LEVEL BY POVERTY AND REGION

Percentage of Students in School Lunch Program	Percentage of Schools in This Category	Urban Discount Percentage	Rural Discount Percentage
< 1	3	20	25
1–19	31	40	50
20–34	19	50	60
35–49	15	60	70
50–74	16	80	80
75–100	16	90	90

Source: Schools and Libraries Corporation Applications Guidelines, December 1997, <http://www.sl.universalservice.org/apply>.

group and administered by the FCC according to criteria it alone defines, all without the approval of a single House or Senate committee. Critics derided the "off-budget" financing arrangement, which they charged was not directly specified within the original legislative language of the Telecommunications Act. The core of their argument has been against further continuing the E-rate program on the basis that it is a taxation device beyond the provincial approval of Congress.[26] "America is not about passing tax increases on to all Americans through a bureaucracy, or for an administration official to decide that, gee, this is really a good program, let us tax all Americans and not tell them about it," accused former Representative Joe Scarborough (R-Fla.) on the House floor.[27] Scarborough later added:

> What America is supposed to be about, what this Chamber, the People's House, is supposed to be about, the epicenter of freedom and democracy across the world, it is supposed to be about a fair and free, open debate.
> Over 200 years ago, Thomas Jefferson was talking about the promise and the dream of America and what would make the American Republic. What Thomas Jefferson talked about was the fair marketplace of ideas and the free marketplace of ideas where Americans from all sides of an issue could come together and debate the issues that affected Americans.
> Mr. Speaker, regrettably, this tax increase on the phone bill of all Americans has not been done openly in this Chamber, but rather has been done in the backrooms of the White House and in bureaucracies across Washington, D.C.[28]

An additional concern is the physical means by which the money is collected. Few consumers are aware that they are paying a small amount out of each telephone bill because the universal service surcharge is buried in the back of multiple-page documents along with state, local, and municipal taxes. The telephone companies enthusiastically embrace this process since by definition this is money that they will receive in the form of enhanced business by public schools. Therefore, consumers, whether they support the goals of the program or not, are taxed by the phone companies at the behest of Congress but not directly by federal government.

Another concern focuses on equity in distribution. Because the application paperwork process has been described as cumbersome and the implementation as restrictive, larger and better managed school districts are more likely to apply and receive awards. This leads naturally to a concern about whether these mechanics undersupport districts with higher proportions of minority students. Moreover, there is an increasing concern that the program has no specific provisions for students with disabilities. The concern is that these two groups of students would be further disadvantaged relative to their nonminority and nondisabled peers.

Taken together, these concerns have prompted a flurry of legislation aimed at terminating the E-rate program because of its indirect effect on constituents. Representative Jerry Weller (R-Ill.), a supporter of the original 1996 Telecommunications Act states that, ". . . the FCC created a whole new bureaucracy, known as the School and Library Corporation to administer the E-rate program without any authorization from Congress to do so."[29] Calling the FCC action "an exercise in futility," Senator John McCain (R-Ariz.) called for legislation to be enacted "immediately to stabilize the schools and libraries program and give the entire telephone industry subsidy system the coherence and permanence the Congress intended."[30] Representative Billy Tauzin (R-La.) who accused the FCC of acting like the "tooth fairy" through E-rate, sponsored a measure to overhaul the program by shifting its funding base from telephone companies' universal service fee to telephone excise taxes, which he believed was a more honest approach.[31] "Telephones are taxed more than tobacco, and we think that is atrocious," said Tauzin.[32] Although failing to muster a winning coalition of support, and more draconian than alternative bills, Tauzin's measure signaled sharp congressional protests against the FCC's administration of the E-rate program, which in turn prompted the commission to substantially scale back the program, cutting funding nearly in half.

Various Democrats quickly portrayed the Republican-led bid to alter the E-rate program as a move against improving education, creating more useful libraries, and investing in the nation's future workforce. "Those who attack the E-Rate undercut the future of our children and our country," said Representative Silvestre Reyes (D-Tex.), adding, "Americans want to provide their children the skills and tools of the twenty-first century. Through the E-rate, this is one way we can accomplish this goal."[33] On another occasion, Reyes noted how the E-rate is for leveling the playing field between rich and poor schools:

> The genius of American education is that whether rich or poor, our children are given the opportunity to gain that knowledge. Today, the Internet is a tremendous tool to acquire that knowledge. It brings people and ideas thousands of miles apart to a child's desktop. We cannot afford to have this technology available only in financially strong schools. Through the E-rate, those schools and libraries with limited resources are given the necessary discounts to link up with everybody else.[34]

"It seems like every week we hear more and more about the year 2000 problem," then Senate Minority Leader Tom Daschle (D-S.Dak.) added. "What about the year 2010 problem? This is when—if we do nothing—children who are in kindergarten now will be graduating from high school without the technological skills they need to get a decent job or get a good college education."[35] Congress, argued Daschle and others, understood the slippery funding authority it granted to the FCC.

E-RATE AND THE NEW ADMINISTRATION

Despite President George W. Bush's campaign promise to end the E-rate program, his first legislative proposal, the "No Child Gets Left Behind" initiative, included only an alteration of the current program. Among other policies, the proposal called for widening the class of expenditure allowed to include software, filtering technology, and training for teachers, all of which are specifically excluded in the current program. Additionally, the president's proposal would reduce the paperwork burden by allocating funds to schools automatically rather than by formula, thus eliminating the application process.

The core of this (partial) reversal in policy positions is the realization that the E-rate program garners political support in a wide swath of key constituencies that the Bush political team values: mothers, Hispanics, working-class families, and suburbanites. One contributing factor to the local political salience of the program is the publicity generated from district and school officials bragging about awards and implementations.[36] In a little understood shift, Bush said during the presidential campaign last year that he would combine the E-rate with other educational technology programs already managed by the department of education and other federal agencies, essentially giving the combined funding directly to the states in the form of block grants. The idea was to eliminate bureaucratic waste and create "greater flexibility," an Education Department spokeswoman said.[37]

The more overtly political aspect of the Bush proposal is to tie together various education technology programs, including E-rate, into one single program to, according to the legislation's creation language, provide a performance-based technology grant program that sends more money to schools. The operative phrase here is "performance-based"—in other words tying technology support to standardized testing. Standardized testing on a national level is one of the cornerstones of the Bush administration's educational reform plans, and one of the most controversial proposals to Congress.

A key concern is whether a program run out of the Department of Education that is funded through the normal appropriations process, as suggested by the Bush administration, can provide the predictability and stability of the current process, which is highly formulaic and separated from the parochial whims of Congress. In particular, since the Republican take-over of the 104th (1995–1997) House of Representatives, Republican lawmakers have maintained a rather jaundiced view of funding for the Department of Education. Nonetheless, during a hearing of the House Education and Workforce Committee on March 7, 2001, President Bush's Education Secretary Roderick Paige announced that the administration was reversing itself and leaving the E-rate program in place. The so-called "Gore tax" had now fully survived a change in administration, appearing robust enough to continue operating exactly as it had in the past. This offers the obvious question: How can a program with so many natural enemies and possible constitutional problems survive in a Washington environment hostile to such spending programs?

Something Just Too Tempting

Since its inception, the E-rate program has amassed $1.3 billion in unspent but allocated funds.[38] This is not surprising given that the funding formula and the disbursement process are completely unlinked. That is, there is no market or structural mechanism that ties the universal service surcharge on long-distance calls to the volume and scope of applications from schools for Internet service. So while the program is forbidden to run a deficit (all applications are returned when the size of the fund reaches $250K, for instance), there is no prohibition against running a surplus.

Nothing tantalizes lawmakers more than a surplus in any form. In addition, Congress has shown an enthusiasm for spending on science and technology, distributive programs that impose only general costs on society while delivering plentiful group and geographic benefits, which make many interests better off and few, if any, obviously worse off.[39] Moreover, congressional spending on education represents an outlet from the public's conventional balance of fiscal conservatism with the desire for particularistic benefits.[40] Arguments for "investing in our future" along with appeals to the now-infamous "soccer-mom" mentality provide convenient excuses for members of Congress to break out of normally austere voting patterns with regard to spending. Subsequently, the effects of E-rate, as a direct taxation device, are ameliorated because of the political appeal of the result.

Strong evidence suggests that congressional leaders use district projects to build coalitions to ease the passage of priority legislation despite what their ideal policy preferences might be.[41] Education policies, especially ones with obvious and visible tangible results, are particularly easy to use in this regard since the issue is important in every single congressional district. Members generally factor in the level of the federal bureaucratic presence in their district as a means of gauging constituent awareness of relevant congressional activity.[42] Therefore, the near-universal geographic distribution of E-rate largesse has direct value to members in a classic constituent service context, completely independent of its policy value to members.

The Politics of Survival

The E-rate program endures because Congress and the presidency lack the political will to terminate it even though they would prefer to do so. Arnold defines politically compelling policies as those that lawmakers feel obligated to support because the intended effects are popular, even if the program in question will not meet those objectives.[43] We could hypothesize that E-rate continues to exist because it is a politically compelling policy except that it is clearly and even inarguably successful. Instead, E-rate can be termed a politically compelling policy because of congressional and presidential obligation for a program that meets its objectives in the face of unpopular support by core constituencies.

This paradoxical phenomenon is rare perhaps because it is not often that a federal program can be unambiguously categorized as successful.[44] Further, public-policy programs typically receive greater public support when they blend public satisfaction with public trust.[45] Satisfaction among many citizens is likely to be high since the program is implemented close to them and provides tangible, physically observable benefits. This effect is amplified since school and district officials typically publicize E-rate awards to the greatest extent possible as a means of demonstrating their administrative skills and forward-thinking perspective on education and technology. Trust among citizens is inclined to be high because teachers and administrators are often among the most trusted public servants.

Distributive policies tend to foster a high degree of cooperation between executive branch bureaucrats in the implementation agency and the congressional committees with jurisdiction.[46] This is because both actors have motivations to keep the policy subsystem contained and stable.[47] However, when Congress plays no fiscal role whatsoever, this dynamic is changed.

Since E-rate is a self-perpetuating "quasi-entitlement" run by a semigovernmental organization in cooperation with a colluding industry group, Congress is left with the all-or-nothing choice provided by coercive budgeting tactics on the part of the agencies.[48] This forces Congress to make the decision to either terminate or tolerate the continuation of the E-rate program. A third option, amending the program with new legislation, has proven to be difficult since there is no clear agreement on details or priorities. While the administration has greater leverage over changes in the program due to executive privilege, the cost to the Bush administration in terms of public opinion exceeds their often-stated desire to consolidate or eliminate the program.

Congress has tried on many occasions to control or eliminate these off-budget, so-called "backdoor," appropriation methods. The landmark Congressional Budget and Impoundment Control Act of 1974 originally included provisions to bring all off-budget programs under control of the appropriations committee, but political reality prevailed and the final language was changed. Even so, this has failed to restrain congressional protection of favored programs. As one student of the budget process notes, on many backdoors, the Appropriations Committees puts up no fight at all, but bows to the tide of events within Congress.[49] Backdoor spending is much more than a technical deviation from standard legislative procedures. It represents a congressional determination to shelter certain programs from appropriations review and control, giving such programs an advantage in the competition for federal dollars.

Traditionally there have been three types of off-budget appropriations: entitlements (automatic, formulaic payments to individuals), borrowing authority (executive branch agencies spending borrowed money), and contract authority (executive branch agencies executing contracts that later get funded through the appropriations process).[50] The E-rate program does not really fit within any of these three categories; it is like borrowing authority except the money is not borrowed from the Treasury or the public at large. As a direct tax, but one that is industry implemented, it represents legislative "innovation" in backdoor appropriations.

So E-rate survives largely because it shows easily measured results, because it is highly visible to the public, because it is implemented at the grassroots level by trusted public officials, because it enjoys protection from the whims of the annual congressional budget process, and because it addresses an historically important perceived public need. Taken together, this amounts to a recipe for continued existence in even the harshest and inimical political environments. Additionally, independent of congressional tolerance for the program, E-rate has steadily constructed a powerful clientele—hardware manufacturers, vendors/integrators, and the phone companies—with a vested interest in the program, who collectively possess an effective lobbying group to ensure its survival.

IMPLICATIONS FOR THE FUTURE

Since Congress cannot generate the political will to kill the E-rate program, how will the program be revised by specific legislation and how will the administration of the program adjust to the changing needs of the schools? As the election campaign of 2002 nears, it is clear that education will continue to remain foremost in the minds of voters and, therefore, congressional candidates. The road map for E-rate and other technology programs is outlined in the *Kerrey Commission Report*, which identifies four primary challenges remaining: more trained, professional guidance on using the Internet as learning tool; a more detailed understanding on how students are making use of the Internet and what can done to improve their use; a focus on informational value unique to the Internet as a transmission medium; and the need to move more schools from narrowband access to broadband access, particularly to facilitate the transmission of graphical images. What the Kerrey Report suggests by implication is that the E-rate program has succeeded in its initial mission and needs to be reoriented.

TABLE 8.5   PERCENTAGE OF CHILDREN WITH HOME COMPUTERS

INCOME	1994	1997	1998	2000
< $20,000	10	18	21	31
$20,000–$35,000	24	41	42	51
$35,000–$50,000	41	60	63	72
$50,000–$75,000	57	74	76	83
$75,000 +	76	89	91	94

Source: *E-Learning Report* (Washington, D.C.: Department of Education, 2000).

While the first and most critical barrier to full exploitation of the Internet as a learning tool is physical access, the subsequent challenge is twofold: maximizing the experience through well-thought-out integration into lessons, and ensuring equitable support. Much of the funding from the E-rate program goes to high-need schools because of the allocation guidelines. These schools are often less likely to have highly involved parental organizations. There is thus a tendency to consider such federal support as a replacement for critical support mechanisms within schools.

The equity issue in schools is important because of the general concern that there is a technology capability gap between poorer students and students from wealthier families. This has significant societal implications for both sociological and economic reasons. The effect is further magnified because middle-class and wealthier families are far more likely to have a computer in the home. Thus, if schools are not providing adequate and productive training on computers and Internet usage to low-income students, they may never get such education. Table 8.5 shows that while all income categories demonstrate improved proportions of computers in the home, lower-income groups lag far behind higher-income groups.

NOTES

1. The authors wish to thank the Center for Congressional and Presidential Studies at American University, the Pew CharitableTrusts, and Colton Campbell and Jim Thurber for their useful comments and suggestions during the preparation of this chapter.
2. Mike Mills, "FCC Pares School Internet Program; Funding for Program Cut Nearly in Half," *Washington Post*, 13 June 1998, p. D-1.
3. National Center for Education Statistics, 1999.
4. See comments by the Center for Democracy and Technology Subcommittee on Telecommunication and the Internet Hearing on "E-Rate and Filtering: A Review of the Children's Internet Protection Act," April 4, 2001 and also the April 13, 1999, letter from the head of the National Telecommunications and Information Administration (part of the Department of Commerce) to FCC Chairman Kennard.
5. John Schwartz, "Internet Filters Used to Shield Minors Censor Speech, Critics Say," *New York Times*, 19 March 2001, p. A-15.

6. Technical filtering issues are actually more complicated than one would think. Although a great many sites fit into the obviously excludible category, some have sufficiently overlapping keywords that it is difficult to make highly certain filtering decisions. For example, some have noted this difficulty when doing personal medical research on the Internet and typing "breast cancer" into a search engine.
7. Deborah Sontag, "West Bank Slaying, Via Internet," *New York Times*, 19 January 2001, p. A-6.
8. Rebecca S. Weiner, "Group Aims to Fine Tune Wired Schools," *New York Times*, 4 April 2001, <www.nytimes.com>.
9. Margaret W. Goldsborough, "Facing History," *New York Times*, 21 February 2001, <www.nytimes.com>.
10. Matthew Mirapaul, "Guggenheim's Latest Branch Is to Open in Cyberspace," *New York Times*, 30 April 2001, p. E-1.
11. See the THOMAS Web site of official congressional information for example: <http://thomas.loc.gov/home/thomas.html>.
12. Jay Mathews, "Students Embrace Technology," *Washington Post*, 5 June 2001, p. A-9; and Mirapaul, "Guggenheim's Latest Branch Is to Open in Cyberspace."
13. Carey Goldberg, "Auditing Classes at MIT, on the Web and Free," *New York Times*, 4 April 2001, p. A-1.
14. Rebecca S. Weiner, "When School Is Held on Snow Days," *New York Times*, 14 March 2001, <www.nytimes.com>.
15. Rebecca S. Weiner, "Online Courses to Improve Teacher Technology Skills," *New York Times*, 25 April 2001, <www.nytimes.com>.
16. Lisa Guernsey, "Adding Options to Traditional Classrooms," *New York Times*, 17 February 2001, p. G-8; and Lisa Guernsey, "Teenagers Try Online Learning," *New York Times*, 15 February 2001, p. G-1.
17. Bob Kerrey, *The Power of the Internet for Learning: Moving from Promise to Practice* (Washington, D.C.: Web-Based Education Commission, December 2000).
18. Anne Cattagni and Elizabeth Farris Westat, "Internet Access in U.S. Public Schools and Classrooms," in *Statistics in Brief* (Washington, D.C.: National Center for Education Statistics, U.S. Department of Education, Office of Educational Research and Improvement, 2001).
19. Ibid.
20. Equating schools by the aggregate number of wired computers is somewhat deceptive in that there can be substantial differences in the speed of that access. These rates vary from narrowband access at 28.8 Kbps to a DS-1 (1.544 Mbps) to broadband ranging between the DS-1 to a full DS-3 at 44.736 Mbps (equivalent to 672 telephone channels). Therefore, speed ranges can differ by a full 1,000-fold. In addition, there still exist rural schools unable to use standard telephone lines to connect with the Internet due to distance to the nearest central office of the phone service provider.
21. Ibid.
22. There are also administrative incentives and barriers that affect how successful teachers can be at using the Internet as a learning tool. The *Kerrey Commission Report*, a study by an ad hoc congressional commission, identified several key policy issues here: determination of whether or not classroom credit is given for work done on the Internet; whether or not states are explicitly providing financial support through the budgeting process; making the Internet access part of the education process rather than a means of doing less work for the teachers; the existence of enlightened policies with regard to attendance versus distance learning; certification of teachers with regard to computer expertise; student/teacher ratios in laboratories and other computer applications; and compensation for teachers that spend time retooling their skills. These issues mainly focus on the role of the teacher as a qualified and compensated guide to the new technology. It is clear to many observers of educational reform that not considering the key role of teachers dooms any policy to certain failure.
23. *E-Learning Report* (Washington, D.C.: Department of Education, 2000).
24. Because of constitutional issues with the distribution of federal benefits, as of January 1, 1999, the SLC and Rural Health Care Corporation (RHCC) became divisions of the USAC: the Schools and Libraries Division (SLD) and the Rural Health Care Division (RHCD).
25. The classification system is based on the definitions determined by the U.S. Department of Health and Human Services in which counties are determined to be rural or urban based on their U.S. Census Metropolitan Statistical Area (MSA). All applicants in rural MSAs are

classified as rural. All applicants in metropolitan MSAs are classified as urban, except those falling in a census block subject to the "Goldsmith Modification," which identifies rural pockets in urban MSAs.
26. In July of 1999 the 5th U.S. Circuit Court of Appeals ruled that E-rate was constitutional because although the language and legislative history of the 1996 Telecommunications Act do not describe or support the manner in which the E-rate program was designed, Congress left the implementation wording sufficiently abstract and underspecified as to delegate such decisions to the executive branch. Short of action by the Supreme Court, this is likely to be the final word on the constitutionality of the E-rate program.
27. *Congressional Record*, 105th Cong., 2nd sess., June 16, 1998, H4575.
28. Ibid.
29. U.S. Congress, House Subcommittee on Telecommunications, Trade and Consumer Protection Legislative Hearing, *H.R. 1746—Schools and Libraries Internet Access Act*, 106th Cong., 1st sess., 30 September 1999.
30. Quoted in Mills, "FCC Pares School Internet Program; Funding for Program Cut Nearly in Half."
31. John Schwartz, "FCC to Expand 'E-Rate' Funding; Some Lawmakers Deride Program that Aids Schools, Libraries," *Washington Post*, 26 May 1999, p. E-1.
32. Quoted in Dan Egbert, "Rep. Tauzin Challenges Administration on School Internet Program," *States News Service* (July 23, 1998).
33. *Congressional Record*, 105th Cong., 2nd sess., July 21, 1998, H5968.
34. *Congressional Record*, 105th Cong., 2nd sess., July 21, 1998, H5504.
35. *Congressional Record*, 105th Cong., 2nd sess., July 10, 1998, S6005.
36. Jack Torry, "At Whose Expense: E-Rate Program an Educational Boon or Boondoggle?" *Pittsburgh Post-Gazette*, 31 January 2000, p. A-1.
37. Anne E. Kornblut and Robert Schlesinger, "Bush Yields on 'E-Rate' to Wire U.S. Schools," *Boston Globe*, 17 March 2001, p. A-3
38. General Accounting Office, *Schools and Libraries Program: Update on E-Rate Funding*, Report GAO-01-672 (Washington, D.C.: General Accounting Office, 2001).
39. Alfred E. Cohn, "Federal Legislation in Support of Science," *Political Science Quarterly* 62 (1947), pp. 228–240 and Colton C. Campbell, *Discharging Congress: Government by Commission* (Westport, CT: Praeger Publishers, 2001).
40. Andre Modigliani and Franco Modigliani, "The Growth of the Federal Deficit and the Role of Public Attitudes," *Public Opinion Quarterly* 51 (1987), pp. 459–480.
41. David P. Baron, "Majoritarian Incentives, Pork Barrel Programs, and Procedural Control," *American Journal of Political Science* 35 (1991), pp. 57–90; and Diana Evans, "Policy and Pork: The Use of Pork Barrel Projects to Build Policy Coalitions in the House of Representatives," *American Journal of Political Science* 38 (1994), pp. 894–917.
42. Morris P. Fiorina, "The Case of the Vanishing Marginals: The Bureaucracy Did It," *American Political Science Review* 71 (1877), pp. 177–181.
43. R. Douglas Arnold, *The Logic of Congressional Action* (New Haven, CT: Yale University Press, 1990), p. 78.
44. Jeffrey L. Pressman and Aaron B. Wildavsky, *Implementation: How Great Expectations in Washington Are Dashed in Oakland* (Berkeley, CA: University of California Press, 1973).
45. Richard L. Cole, "Citizen Participation in Municipal Elections," *American Journal of Political Science* 19 (1975), pp. 761–781.
46. Randall B. Ripley and Grace A. Franklin, *Congress, the Bureaucracy, and Public Policy* (Homewood, IL: Dorsey Press, 1984). See Chapter 4.
47. James A. Thurber, "Dynamics of Policy Subsystems in American Politics," in *Interest Group Politics*, 3rd ed., ed. Allan J. Cigler and Burdette A. Loomis (Washington, D.C.: CQ Press, 1991).
48. William A. Niskanen, Jr., *Bureaucracy and Representative Government* (Chicago: Aldine Atherton, Inc., 1971).
49. Allen Schick, *Congress and Money* (Washington, D.C.: Urban Institute, 1980), p. 426.
50. Roger H. Davidson and Walter J. Oleszek, *Congress and Its Members*, 4th ed. (Washington, D.C.: CQ Press, 1993), p. 397.

9

THE INTERNET, CONGRESS, AND EDUCATIONAL OUTREACH[1]

GRAEME BROWNING

In horse racing even the fastest colt will falter if distracted by horses running beside him. If that happens the trainer will fit the colt's bridle with half-closed eye cups, to block his peripheral vision and keep him focused on the track ahead.

When employing the Internet to educate and communicate with the American public, Congress could use some of those eye cups. After a slow start from the gate in the early 1990s, most of its members are now charging full-speed toward the Information Age. Everyone in Congress now has a Web site, many have hired Internet-savvy staffers, and more than a few are learning to use e-mail. But even in this rush to become "wired," Congress is still wasting valuable energy trying to prove that it can be as hip and flashy on the Web as the private sector is. At the same time, very few members of Congress seem to be looking ahead to the radical new communications style they will need to communicate with the coming generation.

A BRIEF HISTORY OF CONGRESS AND THE INTERNET

In 1993 only 8 percent of Americans had access to a computer at home, according to the National Science Foundation. Nevertheless, former Representative Charlie Rose (D-N.C.), then chairman of the Committee on House Administration, decided it was time for Congress to venture on to what was then being called "the Information Superhighway." In June 1993 Rose established the first pilot project to study the efficacy of electronic mail in congressional offices. Only seven members of Congress signed up for the experiment.

But e-mail caught on. Within a year, forty members of the House and thirty senators acquired Internet addresses, and the same number of members and committees in both houses requested Internet access.[2] Many members of Congress struggled to comprehend the uses of e-mail in those early days. Newly elected Speaker of the House Newt Gingrich's (R-Ga.) <Georgia6 @hr.house.gov> address, for example, received almost 13,000 e-mail messages in the first six weeks after Congress returned to work in January 1995. Taken aback by the volume, Gingrich's staff asked the House of Representatives' technical staff to delete the e-mail. Eventually, cooler heads prevailed and the e-mails were relegated to a backup tape.

Congress came to the Web somewhat more slowly. At the urging of his young staffer Chris Casey, Senator Edward M. Kennedy (D-Mass.) built the first congressional Web site in early 1994. No one else in the House or the Senate followed suit, however, until a year later. In March 1996, when then Representative Rick White (R-Wash.), founded the Congressional Internet Caucus, approximately one-third of the members of Congress had Web sites. It took four more years for the rest of Congress to catch up: Representative Joel Hefley (R.-Colo.) whom the press called "the last Web holdout in Congress," agreed in January 2001 to establish a Web site.

Some of the technology that the private sector takes for granted still is not acceptable in Congress: In 1997 the Senate Rules Committee refused the request of Senator Michael B. Enzi (R-Wyo.) to bring his laptop into the Senate chamber, and the committee has yet to change its stance. In March 2001, however, the Senate Republican Conference began making the daily delivery of its policy papers, issue briefs, press releases, and schedules available to all fifty Senate GOP members via their Palm Pilot.[3]

"Webcasting," the practice of broadcasting live audio and video via the Internet has also become a popular practice in Congress. As with Web sites, Webcasting technology captured the political imagination early. Ben Brink, a Republican from Silicon Valley who ran the first wholly on-line congressional campaign in 1994, promised voters that he would try to pass legislation requiring congressional committee hearings to be conducted via video-conferencing, so that members of Congress could spend more time in their home districts.[4] But it was not until November 1999 that Representative David Dreier (R-Calif.), chairman of the House Rules Committee, initiated the first live audio broadcast of a House hearing. A little more than a year later, C-SPAN began Webcasting most of the Senate's committee hearings.

The Internet has also begun to affect Congress's legislative perspective. The 104th Congress (1995–1997), for example, considered fewer than ten bills relating to the Internet. When the 105th Congress (1997–1999) closed shop, however, it had considered a record 110 bills relating to the Internet, leading one observer to declare 1998 "the year the Internet came of age." During the 106th Congress (1999–2001) some 476 measures were introduced that had the word "Internet" in them. In a recent "Dear Colleague" letter to House

Republicans, House Speaker Dennis Hastert of Illinois wrote: "Whether we are speaking in such terminology as 'digital age,' 'Information Superhighway,' or the 'knowledge economy,' the success of the Internet is real and it is here."[5]

"Wiring" Congress matters a great deal because the Internet is rapidly becoming the vital link in all of our communications, political and otherwise. In 1996 less than 15 percent of Americans were on-line, according to Jupiter Media Metrix, one of the leading Internet research firms. By early 2001, 60 percent of Americans, or 168 million people, were using the Internet—a *quadrupling* of the on-line public in only four years.

At the same time, the Internet audience—once a group known primarily for its homogeneity—now resembles mainstream America. "Increasingly people without college training, those with modest incomes, and women are joining the ranks of Internet users, who not long ago were largely well-educated, affluent men," the Pew Research Center for the People & the Press reported in early 1999.[6] African Americans, Hispanic Americans, and Asian Americans also now represent significant segments of the Net community, although there is conflicting research about the depth of the "digital divide" in this country. And while some politicians would characterize the Internet as a bastion of far-left ideology, there is evidence that Americans who go on-line are no more partisan than other citizens. A 1995 study of technology in the American household by the Times Mirror Research Center for the People & the Press found that computer users are almost identical to those who do not use a computer in terms of party identification and congressional and presidential voting patterns.[7]

CONGRESS'S CURRENT RELATIONSHIP WITH THE INTERNET

Congress reaches out electronically to its various constituencies through e-mail and sites on the World Wide Web. While both technologies have become standard educational tools for Capitol Hill, neither is being used to its full potential there.

E-mail, which was created in late 1971 for use on the fledgling Department of Defense network ARPANET, has now utterly outstripped its modest beginnings. By 1995 some 35 million people were using e-mail.[8] Today there are more than 500 million e-mailboxes worldwide.[9] Many Americans have also begun to incorporate e-mail into many facets of their daily lives: E-mail is the number one activity for people on-line and the typical e-mail user is on the Internet seven to eight hours per week, the Gallup Organization found in a recent survey.[10] What is more, the majority of the e-mail users in the Gallup survey said they now use the telephone and U.S. mail less often.

At the same time Americans have begun to rely on the Internet for up-to-the-minute information, particularly on topics with political overtones or in times of national crisis. On September 11, 1998, 12 percent of adult Americans—almost 20 million people—went to the Internet to read Independent Counsel

Kenneth Starr's 445-page report on President Clinton's White House peccadilloes.[11] At the time that was the single highest number of people who had ever used a computer to access a single document. Exactly two years later, 12.5 million people logged on to MSNBC's Web site in the twenty-four hours after the first terrorist-controlled airliner crashed into New York's World Trade Center Towers. On average, almost 12 million Americans visited Web-based news sites in the week after the attacks.[12]

E-mail has also become a crucial component in political communications. During the 2000 election season, for example, e-mail became the "killer app" for campaign managers eager to recruit and motivate volunteers. As the campaign season went into high gear last summer, both the Democratic National Committee (DNC) and the Republican National Committee (RNC) initiated e-mail campaigns asking the on-line faithful to send party-generated e-mails to their friends, in an electronic version of the chain letter. "We believe electronic word-of-mouth is the best form of voter contact," Larry Purpuro, deputy chief of staff at the RNC and director of its "e.GOP" project, told the *New York Times*. "It's personalized, it's targeted and it works with lightning speed."[13]

E-mail is also exploding in Congress's electronic in-boxes. According to a March 2001 report by the Congress Online Project at George Washington University, the e-mail volume in the House of Representatives skyrocketed from 20 million messages in 1998 to 48 million messages in 2000.[14] Even now e-mail to the House continues to grow by an average of one million messages per month.

Unfortunately, Congress is floundering in this sea of e-mail. Just as House members were preparing to vote on impeachment in 1998, for example, a glitch in the Microsoft e-mail server software that the House uses sent thousands of constituent messages into a continuous loop.[15] In the Senate, messages from the public are sometimes delayed for a day or more, and occasionally are bounced back as "undeliverable" by the Senate's overloaded system. Even though the Senate e-mail server, which is based on Lotus Development Corporation's cc:Mail, has been upgraded since 1998, it is still inadequate to the load.[16] "Rather than enhancing democracy—as so many hoped—e-mail has heightened tensions and public disgruntlement with Congress," the Congress Online Project noted in its report.

Congress, on the other hand, worries about being overwhelmed by e-mail. "Precisely because it is so easy and quick to use, [congressional staffers believe] it is far more likely that someone will e-mail her or his member rather than taking the time to write a letter, put it into an envelope, put a stamp on it, and mail it," OMB Watch, a Washington-based advocacy group, has reported.[17] Because of this fear, congressional offices take personal letters sent through the regular mail most seriously, followed by personal visits and telephone calls. Faxes and e-mail rank "considerably below" personal visits in terms of effectiveness, while petitions, form letters via regular mail, and postcard campaigns rank at the bottom.

The problem is, Americans who are on-line have come to expect that Congress will heed their e-mails as seriously as it does their letters and phone calls. As the Congress Online Project notes, in a 1999 study of more than 155,000 e-mail users, Juno Online Services and e-advocates, a consulting firm, found that sending e-mail to Congress was preferred over writing letters by a margin of two-to-one. When the survey asked, "Should your Members of Congress treat e-mail as seriously as calls and letters?" only 7 percent of the respondents answered no.[18]

Congress is making more progress on the Web. In a 1996 review of congressional Web sites, except in a handful of instances, politicians in Washington were using the new technology (of the Web) to convey an old message.[19] Five years later, a number of Web sites in both Houses of Congress have turned that critique on its head.

In 1999, the Congressional Management Foundation, a Washington, D.C., think tank, issued *Building Web Sites Constituents Will Use*, a rigorous and objective analysis of congressional Web sites.[20] Two years later, the foundation undertook a similar analysis not only to gauge the sites' effectiveness but also to determine "best practices" for congressional Web design. The foundation's research team identified five key criteria on which the sites were judged—including whether the site clearly defined its audience, whether it provided content specifically targeted to meet visitors' needs, and whether it was interactive, attractively designed, easily navigable and innovative—and convened an expert panel, of which the author was a member, to conduct the final round of reviews.

The more than fifty congressional sites considered in that final round were uniformly attractive and information-laden in terms of the events, issues, and schedules in Congress itself. All made a concerted effort to offer answers to the questions about veterans' benefits, Social Security, visitors' tours, internship programs, and appointments to military academies that are the standard fare for congressional caseworkers. It was also clear that many congressional Web designers were taking cues from the private sector by providing such useful site components as the following:

- Privacy and security policies
- Site indexes
- Search engines
- Spanish-language versions of the site
- Congressional Research Service reports on-line
- High- and low-bandwidth versions of the site
- "Bulletin boards" where constituents could post questions and comment on issues before Congress
- Pages for younger visitors and students, with links to museums, youth-oriented government Web sites, and consumer, educational, media, non-profit, and employment-related sites

However, some of the sites also left cookies without warning, did not include regularly updated material, and, in a few cases, had misspellings.[21] Few included the direct phone numbers or e-mail addresses of key staff members, were designed to be accessible to Americans with disabilities, or offered technical or practical information written in user-friendly language. And while all the sites encouraged constituents to contact their member of Congress via e-mail, many noted that the response would arrive via the U.S. Post Office instead of the Internet.

Most important, a number of the congressional Web sites I reviewed used "flash" applications, complex graphics, and video inserts that require the sort of high-speed Internet connection that, even now, few Americans have on their home computers. Eye-popping design elements such as these are becoming customary on private-sector Web sites, particularly those that cater to a younger audience. But they add nothing to the actual content of the site, and, in my opinion, signify the triumph of form over function when used in a congressional Web site.[22] A set of "roll-over" titles that appear when the user's mouse touches a section of the site, or a separate box that pops up when he or she clicks on an on-line poll, may give the ordinary American the impression that he or she is exchanging information—actually *interacting*—with the site when that is not the case.

THE FUTURE IS A FREIGHT TRAIN

Why is the lack of true interactivity on most congressional Web sites so important? A few statistics will illustrate the problem. According to one well-regarded source, 17 million Americans aged thirteen to twenty-two are on-line today.[23] Another equally substantive source estimates that 73 percent of U.S. kids aged twelve to seventeen are currently using the Internet.[24] No matter what the actual figures, these Americans differ *fundamentally* from almost every current member of Congress in their understanding of electronic communications.

These future voters grew up with computers, and they use the Internet instinctively instead of as a learned response, as their parents and grandparents do. They are the Americans to whom "56K" means a modem speed instead of a math problem, who know as much about RAM and MP3 as they know about skateboarding and the latest boy bands. More than two-thirds of them go on-line at least once a week and 35 percent report that they are on-line "almost every day."[25] In fact, anyone who has a computer and preteen or teenager at home knows that the coming generation is just as likely to be on-line sending instant messages after school as watching television or talking on the telephone. The Internet is a link to friends, a homework buddy, an entertainment center, a shopping mall, and, last but not least, an information resource.

In contrast, adults age fifty and over are print-oriented, and almost always use newspapers, magazines, books, and journals as learning tools.[26] Even younger Baby Boomers—the first generation to grow up with television—are visually oriented, cannot live without cable television, and sometimes struggle to get their laptops to work.

For many Americans who are twenty years old or younger, however, computers are just as natural a communications medium as television, telephone, and radio. "If parents think that their kids are catching on to the new technologies much faster than adults, they're right," Don Tapscott, chairman of the Alliance for Converging Technologies, writes in *Growing Up Digital: The Rise of the Net Generation*.[27] "Because [today's] children are born with technology, they assimilate it. Adults must accommodate—a different and much more difficult learning process. With assimilation, kids view technology as just another part of their environment, and they soak it up along with everything else. For many kids, using the new technology is as natural as breathing."

When the newest generation of computer users comes to the Internet, they expect a true give-and-take instead of the old television-based, one-way information flow that most congressional Web sites now offer. Many sites post an abundance of information—including press releases, newspaper and magazine articles, bios, drafts of legislation and policy statements, still pictures, and video and audio clips—but that information is often offered in a format that only allows the user to read or download it, not respond to it. Some sites with "bulletin board" features post constituent comments in the interactive manner to which most Internet users have grown accustomed, but they are few and far between.

This state of affairs is disconcerting, given the demands for electronic communication that legislators from Capitol Hill to the local county commission will face within the next decade. To go back to statistics, in 2005—less than four years from now—the number of Americans on-line is expected to swell to 194 million.[28] By that time today's thirteen to twenty-two-year-olds will have reached their late teens and early twenties and a whole new generation of technology-savvy youngsters will be "soaking up" the Internet. That means that as much as 20 percent of the U.S. population who regularly use computers to communicate will be those people who have been conducting every aspect of their lives on-line almost since they learned to walk.

Why should Congress care? After all, thirteen-year-olds cannot vote. No, but they will eventually. And they will expect to do it on-line, just as they will expect to conduct other facets of their political business—and other facets of their lives—on-line. As a Forrester Research analyst puts it, "Having grown up in a digital world, young consumers are not simply ahead of adults, they're different from adults."[29]

For example, in an ABC News survey taken during the 2000 election season, only 19 percent of Americans age sixty-five and older supported Internet voting—but 60 percent of the respondents age eighteen to thirty-four said they would vote on-line if they could.[30] More recently, responses to a telephone survey on on-line voting commissioned by Unisys Corp. and the Information Technology Association of America, a leading high-tech trade association, showed a striking generation gap: 60 percent of those people aged eighteen to twenty-four who were surveyed support Internet voting, while only 20 percent of those fifty-five and older back it.[31]

The outcome of these changes is not hard to imagine. In *Next: The Future Just Happened*, his acclaimed analysis of the social impact of the Internet, best-selling author Michael Lewis predicts that in the decades to come an increasingly technological electorate will push the U.S. political system away from representative democracy. "Sooner or later, it will be possible to vote on-line," Lewis writes. "And sooner or later, it will be possible to collect signatures on-line. Together these changes might well lead to direct democracy, at least in states like California where citizens can call votes on an issue simply by gathering enough signatures on its behalf. At which point someone asks, 'Why can't we do the same thing in Washington?' One constitutional amendment later and—poof—Americans are voting directly to decide important national questions rather than voting for politicians and leaving the decisions up to them."[32]

To be sure, many older Americans will find this prospect disturbing. More than half the adults in this country do not have Internet access, and the majority of that group does not want access because they consider the on-line world dangerous.[33] But by 2010 or 2015, as the ranks of the older generation thin, and the new generation of Internet-oriented voters reaches adulthood, it will become reality. Congress should stop hiding its head in the sand, and make ready.

Notes

1. Parts of this paper are adapted from Graeme Browning, *Electronic Democracy: Using the Internet to Transform American Politics*, 2nd ed. (Chicago, IL: Information Today, 2001).
2. William F. Powers, "Virtual Politics: Campaigning in Cyberspace," *Washington Post*, 8 November 1994, p. E-1.
3. William Matthews, "Republican Palm Push," *Federal Computer Week*, 26 March 2001, <http://www.fcw.com/fcw/articles/2001/0326/web-sen-03-26-01.asp>.
4. Graeme Browning, "Prospecting for Votes in Cyberspace," *National Journal* (15 October 1994), p. 2412.
5. "Dear Colleague" letter of March 25, 1999, from House Speaker Dennis Hastert of Illinois, as reported in *National Journal's Technology Daily* on-line news service on the same day.
6. The Pew Research Center for the People & the Press, "The Internet News Audience Goes Ordinary," <http://www.people-press.org/tech98sum.htm>, January 1999.
7. The Pew Research Center for the People & the Press (formerly the Times Mirror Center for the People & the Press), "Technology in the American Household." Summary available at <http://www.people-press.org/tech.htm>, 1995.
8. Quoted in Don Tapscott, *Growing Up Digital: The Rise of the Net Generation* (McGraw-Hill 1998), p. 23 and *Cyberatlas*, found at <http://www.cyberatlas.com>, May 1997.
9. Estimate by International Data Corp., as quoted in Michael Pastore, "More Mailboxes on the Way," *Cyberatlas*, <http://www.cyberatlas.com>, September 17, 2001.
10. Ibid.

11. "20 Million Americans See Starr's Report on Internet," *CNN Online*, <http://www.cnn.com>, September 13, 1998.
12. Melinda Patterson Grenier, "Traffic to News Web Sites over Two Days Sets Records," *Wall Street Journal Online*, <http://www.interactive.wsj.com> (subscription required), September 13, 2001.
13. Leslie Wayne, "E-Mail Used to Mobilize Voters," *New York Times* on-line, <http://www.nyt.com>, November 6, 2000.
14. Kathy Goldschmidt, "E-Mail Overload in Congress: Managing a Communications Crisis," Congress Online Project, <http://www.congressonlineproject.org/publications.html>, March 19, 2001.
15. Sandra Gittlen and Jason Meserve, "Bug Slows Impeachment E-Mail to House Members," *CNN Online*, <http://www.cnn.com>, December 16, 1998.
16. William Matthews, "Slow E-Mail Dogs Senate," *Federal Computer Week*, <http://www.fcw.com/fcw/articles/2001/0219/news-email-02-19-01.asp>, February 19, 2001.
17. *Speaking Up in the Internet Age: Use and Value of Constituent E-Mail and Congressional Web Sites*, OMB Watch, December 1998. Available for order at <http://www.ombwatch.org/ombpubs.html>.
18. "Executive Summary: First Annual E-Politics Survey," Juno Online Services Inc. and e-advocates. Available at <http://www.e-advocates.com/survey/survey2.htm>.
19. Graeme Browning, "New Media, Old Messages," *Media Studies Journal* 10 (winter 1996), pp. 67–74, at p. 67.
20. *Building Web Sites Constituents Will Use*, Congressional Management Foundation, 1999, <http://www.cmfweb.org/pubs.htm#Building>.
21. For example, one site, in a reference to the terrorist attacks on September 11, 2001, noted that it supported "America [sic] United."
22. The author wishes to make it clear that she does not speak for the Congressional Management Foundation when she makes this, or any other, personal observation in this paper.
23. From promotional materials by Forrester Research, Inc., "Reaching and Keeping a Generation That Is Wired Differently" (a conference held December 5–6, 2001, Cambridge, Mass. Available at <http://www.forrester.com/Events/Overview/0,5158,347,00.html>).
24. Pew Internet & American Life Project, *Teenage Life Online: The Rise of the Instant-Message Generation and the Internet's Impact on Friendships and Family Relationships*, <http://www.pewinternet.org/reports/toc.asp?Report=36>, June 20, 2001.
25. Quoted in David Lake, "Youth: Next on the Net," *The Industry Standard, Metrics*, <http://www.thestandard.com/article/0,1902,15636,00.html>, June 5, 2000.
26. American Association for Retired People, "Executive Summary," *AARP Survey on Lifelong Learning*, <http://research.aarp.org/general/lifelong.html>, July 19, 2000.
27. Tapscott, *Growing Up Digital*.
28. Jupiter Media Metrix, "U.S. Online Users: 1996–2005." Available at <http://www.jmm.com/xp/jmm/press/industryProjections.xml>.
29. Gary Langer, "Virtual Voting: Polls Find Most Oppose Online Ballots," ABCNews.com, <http://abcnews.go.com>, July 21, 2000.
30. Ekaterina O. Walsh, quoted in "Young Net Surfers Are Tomorrow's Prime Financial Consumers, According to Forrester Research," Forrester Research, Inc., press release, <http://www.forrester.com/ER/Press/Release/0,1769,424,00.html>, October 26, 2000.
31. Dibya Sarkar, "Americans Support Voting Upgrades," *Federal Computer Week*, <http://www.fcw.com>, April 2, 2001.
32. Michael Lewis, *Next: The Future Just Happened* (W. W. Norton & Company: New York, 2001).
33. Pew Internet & American Life Project, "Who's Not Online: 57% of Those without Internet Access Say They Do Not Plan to Log On," <http://www.pewinternet.org/reports/pdfs/Pew_Those_Not_Online_Report.pdf>, September 21, 2000.

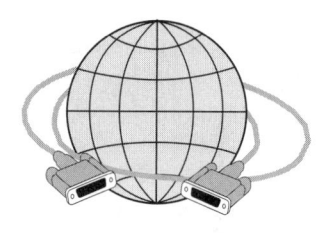

AFTERWORD

CONGRESS AND THE INTERNET: LOOKING BACK AND LOOKING FORWARD

CHRIS CASEY

The phrase "Internet Time" is generally understood to mean "very, very fast." That is, it describes the speed with which new innovations are developed and deployed on the Internet, the speed in which Internet companies frequently experience meteoric rises and often similarly speedy falls, and it can also describe the Internet's amazingly rapid growth rates among the world's population during the 1990s.

Just as the milestone year of 1984 came and went without many of the fearful predictions from George Orwell's novel coming to pass, we are currently halfway through another year for which great leaps forward in computer technology and space travel have been imagined, yet remain unrealized. But having survived the predicted technological doom of the Y2K bug, the year 2001 does provide an opportunity to examine the state of technology in general, to compare the current reality against previously imagined progress, assess advances and milestones passed, and make further attempts to predict what lies ahead.

There are not many things that Congress does on "Internet Time." Congress in general, and the Senate in particular, are institutions that were designed to be deliberative and slow to change. Nevertheless, there is no stopping regular time, and almost ten years have passed since Congress first ventured onto the Net. And ten years of anything is usually enough to rate some review and reflection.

TOP TEN MILESTONES FOR CONGRESS ON THE INTERNET

With no authority other than my own, and with no method other than personal recollection and reading, I offer a listing of "Top Ten Milestones for Congress on the Internet." Originally entitled "Top Highs and Lows for Congress on the Internet," I quickly realized that not every entry on my list could be considered a "highlight," hence "milestones." For better or for worse, therefore, these milestones signify a turning point of one sort or another in Congress's use of the Internet. As the creation of any such list is a purely subjective exercise, I offer this list as my own, and know it is strictly a matter of opinion. And following this look back, I look forward with some predictions for Congress's future use of the Internet.

Senator Robb Accepts E-Mail (Late 1993)

A brave group of seven members of the House of Representatives launched the era of constituent e-mail earlier the same year, but did so with the protection of a cumbersome registration process and filtering capabilities provided by House Information Resources. Senator Charles S. (Chuck) Robb (D-Va.), among the first members of the Senate to provide information from his Senate office on-line (via a Washington area free-net called CapAccess), was also the first senator to share his e-mail address on-line. Reports from his office at the time that the flow of constituent e-mail was "manageable" were reassuring to other offices. But they belied the inevitable fact that every other member of Congress would eventually also open an e-mail pipeline into their offices, and that these pipes would more closely resemble a fire-hose than the trickle Senator Robb originally received.

Senator Kennedy Launches Web Site (May 1994)

<http://www.ai.mit.edu/iiip/projects/kennedy/homepage.html>: How is that for a URL? It was the first for a member of Congress, primarily because at the time there was not yet any such thing as <www.senate.gov> or <www.house.gov>. Benefiting from the good fortune of having some enthusiastic graduate students, attending one of the country's premier technical institutions (Massachusetts Institute of Technology), which happened to be in his state, Senator Edward M. (Ted) Kennedy (D-Mass.) led Congress onto the World Wide Web. Unlike using e-mail, which brought with it the burdensome expectation of a response, Web sites were more quickly understood and embraced by members of Congress eager to inform cyberspace of their good deeds.

House Republicans Restrict Access to Committee Minority Web Sites (June 1996)

It was not just individual members who discovered the Web, but congressional committees as well. Senate committees generally share the services of a single system administrator, and as a result most developed a single Web site. House committees more frequently had separate computer support for their majority and minority staffs, and hence were more likely to develop separate Web sites representing the majority and minority sides for a committee. Initially, both the majority and minority Web sites could be accessed by direct links from the main House Web site at <www.house.gov>. But in a move equivalent to forcing visitors to walk through the majority staff's lobby before visiting any minority staff office, House Republicans passed a rule that minority committee sites would be accessible only from the majority's Web page, and not from the main House page. With this, the Hill Web became a political weapon.

Animations Abound (Early 1997)

Like the much maligned <blink> tag, animated "gifs" brought movement to Web pages of the sort that initially entertains, but ultimately annoys. Congressional Web sites embraced animated gifs with a vengeance. Waving flags, flying letters that folded themselves up, sprouted wings, and flew into mailboxes, and fluttering flames that announced "hot news" that usually was not, turned up everywhere on congressional Webs. Usually these images were copies of others, liberally "borrowed" from other sites on which they could be found. Two original animations, however, stood apart from the rest. The first was former Senator Bill Bradley's (D-N.J.) signature, which wrote itself across the bottom of his welcome message. The second was Representative James Traficant's (D-Ohio) photo that showed him with a large "Buford Pusser"–style wooden club, menacingly held in one hand while being hit into the palm of his other hand, announcing that he was "Bangin' Away" on his constituent's behalf in the nation's capital. Evidence of both development skills and originality were rapidly appearing on congressional Web sites.

Write-Your-Representative and Web Forms (Early 1997)

The problem with e-mail, most members of Congress have discovered, is the sheer quantity of messages received in a given day. In most cases, the majority of incoming e-mail is not even sent by an identifiable constituent. Congressional offices rightly wondered whether it was a waste of time even bothering to reply to "jdoe@aol.com," lacking any other hint of the sender's origin. Added to this fact is that senders frequently e-mail-bombed an individual's office by sending the same message repeatedly, or "spammed" the Hill by copying the e-mail addresses of every member of Congress who had one. The challenge of identifying an actual constituent message in an overflowing in-box was akin to the hunt for the proverbial needle in a haystack.

While the House of Representative's initial attempt to deal with this predicted problem by requiring senders to preregister was quickly scrapped, new efforts were made to deal with the problem. The House initiated "Write Your Rep.," a system by which lawmakers could elect to be reachable via e-mail only by senders who had first found their way through a zip code look-up form. Many members quickly adopted the system. Other legislators switched from traditional e-mail addresses to Web-based Web forms, which offer many mail management advantages for congressional offices, such as a protection Web form against "spam," as well as the ability to sort and data enter these incoming messages.

SENATOR DASCHLE'S CHRISTMAS TREE WEB CAM (NOVEMBER 1997)

From locations around the world, ranging from the mundane to the exotic, Web cams typically take frequent pictures of their subjects at short intervals and upload the image to a Web site, offering visitors an up-to-the-minute Web window on the world. This new net technology was combined with another congressional holiday tradition, the Capitol Christmas Tree. Each year a different National Forest or individual donor is selected to provide an appropriately impressive tree, which is brought to Washington, either by train or by truck, decorated and lit on the West Lawn of the U.S. Capitol.

In 1997, such a tree came from the Black Hills National Forest of South Dakota, and Senator Thomas A. (Tom) Daschle (D-S.Dak.) sought a way to share the tree from his home state with folks beyond the beltway. Enter "TreeCam"—a Macintosh computer, connected to a television camera and the Internet, with an impressive view of the West Lawn and the Christmas tree from a third floor window in the Capitol. Immediately popular, "Netizens" around the world frequently logged on to check the tree and enjoy its colorful lights. Congress learned that it does not have to be just about politics online, and a new Holiday tradition was born. Senator Daschle's office has brought the TreeCam back every Christmas since.

THE *STARR REPORT* GOES ON-LINE (SEPTEMBER 1998)

It is interesting to note that the first document to create such a great demand on congressional Web servers to literally grind them to a halt did not originate in Congress. Rather, it was Independent Counsel Ken Starr's salacious report that ultimately led to the impeachment of President Bill Clinton that caused such a stir. As the much-anticipated report was made available by the House Judiciary Committee, the Library of Congress's THOMAS server, and the Government Printing Office, each of these Hill servers strained under the overwhelming demand. The Senate's Web site, one of the few Hill Web servers that did not have the report, received so much traffic that its regular front page was temporarily replaced with a road-sign page, which warned visitors that the Starr Report was not available on <www.senate.gov> and subsequently directed them to other locations. While the *Starr Report* was certainly not the usual congressional on-line offering, its availability on congressional Web sites marked a loss of Congress's on-line innocence in more ways than one.

The Senate Gets Hacked, Twice (May 1999, June 1999)

Perhaps the most surprising thing is that it took so long to happen, but hackers made up for lost time in 1999 by defacing the Senate's official Web page twice in just two months. Hacking had already happened to many other prominent government Web sites, including the Federal Bureau of Investigations (FBI) and Central Intelligence Agency (CIA) sites, but this was the first Hill hack. In each instance, the intrusion was quickly detected and corrected. As a result senate staff access to Web pages they maintained was subsequently placed under new restrictions.

All 100 Senators On-Line (March 2000)

It took six years, a whole Senate term, before it happened, but when Freshman Senator Peter Fitzgerald (R-Ill.) finally got around to launching his Web site, he became the 100th senator to go on-line. While some senators may have hoped that the Internet was a passing fad that could be ignored, the Internet proved itself to be an effective communications medium on Capitol Hill. Senators and representatives alike are now expected to have individual Web sites and e-mail addresses; those who do not are the exception rather than the rule.

Senator Clinton's Day One Web Launch (January 2001)

Proving the previous point, the freshman members of the Senate class of 2000 knew that their constituents expected to be able to find them on-line, and they sought to get there quickly. None was quicker than Freshman Senator Hillary Rodham Clinton (D-N.Y.), who launched her official senate Web site within hours of being sworn in as a member of the world's most deliberative body. Other freshman senators were similarly quick to establish their on-line presence, demonstrating that perhaps the Senate's newest members understood something about working on "Internet Time."

Three Predictions for Congress's Future on the Internet

Making predictions is a tricky business. The safest predictions are generally the most obvious and easiest to make—such as the sun will rise tomorrow—but these are also the most meaningless. Daring predictions are ones that seem unlikely when initially made, but prove to be accurate, demonstrating some true insight by the predictor. Because the following three predictions are probably much more safe than daring, the question is really how quickly they will come to pass. For each, however, I include a slightly more daring, related add-on prediction.

Outbound E-Mail Takes Off

The number of congressional offices that maintain electronic mailing lists to which they send regular updates is small, but growing. These numbers will grow more quickly and eventually be recognized as a fundamental part of any member's on-line presence. Campaigns have already discovered the power of using their Web site to develop such opt-in mailing list of subscribers who ask to receive updates via e-mail, as illustrated in the chapter by Campbell and Dulio. While even the most interested Web surfer may not find his or her way to any particular lawmaker's Web site with great frequency, most people deal with their e-mail daily. Thus as congressional offices learn to keep their Web sites updated with current information, they will likewise develop electronic mailing lists as a means to lure interested Netizens to their sites.

As an add-on prediction, some congressional candidate or member of Congress will find him or herself in political trouble for abusing their mailing list or "spamming" individuals who never joined them to begin with.

Greater Real-Time Access

With C-SPAN, House and Senate floor proceedings can now be viewed on the Web. And there have been a growing number of successful examples of committee hearings broadcast live on the Internet, and members who have participated in live on-line chats. Such real-time events will certainly increase in both frequency and complexity. This may take the form of remote participation in committee hearings by witnesses, or by members themselves. Or perhaps visitors to the Capitol will be able to follow House and Senate floor proceedings from a virtual gallery that immerses them in the debate around them from the comfort of their own homes. However it evolves, we can expect the on-line Congress to become a "livelier" place than we know today.

As an add-on prediction, some member of Congress will be found to have let a staff assistant impersonate him or her in an on-line chat, while they were in fact somewhere else.

Greater Interactivity on Congressional Webs

Seven years since the first congressional Web site was created in 1994, most House and Senate Web sites remain static. They are frequently treated as on-line newsletters, intended to utilize the Internet as a one-to-many broadcast medium. This is not very surprising. Often working under technical and talent constraints that limit what they can accomplish on-line, such brochure-ware sites are sometimes the best a congressional office may produce. But as the sophistication of commercial Web sites continues to develop, the public's expectations from congressional Web sites will likewise increase. If commercial sites such Amazon.com can recommend books to individuals based on customers' shopping history, congressional Web sites should remember their customers' interest in particular issues and keep them posted on related legislation, or let them initiate casework inquiries with their representative that automatically track progress on an issue of concern and keep them posted on its progress. Such technology currently exists. The question is just how long it will take before it finds widespread use by members of Congress.

As an add-on prediction, the use of cookie files and other such technologies that permit such personalization are also the focus of privacy concerns that are often amplified when such tools are used by the government. As Congress considers what legislative steps are needed to protect individual privacy on-line, some members will be subject to criticism for their own intrusive tracking of individuals through their Web sites.

Conclusion

Initially slow to harness the technology available to them and to open their institution to the kind of scrutiny and interaction that technology allows, nearly every member of Congress now embraces the use of the Internet, and once less technologically inclined congressional districts are getting new avenues of access. Still, the use of the Internet may fall short of the demands of computer aficionados, largely because tradition dies hard on Capitol Hill. What one can safely conclude is that while the Internet's impact on Congress remains an open question with untested results, particularly given the ever-evolving nature of the Internet, it clearly has been a force for those with their palm on a mousepad.

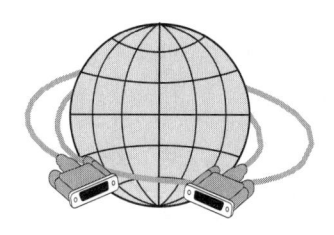

Index

A
Abraham, Spencer, 153
Accountability, 132–133
Activism. *See also* Interest groups; Lobbies,
  international electronic, 126–128
  Internet, 34–36, 118
  snail mail vs. e-mail, 37–38
Adobe Acrobat®, 56, 67
Advisory Council on the National Information Infrastructure, 143–144
AFL-CIO, 127
Age, 17, 182–184
Agenda for Action, 140
Agendas, legislative, 112–113
Allard, Wayne, 4
Alliance for Converging Technologies, 183
American Technology Honor Society, 166
Animations, 188
Anticopying technology, 150
Armey, Richard, 149
ARPANET, 179
Asbestos removal, 167
Audience, 39

B
Backdoor appropriations, 172–173. *See also* Off-budget financing
Bliley, Thomas J., 153
Boise Cascade Corporation, 127
Boucher, Rick, 141
Bradley, Bill, 188
Broadcasting, 39
Brown, Ron, 143–144
Buck slip, 36
Budget and Impoundment Control Act of 1974, 172
Building Web Sites Constituents Will Use, 181
Bulletin boards, electronic, 181, 183
Bumpers, Dale, 141
Bush, George W., E-rate and, 170–171

C
Campbell, Ben Nighthorse, 4
Candidates, 13, 15
Capitol Advantage, 36, 126
Capitol Correspond, 130
congress.com, 36
Censorship, 43
Censure and Move On, 38
Child Online Protection Act (COPA), 155
Circumvention devices, 150
CitizenDirect, 36
Classroom, Internet in, 163
Clinger-Cohen Act of 1996, 144
Clinton, Bill, 139–145, 153–155, 166
Clinton, Hillary, 25, 190
Clinton TechCorps, 166
Coats, Daniel R., 155
Coble, Howard, 149–150
Cold sweat letter, 37
COMIS. *See* Committee Information and Scheduling System (COMIS)
Commerce, Internet, 147–149
Committee Information and Scheduling System (COMIS), 31–32
Committee system. *See also* Hearings, attendance of
  COMIS and, 32

193

Committee system (*cont.*)
  deliberative process and, 82–83
  effects of Internet on, 5, 70–73, 107–112
  voting, remote, 92
  Webcasts, 64
  Web sites, 59–61, 89–90, 112, 187–188
Communications Decency Act, 43, 155
Computer access, 164–165, 177
Computers, Congress and, 104–105
Computer Systems Policy Project (CSPP), 142
Congress, virtual, 47
Congressional Accountability Project, 45, 117–118
Congressional Budget and Impoundment Control Act of 1974, 172
Congressional Internet Caucus, 88–89, 178
Congressional Record
  access to, 43–44, 54
  communication, types of, 38
  memorandums of understanding in, 110
  revision of, 40–41
Congressional Research Service (CRS), 44, 69, 90–92, 105, 181
Congressional Staff Fellowship Program, 85–88, 93–94
Congress Online Project, 86–87, 129, 131–133, 180–181
Connections, last mile, 165, 167
Constituents. *See* Representation
Constitutionality, of E-rate, 167–170, 176n26
Consumer Internet Privacy Enhancement Act, 154

Content, Web site, 132, 181–182
Contract with America, 45
Cookies, 154, 182, 192
COPA. *See* Child Online Protection Act (COPA)
Copyright, 149–150
Cox, Christopher, 148
Credibility
  of interest groups, 35–36
  mudslinging and, 115
CRS. *See* Congressional Research Service (CRS)
C-SPAN, 39, 46, 103, 178
CSPP. *See* Computer Systems Policy Project (CSPP)
Cybersquatting, 25–26

D
Daschle, Tom, 189
Dear Colleague letters, electronic, 6
Delegate-trustee issue, 5
Deliberations, 78–95
  CRS and, 69
  document production and, 68
  effects of Internet on, 5, 119–120
  electronic, 48–49
  electronic democracy and, 66–67
  flaming and, 45–46
  hearing attendance and, 70–71
  values and, 47
  voting machine and, 101–102
Democracy, direct, 75, 184
Democracy, electronic, 48–49, 66–67, 78–79, 88
Democracy, representative, 80–82
Digital divide. *See also* Income; Race
  among legislators, 146

deliberations and, 87
E-rate program and, 161
message politics and, 113
NII and, 140
race and, 5, 179
Digital signature technology, 68, 92
Discount levels, E-rate, 168
Documents
  electronic, 91
  legislative, 67–70, 71
  official, 40–41, 68–69
Dorgan, Byron, 149
Dornan, Robert, 114

E
EchoMail, 130
E-Congress, 47
E-Contract 2000, 113
Edison, Thomas, 101–102
Educate America Act, 166
Education, 162–166
Education rate pricing (E-rate), 166
e.GOP, 180
Effort, hierarchy of, 37
Electioneering, 17–20
Elections, 11–27
Electronic postcards, 130
Electronic precincts, 13
Electronic Signature in Global and National Commerce Act, 153
E-mail
  activist, 125–128
  after anthrax, 4, 6
  campaign lists, 13
  flaming, 45–46
  franking, 22
  House regulations, 23–25
  increased use of, 2, 179–180
  introduction of, 177–178, 187
  mailing lists, congressional, 191
  management of, 42, 128–130, 180–181, 188–189

INDEX

representation and, 33–38, 61–64, 118
resistance to, 4, 40
Senate regulations, 22
standardized, House of Representatives, 54
Stennis Fellows on, 86
Encryption technology, export of, 152–153
Energy crisis, 116
Entrepreneurship, policy, 136–139
E-rate program, 161–174
E-signatures, 153–154
Executive orders, 143–144

F

Fax communications, 124–125
FEC. *See* Federal Election Commission (FEC)
Federal Election Commission (FEC), 25–26
Federal Information Technology order, 144
Federalist, 33, 80–81
Federal Reserve, 5
Federal Trade Commission, 154
Filtering software, e-mail, 129–130, 187
Filtering software, Internet, 162, 175*n*6
Firstgov.gov, 132
Fitzgerald, Peter, 190
Flaming, 45–46
Flash applications, 182
Floor proceedings, televised, 102–104
Format, information, 46–49
Forms, Web, 188–189
Foundation for Public Affairs, 127
Founders, the, 80–82, 94–95
Franking, 22, 23, 64
Free speech, 43, 155
Funding, for E-rate, 166–170, 171
Fundraising, 13

G

Gambling, 150–151
Geography
  campaigns and, 26
  pornography and, 155
  representation and, 32–36
Gingrich, Newt
  computers and, 105
  deliberative process and, 120
  e-mail and, 178
  information, access to, 52
  Internet infrastructure and, 54
  THOMAS and, 88
  Web site, 6
  Y2K and, 111
Global Disaster Information Network, 143
Globalization, 79
Global Trends 2015, 79
Goodlatte, Bob W., 149, 151, 152–153
Gopher systems, 32
Gore, Al, 111, 139–145, 155, 166
Gore tax, 171
Government Performance and Results Act of 1993, 144
Gramm, Phil, 153
Greenspan, Alan, 5
Gregg, Judd, 154
Growing Up Digital, 183
Guiliani, Rudy, 25

H

Hackers, 18, 152, 190
Hamilton, Alexander, 81, 95
Hardware, House, 65–66
Hatch, Orrin, 149–150
Health care, 116
Hearings, attendance of, 70–71, 83, 178. *See also* Committee system
Hearings, Internet broadcast of, 6
Hefley, Joel, 4
Hierarchy of effort, 37

High Performance Computing Act of 1991, 140–142
High Performance Computing and Communications Program (HPCC), 142
HillaryNo.com, 25
HMOs, 116
Hollings, Ernest, 141
Hollywood, 149–150
House
  campaign regulations, 23–25
  electronic upgrade of, 52–55
  representation and, 33
House Franking Commission, 23
HPCC. *See* High Performance Computing and Communications Program (HPCC)

I

IITA. *See* Information Infrastructure Technology and Applications Program (IITA)
Income. *See also* Digital divide; E-rate program
  E-rate program and, 164–165, 169, 174
  e-voting and, 12
  Web site quality and, 5
Information
  access to, 117–118
  campaign, 15–17
  control of, 5–6, 39–44
  Federalist on, 81
  format of, 46–49
  majority control of, 71–72
  overload, 118–119
  unofficial, posting of, 68–69
Information Infrastructure Technology and Applications Program (IITA), 142
Information superhighway, meaning of, 145

Infrastructure, electronic committee rooms, upgrade of, 72–73
House, 52–55, 65–66
Initiatives, 75
Institutions, tandem, 136
Intellectual property rights, 149–150
Interactivity, 182–184, 191–192
Interest groups
  advocacy, Internet, 118
  communication, types of, 37–38, 123–125
  electronic democracy and, 67
  geographical vs. Internet, 34–36
Internet industry, 113
  message politics and, 112
  spamming and, 62
Internet Caucus, 3, 146–147
Internet Tax Freedom bill, 148
Internet Time, 186, 190
Intranet, congressional, 40, 112
Intranet Quorum (IQ), 130
IQ. *See* Intranet Quorum (IQ)
IRS, 114–115

J
Jefferson, Thomas, 45, 83, 168
Jeffords, James M., 116
Jell-O, 149
Junk mail, electronic, 127–128
Jurisdiction, committee, 107–110, 140–141

K
Kennedy, Edward M., 178, 187
Kerrey Commission Report, 173–174, 175n22
Kyl, John, 150–151

L
Laptops
  Greenspan, Alan and, 5
  House use of, 65
  in state legislatures, 73
  use of, on floor, 91–92, 98n49, 106, 178
Last mile connections, 165, 167
Law enforcement, encryption technology and, 152–153
Lawmaking
  committee Web sites and, 60–61
  documents, access to, 67–70
  electronic, 66–67
  Internet policy and, 145–156, 178–179
  public input, real-time, 45–46
  stagecraft of, 115–116
  in state legislatures, 74–75
  technology and, 54–57
Leahy, Patrick, 150
LEGIS, 108
LEGI-SLATE, 43
Legislative Information System (LIS), 2
Legislatures, state, 73–75
Lewis, Michael, 184
LEXIS-NEXIS, 43
LIS. *See* Legislative Information System (LIS)
Lobbies, international, 35

M
Madison, James, 78, 80–81, 94–95
Mail, surface
  activism and, 37
  vs. flaming, 45–46
  management of, 123–124
  misdirected, 36
  representation and, 38
  as response to e-mail, 130
Manual of Parliamentary Practice, 83

McCain, John
  on CRS access, 44
  E-rate program and, 169
  privacy and, 152, 154
  Web campaigning, 11
  Y2K and, 111–112
McCloskey, Frank, 114
McInnis, Scott, 4
McIntyre, Richard, 114
McLuhan, Marshall, 38, 41, 45
Media, traditional, 39–40
Memorandums of understanding, 110
Message politics, 112–113

N
National Competitiveness Act of 1993, 140
National Exchange Carrier Association (NECA), 166
National Governors Association (NGA), 148–149
National Information Infrastructure Act, 141
National Information Infrastructure (NII), 140–145
NECA. *See* National Exchange Carrier Association (NECA)
Netiquette, 6
Newsletters, electronic, 24, 63–64
Next: The Future Just Happened, 184
NGA. *See* National Governors Association (NGA)
Nielsen NetRatings, 125
NII. *See* National Information Infrastructure (NII)
Nixon, Richard, 103
No Child Gets Left Behind, 170

O
Off-budget financing, 168, 172–173
Oversight, 106

P

Palm Pilots, 178
Panels, *ad hoc*, 110–112
Paperwork Reduction Act of 1995, 144
Parker, Susan, 12
Parties, political, 13–15, 112–116, 180
Partisan politics, 5–6, 44, 114–115, 169–171
Patch-through technology, 124
Phone communications, 124
Phone companies, E-rate and, 168–169
Plebiscite, electronic, 48–49
Policy entrepreneurship, 136–139
Political parties, 13–15, 112–116, 180
Politics, criminalization of, 115
Politics, partisan, 5–6, 44, 114–115, 169–171
Polls, online, 132
Pornography, 43, 155–156
Postcards, electronic, 130
Precincts, electronic, 13
Presidency, Internet policy and, 139–145
Pressler, Larry, 3
Privacy, 152–155, 181
Property rights, intellectual, 149–150
Public opinion, 80–82, 172

R

Race
  computer access and, 164–165
  digital divide and, 179
  election practices and, 28n33
  E-rate program and, 169
  Web site quality and, 5
Radio, floor proceedings and, 103
Rainforest Action Network, 127

Real-time information
  deliberative process and, 5, 69
  lawmaking and, 45–46
  Webcasts and, 191
Referendums, 75
Referrals, committee, 110
Regulations, campaign, 22–26
Reinventing government, 144
Reno v. ACLU, 155
Representation, 31–50
  congressional Web sites and, 131–133
  effects of Internet on, 106, 118
  electronic, and deliberation, 92
  interactivity and, 191–192
  of minority views, 71–72, 101–102, 187–188
  technology and, 57–66
  Web site quality and, 5
Research, legislative, 54–57
Retired Officers Association, 126
Right click acquisition, 41
Robb, Charles S., 187
Roll-over titles, 182
RudyYes.com, 25

S

Sales tax, 148
Sanchez, Loretta, 114
Schools and Library Corporation (SLC), 166–167, 169
Search engines, 42–43, 88, 132, 181
Secure socket layer (SSL), 13
Self-promotion, congressional, 132
Senate
  campaign regulations, 22–23
  C-SPAN and, 103–104
  deliberative process and, 45

hackers and, 190
laptops and, 178
representation and, 33
Sensenbrenner, James, 108–110
Separation of powers, 136
Servers, House, 65–66
Signature, digital, 68, 92, 153–154
Skills gap, 162. *See also* Digital divide
SLC. *See* Schools and Library Corporation (SLC)
Snatch and grab, 41
Soak and poke, 33
Solomon, Gerald, 152
Spam
  congressional, 191
  deliberative process and, 86–87
  representation and, 38, 62–63
  vote.com and, 127–128
  Web forms and, 188–189
Spanish-language, 107, 181
Speech of Debate clause, 44
Spin, 17
SSL. *See* Secure socket layer (SSL)
Staffing, Internet, 55, 66, 131
Standardized testing, 170
Starr Report, 42–43, 180, 189
State legislatures, 73–75
Stennis Fellows, 85–88, 93–94
Streaming, 64–65
Surfing, Internet, 39–40
Surveys, electronic, 92

T

Tandem institutions, 136
Tauzin, Billy, 108–110, 151, 169
Taxation, E-rate and, 168–169
Taxation, Internet and, 147–149

Teachers, role of, 163, 165–166
TechCorps, Clinton, 166
Technology, educational, 163–167
Technology Honor Society, American, 166
Telecommunications Act of 1996
  committee jurisdiction and, 109–110
  education technology and, 166
  E-rate program and, 168–169, 176n26
Telephone communications, 124
Telephone companies, E-rate and, 168–169
Televised floor proceedings, 102–104
Television, 39
Term limits, 73
Testing, standardized, 170
THOMAS
  information, access to, 44
  introduction of, 54, 105
  legislative schedule and, 40
  URL, 2
Thomas, Bill, 54
Thurmond, Strom, 6
Time-out period, 148
Traficant, James, 188
Transparency, 117–118

Treaties, intellectual property, 149–150
TreeCam, 189
TROA, 126
21st Century Congress Project, 54, 73, 90–91, 93

U
Universal Service Administrative Company (USAC), 166
Universal Services Order, 166
USAC. *See* Universal Service Administrative Company (USAC)
Users, Internet
  demographics of, 11–12, 179, 182–184
  information sources, preferred, 15–17

V
Values, deliberative process and, 47, 119–120
Video, e-mailing of, 12
Video conferencing, 70
Video phones, 101
Vietnam War, 103
Volunteers, campaign, 13
Vote.com, 127–128
Voters, 15–20
Voting, online, 12, 18–20, 183–184

Voting machine, electronic, 101–102

W
Washington, George, 45
Web cams, 189
Webcasts, 64, 71–73, 178
Web sites
  candidate, 13, 25–26
  congressional, 130–133, 178, 181–182, 187–188
  e-mail through, 62–63, 188–189
  interest group, 126–127
  partisan, 114–115. *See also* Guiliani, Rudy
  representation and, 57–61
  Senate, 190
  Spanish-language, 107, 181
  spoof, 25–26, 42
  underutilization of, 40, 89, 90
  Write Your Representative, 36
Webster, 2
Welcome Wagon, cyber, 3
Wilson, Woodrow, 83
Write Your Representative, 36, 188–189
Wyden, Ron, 148

Y
Y2K, 94, 111–112, 186
YesRudy.com, 25